The American Dream
and the
Power of Wealth

The American Dream
and the
Power of Wealth

Choosing Schools and Inheriting Inequality in the Land of Opportunity

Heather Beth Johnson

Routledge
Taylor & Francis Group
New York London

Routledge is an imprint of the
Taylor & Francis Group, an informa business

Routledge
Taylor & Francis Group
270 Madison Avenue
New York, NY 10016

Routledge
Taylor & Francis Group
2 Park Square
Milton Park, Abingdon
Oxon OX14 4RN

© 2006 by Taylor & Francis Group, LLC
Routledge is an imprint of Taylor & Francis Group, an Informa business

Printed in the United States of America on acid-free paper
10 9 8 7 6 5 4 3 2 1

International Standard Book Number-10: 0-415-95239-5 (Softcover) 0-415-95238-7 (Hardcover)
International Standard Book Number-13: 978-0-415-95239-2 (Softcover) 978-0-415-95238-5 (Hardcover)

Library of Congress Cataloging-in-Publication Data

Johnson, Heather Beth, 1972-
 The American dream and the power of wealth : choosing schools and inheriting inequality in the land of opportunity / Heather Beth Johnson.
 p. cm.
 Includes bibliographical references.
 ISBN 0-415-95238-7 (hardback : alk. paper) -- ISBN 0-415-95239-5 (pbk. : alk. paper)
 1. Wealth--United States. 2. Educational equalization--United States. 3. Equality--United States. 4. United States--Economic conditions--2001- 5. United States--Social conditions--1980- I. Title.

HC110.W4J64 2006
339.2'20973--dc22   2006004716

Visit the Taylor & Francis Web site at
http://www.taylorandfrancis.com

and the Routledge Web site at
http://www.routledge-ny.com

To Braydon, who, with me, is always asking,
How can this be?

Anything could happen, this was America.
He gave himself up to the country and dreamt.

— **Gish Jen,** *Typical American*

Table of Contents

Preface and Acknowledgments   xi

1. The Wealth Gap and the American Dream   1

2. Meritocracy and "Good" Schools   19

3. Buying In and Opting Out   53

4. Making Do and Feeling Stuck   79

5. Wealth Privilege   101

6. Inequality and Ideology   129

7. An Unresolved Conflict   157

Appendix: Methodology   175

Notes   183

Bibliography   199

Index   223

Preface and Acknowledgments

I would like to open my first book with three acknowledgments.

The first is that my goal in all of my scholarship and teaching— including that in this book—is to get people to think in new directions. On one balmy August night in the summer that I conducted the second phase of interviews for this book, I received a phone call at home. I had to run inside from our back porch and when I got to the phone, out of breath, I was surprised to find that on the other end was a woman I had interviewed a few days earlier. Although we had always given phone numbers to every family we interviewed (saying that they could always call us for any reason at all), never, until then, had a family called. The woman said that she felt she needed to tell me that she had been thinking "nonstop" about her interview ever since I had left her house. She explained that she and her husband were suddenly "noticing things" they had not before, that they were "talking and talking about it at home," and she gave an example. She told me that the same day of our interview her in-laws had sent her "out of the blue" a gift card for a new mattress set. Apparently they had recently visited, discovered that the bed in the guest room was not very comfortable, and thought it would be nice if they helped out by sending this gift to their son and daughter-in-law. My interviewee exclaimed that before her interview she had "just never thought about how much this stuff happens!" She said that she had gotten to thinking, "This doesn't really happen to everyone," that "others surely do not have this same kind of financial support in their families"; "but," she said, "everyone thinks that we're all competing in a fair game together."

I want to make clear that this story represents exactly what I hope for; that my work in this book will get people to think about the paradoxes and dilemmas I have written about, that they will begin to notice things that they might not have before, and that they will talk about it at home and in the world. That, simply, is my goal. I do not claim to solve problems; rather, I see my job as to explain and clarify sociological paradoxes and dilemmas, to get people to notice things they otherwise might not, and to raise questions for people to take away with them.

The second acknowledgment is of the significance to me and to my work of all of those people whose interviews, perspectives, and experiences frame this book, and of my friends, family, and colleagues who have supported the writing of this book. The families we interviewed were gracious in sharing their views and their stories, and I continue to be amazed at everything I am learning from them. They are the true foundation of this work. The bulk of their interviews come out of a much larger project, of which this book is just one small part. I am grateful to Thomas Shapiro, principal investigator of the Assets and Inequality Project, for allowing me to use the data from that project, which was funded by two generous grants from the Ford Foundation. Those grants also funded graduate research assistantships that supported me during my years at Northeastern University as a doctoral student in sociology. The other interviews herein I conducted independently during my second year on the faculty at Lehigh University. Exceptional financial support from Lehigh in the form of two faculty grants and a pretenure endowed chair, as well as exceptional encouragement from my department and the university administration, made it possible for me to finish my research.

In my first four years at Lehigh I have worked with many impressively talented students who have helped with various aspects of the research for this book. I cannot name them all, but these students include five who especially stand out as research assistants: Sara Barker, Troy Boni, Maggie Hagerman, Julia Schulman, and Shahin Shaghaghi; each has been invaluable to me as I pushed to complete this project. Colleagues and friends who have read the manuscript in its various renditions over time have offered important insight and made contributions for which I am grateful. The committee members for my original dissertation—Maureen Kelleher, Melvin Oliver, Gordana Rebrenovic, and Thomas Shapiro—were instrumental in shaping my project, not to mention my career. My editor at Routledge, David McBride, read my dissertation and helped me to turn it into a manuscript. Lisa Keister reviewed my book early on, before it was even really a book, and gave me helpful comments that pushed me forward. Later, Dalton Conley and an anonymous reviewer gave me valuable feedback that pushed me even further. My mother and my husband graciously read my manuscript and helped me—notably—to see it through the eyes of nonacademics. And finally, toward the end of my writing and revising, I asked several of my most trusted comrades to give me feedback, and their insights have been instrumental in turning the book into something of which I am finally proud. They are Karen Albright, Patricia Arend, Jessica Kenty-Drane, Thomas Shapiro, and Jessica Holden Sherwood.

I want to thank my "inner circle" for all of the various ways they have supported me. Braydon Johnson-McCormick, my partner in all that I do, was my boyfriend when I started all this, and is now not only my husband but co-parent to our children. He has been there through it all—through every stage and phase of this project, and I am forever indebted to him; "thank you" just does not cut it! My parents Don and Janet Johnson, who first shaped me to be concerned with social justice in the world, continue to influence my orientation and support me in the most tangible ways to make my life so rich. Jessica Kenty-Drane (especially in her talks with me during millions of phone calls), and Beth Anderson (especially in her talks with me during millions of Wednesday night dinners), have been pillars of support. And the children in my life—first Maria, and now Kyle and Owen, too—have been, and are, my inspiration and my grounding presence. Finally, and truly most important, I want to thank my advisor, friend, and mentor Thomas Shapiro. I owe a great debt to Tom for all he teaches me, and for all he does for me. Whatever is good here is partly his, but whatever is bad here is all mine.

Third, I want to acknowledge that my hope for all of my scholarship and teaching—including this book—is that the dissolution of the social problems at their core will someday make them obsolete. On a bitter January night during the final winter of writing this book, my husband and I had dinner with my favorite sociology professor from college. It was our first reunion in ten years, and it was a special evening. As we sat around the table, the professor asked me what I was currently working on. I told her that it was, basically, exactly the stuff that I had been thinking about in college, that some of the specifics had changed, but the basic social problems that had then engaged me were the same things I was working on now. It strikes me that for as much as I know that a decade is only a very short time in the context of social change, I nonetheless feel unnerved by the idea that so little has been altered. For as much as I am passionate about my work, I do hope that a day will come soon when I will not need to be so concerned with the social problems central to it. I love my work, but the problems I work on are not problems I love. I do hope there is a day when all of us who work in these areas can move on to other topics.

This last point is especially poignant for me now, because in the final year of work on this book my husband and I were also in the process of adopting twin baby boys. I do not want my sons to have to face the structural inequalities and the basic injustices that I see in the world. As idealistic as it might seem, I genuinely do hope that there is a day—not so far in the future—when all of us who are asking "How can this be?" can shift our focus to different questions.

Heather Beth Johnson

1

The Wealth Gap
and the American Dream

The wealth gap between white and black families in the United States is increasing, not decreasing. When I state this in a lecture, I watch students' faces look up from notebooks with expressions of skepticism or full-blown disbelief. They come to talk to me after class, then walk with me, slowly moving out of the classroom building along the winding paths of the university to my office, asking me, "How—how can this be? The racial wealth gap is *increasing*?"

I know it is hard to believe. My students have been told their whole lives that everything is getting better, not worse, where race and class inequality is concerned. They have learned that the civil rights battle was won years before they were born. They know the story of Martin Luther King, Jr., and many can recite sentences of his famous "I Have a Dream" speech. They have grown up believing that the general principles of equal opportunity, egalitarianism, and inclusiveness are the basis for how our system operates. The concept of an increasing black-white wealth gap in the present-day United States is a hard pill for college students to swallow, not because it reveals that inequality exists—they know that it does—but because it implies a fracture in the American Dream, a recognition of real advantage and disadvantage being passed along categorically to each new generation. To know that certain individuals own less or have achieved more than others is one thing, but to know that whole groups of people are increasingly privileged or constrained by their families' wealth histories suggests that inequalities are somehow happening systematically. This is contrary to what my students have been taught—that inequity among us is simply the result of differences in individuals' achievements, that it is not patterned, organized, or structural.

I understand their confusion because I, too, grew up thinking that America was moving closer and closer to resembling a level playing field—especially in regard to race, class, and gender. The message was straightforward and compelling: in the Post–Civil Rights Era we were competing in a fair game with equal chances for success so that, regardless of our backgrounds, whoever worked the hardest would go the furthest. Growing up, my perception was that if it were not entirely true, this message was at least mostly true, and surely truer then than at any time in the past. My parents, my teachers, and everyone else in their generation who conveyed to me this message were justifiably proud of the strides that had been made toward racial justice, equal opportunity, women's rights, and civil rights. Optimism was high and—notably—not unfounded. Much progress had been (and continues to be) made to dismantle the many forms of injustice.

Not unlike the generations of Americans before us, my students and I have been immersed in the culture of a deeply held American Dream. We were told that in this country an individual rises and falls based on personal achievement or lack thereof; that one's background or family of origin is neither a significant help nor hindrance in the quest for success; and that each of us earns and deserves our relative social positioning. Many a child has been told these things, and the American Dream has surely evolved in various ways over time, but those of us born since the 1950s have grown up in the wake of social movements, groundbreaking court decisions, and unprecedented cultural shifts that have led to a particularly literal interpretation of the American Dream's theme. Equal opportunity has been presented to us not so much as an ideal but as an achieved reality. A level playing field has been held out to us not so much as a goal but as an actual, legitimate explanation for how our system operates. So, it is not hard to imagine our surprise when we realize that regardless of all we have been taught, despite all our beliefs, things are not exactly what they seem.

To learn that race and class inequality is still happening systematically, and that in fact an historic cleavage such as the racial wealth gap is getting deeper, is to realize that significant sociostructural problems have yet to be solved, and to suspect that there is something wrong with the *system*. This may force us to examine how much of our own stories are entwined with the privileges or disadvantages that we were born into. To do this is to face the legacies—good and bad—that we have inherited from past generations. This is hard to do in a society so focused on the principle of rising or falling based on individual merit.

This book is about two seemingly paradoxical elements of American life: First, it is about the race and class inequalities related to family wealth that continue to be structured in ways that systematically and categorically advantage some groups while disadvantaging others. Second, it is about the American Dream's ideology of meritocracy that tells us that everyone—regardless of background—ends up where they do based on their own individual achievement. Both of these are major dimensions of social life in the contemporary United States. Despite how much or little we notice them in our daily lives, each is entrenched in our culture and foundational to life as we know it. In this book I take on what is an often unproblematized contradiction: I ask how Americans make sense of the power of wealth (specifically inherited wealth) given its incompatibility with the principles of the American Dream. While perspectives from across the socioeconomic spectrum are included here, I focus especially on wealthy families, seeking to discern how they reconcile the substantial advantages they confer upon their children with their bedrock belief in meritocracy.

Previous literature has documented the patterns of wealth ownership and the statistical contours of the wealth gap. I am not interested in replicating these studies; rather, I am interested in how people *make sense* of the structure of wealth inequality—especially the intergenerational transfer of wealth in families—given that it flies in the face of the American Dream. How can we claim a commitment to meritocracy even when our own lived experiences often contradict it? How do we acknowledge structured inequality as we teach our children that individual achievement determines life chances? For me, what is most sociologically fascinating is not the ideology of meritocracy itself nor the structure or power of wealth. What is so intriguing is how foundational both are to our society, yet how irreconcilable each is with the other—and, perhaps most important, how rarely we question this paradox. An analysis of how Americans reconcile the American Dream with the power of wealth addresses an important lacuna in the emerging sociological literature on wealth and stratification: the role of ideology. Ideology is a critical component in understanding how race and class inequalities are perpetuated in the contemporary United States because ideology—in how it helps to mask and justify systems of inequality—contributes to the collective denial, and thus maintenance, of structural inequities.

At its heart, this book is about the same basic issues of inequality, power, and consciousness that preoccupied Émile Durkheim,

Karl Marx, and Max Weber in what is now known as the canon of "classical social theory" they pioneered in the 1800s. It is also about the same fundamental questions of structural inequality that lie at the heart of much sociology today. It is about my students' question: How can this be?

How are race and class inequality perpetuated through generations in contemporary American society, despite deep belief in equal opportunity and great efforts to dismantle injustice? In a country that takes pride in being the land of opportunity, how do we continue to justify legacies of wealth inequality that grant opportunities to some groups over others? These questions are important because our beliefs and our actions—what we think and what we do—will impact the extent to which we perpetuate historic dilemmas into the future. Given what we have inherited, what will *we* pass along to the generations after us?

Race, Class, and Hard Work

In the United States today, approximately 20 percent of children under the age of six are living below the official poverty line.[1] Many of these children's parents are desperately impoverished and unemployed, and the plight of these families—often single mothers and their children—is harrowing.[2] Perhaps even more troubling, because of the irony, is how many poor children live in homes with at least one working parent; 40 percent of impoverished adults hold at least one job.[3] Many of these families have worked hard, they have played by the rules, and they are still coming up short. The working poor challenge our thinking about inequality in America: if people wind up where they do based on how hard they work, and if 40 percent of the poor are working hard, then why is it that those families are struggling so to even stay afloat? Such questions have been asked often and social scientists have revealed some of the structural arrangements contributing to the predicaments of the working poor;[4] only recently, however, have we begun to seriously consider ways that the structure of *wealth* ties into the dynamics of intergenerational inequality in the contemporary United States.

The sociology of wealth is both an old and a new way to study inequality. For the theorists who pioneered the discipline of sociology, unequal distribution of valued resources and unbalanced relations of property were at the theoretical core of their studies. Marx's *Capital* is probably the most famous example.[5] Private property ownership was critical to such traditional analyses of inequality because of the command over resources and the power to propel life chances that it granted an individual, family, or group. But over time, especially in the United States, the study of social stratification became almost completely dominated by analyses of labor market dynamics and income inequalities. As a result, in both the academic literature and the mind-set of the American public, the concept of socioeconomic class has been tied almost exclusively to achievement in education, success in the labor market, and earned income. This is so much the case that today we often think of class as equated with household income; and indeed, socioeconomic class is often measured this way. Certainly income greatly impacts most American families' basic living standards; but, within the framework of traditionally defined socioeconomic status, many questions about the *perpetuation* of class inequality have remained elusive. To obtain a more comprehensive understanding of class status and class inequalities, researchers have recently begun to look outside the dominant paradigm of income inequality with a renewed interest in examining private family wealth and its impact on framing life chances and basic capacities for an individual or family.[6]

Class is a fundamental category in social theory. Social class inequality is generally understood as hierarchical cleavages that exist between individuals or groups relative to their economic well-being, status, and life chances in society. But in most recent empirical research, theory, and policy work, class has been measured almost exclusively by education, occupation, and income. A more comprehensive understanding of social class takes multiple dynamics into consideration.[7] In addition to level of education, occupation, and income, social class is about the sharing of identities and practices, the ways in which resources are mobilized across generations, and the norms and values that shape behavior.[8] Wealth is an important part of such an understanding because wealth involves, for example, inheritance, which is not earned but which has serious implications for resource mobilization, worldviews, life chances, and the intergenerational transmission of inequality.

In the early 1990s, with the publication of *Assets and the Poor*, Michael Sherraden reintroduced the concept of wealth as a fundamental variable in understanding social class inequality—specifically, the perpetuation of poverty.[9] Since then, the study of wealth as a contemporary scholarly subject has fully emerged across disciplines. This work has begun to reveal that, while we typically equate money with earned income, many American families acquire a substantial portion of their financial portfolios through nonmerit sources, mainly in the form of intergenerational transfers of financial assets. While most American households use job earnings to pay for day-to-day necessities (for instance, food, housing, and clothing), wealth, in contrast, often originates from family financial assistance, gifts, or inheritance and becomes a way to create opportunities, shape life experiences, and ensure the future. Family wealth can propel a family's mobility, access important resources for the next generation, and cultivate a sense of security. A focus on wealth creates a new paradigm for understanding social inequality in fundamentally important ways. It sheds light on some of the dynamics and patterns of contemporary inequality that are masked if we study income alone. It reveals certain advantages that are not earned by individuals per se, but received through families. It allows us to see an historic and persisting wealth gap as a significant sociostructural problem.[10]

The structure of wealth inequality in the United States is, and always has been, extremely unbalanced; more unbalanced than income inequality. Wealth inequality is more extreme in this country than in any European country or industrial society.[11] In her analysis of wealth patterns in the United States, sociologist Lisa Keister found that "while disparities in income and educational attainment are extreme, disparities in the ownership of wealth are likely worse and apparently more enduring across generations."[12] The top 1 percent of wealth holders in the United States own almost 40 percent of all wealth, and the top 20 percent own approximately 80 percent of all wealth.[13] Due to the intergenerational dimension of family wealth, these holdings are continually expanding and amassing.[14] In this, the wealthiest country on earth, some children grow up with luxuries that others cannot even imagine; the average net worth for the top 1 percent of families is about $6.7 million.[15]

Meanwhile, asset poverty is just as extreme: almost 40 percent of American families do not own enough assets to last three months if they were to lose their jobs,[16] and 20 to 30 percent of all households have zero or negative net worth.[17] Asset poverty has serious ramifications for a family, but particularly for the well-being and life chances of a child. It means that, for example, the security that can be provided to a child through owning a home is out of the question. Paying for a college education in the future, or helping a child get started on the purchase of a car, a home, or a business, is impossible. Moreover, with no assets to liquidate and nothing to fall back upon, a situation such as the loss of a parent's job, a family medical crisis, or another emergency can be totally devastating.

The wealth gap in the United States holds dire implications when we consider its interrelationship with other social inequalities. Perhaps most acute is the relationship between wealth and race. In the past decade, research on the intersection between the two has unveiled a strong connection, leading wealth scholars to conclude, as sociologist Lisa Keister has, that race in fact "may be the single dimension along which wealth is most unequally distributed."[18] The cleavages of the racial wealth gap are especially deep between black and white families.[19] In their 1995 book *Black Wealth/White Wealth,* Melvin Oliver and Thomas Shapiro fully exposed this divide by revealing that college-educated whites possessed approximately four times as much wealth as similarly situated college-educated blacks.[20] Oliver and Shapiro showed that regardless of education, achievement in the labor market, or level of income, the wealth gap makes it virtually impossible for disproportionately asset-poor black families to socioeconomically keep up with their disproportionately asset-wealthy white counterparts.[21]

Though the income gap between blacks and whites is by no means unsubstantial, the racial wealth gap is even more extreme. The annual income for white men with bachelor's degrees averages $65,046, compared to $46,511 for black men,[22] but within every income bracket and at every level of educational attainment, black families have substantially less wealth than do white families.[23] In *The Hidden Cost of Being African American,* Shapiro finds that a typical black family's net worth is only $8,000, compared to the $81,000 net worth of a typical white family.[24] The picture this paints for the future is troubling: Not only are 26 percent of white children growing up asset poor, but so are 52 percent of black children.[25] Since wealth-holding families have always tended to pass significant portions of their assets along to the next generation, the disparities have escalated over time. And, as wealth is inherited, maximized, and built upon, this racial wealth gap continues to increase, and the divides between black and white families continue to grow.[26]

The historical roots of the racial wealth gap have been well documented and theorized in the research literature. A history of slavery originally made it illegal for black families to own property, develop capital, accumulate wealth, and pass assets along to their children—a practice that has always been available to white families. Compounding this initial imbalance further, over time, racially discriminatory public policy, which impacted nearly every arena of social life, made it virtually impossible for black families to acquire, grow, and transfer wealth to the same degree as white families. Due to the nature of wealth accumulation, these historic realities have resulted in a legacy that persists to this day. Wealth is accrued through investments and planning, but without an initial base of wealth, asset-poor families cannot catch up to their asset-rich peers.[27]

It is estimated that between one-half to more than 80 percent of all accumulated wealth is received through intergenerational transfers of assets,[28] and about 90 percent of these transfers come directly from parents.[29] Sociologist Dalton Conley's analysis of the black-white wealth gap concluded that in fact "parental wealth is the strongest predictor" of racial differences in net worth.[30] The historic legacies play out today so that black families are able to give and receive inter-generational transfers much less often (and in much lesser amounts) than are white families.[31] For instance, less than 8 percent of black families receive any inheritance, compared to over 28 percent of white families, and the median inheritance for blacks is less than $1,000, while it is approximately $10,000 or more for whites.[32] We tend to think of intergenerational transfers of wealth as isolated primarily to inheritances given or received upon death; however, the passing along of financial assets within families commonly occurs at other times as well. Estimates show that somewhere between 40 and 70 percent of intergenerational transfers are received not in the form of bequests, but through gifts or financial assistance throughout the life course.[33]

In the academic terminology of the social sciences, *intergenerational transfers* refer to the passing along of assets both at death and throughout one's life. Throughout this book, intergenerational transfers are conceptualized as anything of economic value received or passed along in a family over the course of a lifetime. This might include anything from large bequests, monetary gifts, or loans, to the financing of education, a down payment on a home, or help starting a business. It might also include such financial assistance as the receiving or passing along of new or used furniture, appliances, or cars. Such things, while not normally considered remarkable "intergenerational transfers" are remarkably financially advantageous to individuals and families since they do not then have to afford them on their own.

The racial wealth gap and families' abilities (or inabilities) to pass intergenerational transfers forward to the next generation are enormously consequential for individuals of different backgrounds. While it is certainly true that not all white families have assets and that all black families have none,[34] the structure of wealth inequality has real implications in terms of opportunities and life chances for families and children. Wealth gives parents the capacity to provide stable homeownership, safer neighborhood environments, better educational experiences, and more expansive opportunities to their children.[35] Family wealth can also potentially foster other, less tangible, advantages for children such as self-confidence and positive worldviews.[36] The racial wealth gap ensures that some children have beneficial circumstances and resources that others do not. This is a reality with which we are all faced; yet, despite this, our dominant cultural logic tells us that we each independently earn our stations in life and that no group is systematically advantaged or disadvantaged.

The message that social positioning is the result of individual hard work, effort, and achievement comes from every arena. Survey data consistently show that Americans overwhelmingly believe that widespread opportunity exists for all individuals to succeed, that we achieve what we deserve, and that the ideology of individualism is fundamentally strong.[37] Indeed, Americans associate "hard work," more than any other factor, with "getting ahead."[38] These ideas lie at the core of our cultural identity and help to cultivate a national creed for which we are known throughout the world: the American Dream. At its most fundamental level, the American Dream is about meritocracy: the notion of a system in which we advance based on individual merit, wherein no person is unfairly privileged or disadvantaged by the circumstances into which he or she is born. At some level most of us probably believe in this ideology,[39] or at least in the basic values of it, and many Americans surely take great pride in these principles. These principles are, after all, at the heart of what America represents for many people. In some ways, the American Dream of meritocracy may be true, but it is glaringly false in at least one way: inherited wealth is not earned through the beneficiary's individual achievement, and many individuals in wealth-holding families (disproportionately white families) inherit wealth. One cannot "earn" something that he or she inherits.

In looking at race and class inequalities, patterns and group dynamics are revealed through the lens of wealth that stand as a direct contradiction to the American Dream. It would be hard to argue, for example, that a first grader from a wealthy family has earned her coveted spot in an excellent, exclusive elementary school. Although her parents may have worked hard to place her there, few six-year-olds have individually achieved this head start in life. Moreover, as we will see, many of the parents we spoke with who had placed their children in such schools had, at least in part, done so by relying on family wealth originally received through intergenerational transfers. Structural wealth inequality creates advantages for children that are often unearned through individual accomplishment or merit; it virtually ensures that some people have advantages that others do not.[40] Yet, the American Dream of meritocracy promises that individuals get ahead or behind based on their own hard work, achievement, or lack thereof. While this paradox is transparent in the experiences of most of us, we normally do not even question it. The structure of wealth poses a direct challenge to the American Dream without most of us so much as even raising an eyebrow.

The critical point is not that inequalities *exist*, but that they are being perpetuated in recurrent patterns—they are not always the result of individual success or failure, nor are they randomly distributed throughout the population. In the contemporary United States, the structure of wealth systematically transmits race and class inequalities through generations despite deep-rooted belief otherwise. In the Post–Civil Rights Era, the growing racial wealth gap defies our conviction in the principles of individual hard work and achievement at the heart of the American Dream. How do we reconcile that? Addressing that question is critical to understanding the inside-workings of the intergenerational transmission of inequality, and thus critical to understanding how to change its path.

Core Questions

Several questions stand at the core of this book. Central to them all is the intergenerational transfer of inequality in contemporary American society. Questions about the transmission of inequality across generations are core questions for the social sciences generally and sociology specifically. More important, they are core questions for any person interested in understanding how to further advance the interests of the greater good. Given the centrality of this subject in research and in social justice agendas, it is remarkable how little we know about how social reproduction actually unfolds. We know that structured inequality exists and that social reproduction is occurring—in other words, we know that it *is* happening—but *how* is it happening? Understanding dominant ideological beliefs about inequality is an important inroad to approaching this question. It is generally agreed that social stratification is a persistent feature of human society in part because of the role that ideology plays in its maintenance: structured inequality must be supported by broad-based legitimization in order to be maintained.[41] However, while virtually all of social theory assumes this, scholars rarely attempt to describe the mechanisms involved.[42] As researchers of stratification have noted, "the task of contemporary stratification research is to describe the contours and distribution of inequality and to explain its persistence despite modern egalitarian or anti-stratification values."[43] If people's beliefs and values impact their behaviors and actions at all, then understanding dominant ideology is an important component in understanding the social reproduction of inequalities.

Although we are becoming aware of the significance of structured wealth inequality, we know little about how people perceive it. In the United States, where polls show that the vast majority of people believe in the principles of the American Dream, it is especially perplexing to examine how inherited wealth is viewed, legitimized, or justified. How do we make sense of the structure of wealth inequality in the context of our dominant cultural ideology? How do people explain the inherited advantages of family wealth in light of the underlying values of the American Dream? Though extensive literature exists on Americans' class-consciousness and awareness of class distinctions,[44] we know little of their beliefs about class inequality, and almost nothing of how they perceive wealth. While some recent research has focused on the American Dream and Americans' belief in meritocracy,[45] no prior research has asked people directly about how they reconcile those beliefs with the structure of wealth inequality. This is the major purpose of this book.

I look at the institution of education as a focal arena in which to analyze wealth inequality. Education is an important focus for many reasons, primarily because schooling plays a crucial role in the socialization and life trajectories of children. The schools parents choose for their children affect not only the everyday lives of their kids, but significantly impact their life chances, their future prospects, and their identities. Despite decades of court orders, America's schools are not only unequal but increasingly segregated by race and class.[46] Yet education is, ironically, the arena in which our beliefs about meritocracy are perhaps the strongest. Education is the institution that is supposed to perform the "great equalizer" task in our society; where, regardless of background, all children will be given equal opportunity for success based on their own individual achievement and merit. It is a site where ideology and inequality fully converge. The focus on education is partly methodological as well: interviewees needed something concrete to talk about in order to focus their interviews, to access their views in depth, and to engage them fully in a topic as complex as the intersection of inequality and ideology. Education was something for parents to latch onto in their conversations and was something they all had in common since schooling is required for all American children. Narrowing the focus on education even more precisely, this book examines how parents make decisions about where to send their children to school, looking particularly at the roles that wealth and ideology play in guiding those choices.

A special emphasis is placed on wealth privilege, and while parents of various socioeconomic backgrounds were interviewed, I focus the analysis on middle- and upper-class white parents who have experienced the benefits and advantages of family wealth. Scrutinizing privileged populations, positions of relative power, and structures of advantage should be an important piece of any research or policy agenda aimed at furthering our understanding of inequality. Yet rarely in the mainstream academic literature, or even in the popular media, are privileged groups scrutinized with the same intense focus as are disadvantaged groups. Sociology is just as culpable of this bias,[47] and even sociological studies of wealth have focused much more on those disadvantaged by structured inequalities than those privileged by them. The patterns, dynamics, and policy implications of the reproduction of wealth in families are just as important as the patterns, dynamics, and policy implications of asset poverty to our understanding of the social forces contributing to the wealth gap's continual growth and potential future decline. As other sociologists have noted, "Hardly ever do social scientists ask: 'Why are the rich wealthy?' in the same way we often ask why the poor are poor."[48] Furthermore, even in those studies that do spotlight privilege, the vantage points of individuals and groups in privileged positions—their worldviews, perspectives, and beliefs—are rarely considered in regard to the perpetuation of inequality. Studies of inequality have almost uniformly focused attention on "what the social structure looks like from the bottom" rather than the top.[49] This study not only looks closely at the intergenerational transmission of privilege in wealth-holding families, but asks a question that has rarely, if ever, been directly asked of them: How do they understand and justify the privileges of family wealth vis-à-vis their conviction in the values of meritocracy?

Finally, this book looks at race and class inequality with a particular theoretical goal: to expand our understanding of how we—in our day-to-day lives—are impacted by the inheritance of, and participate in the maintenance of, the structures, processes, and mechanisms that uphold these intergenerational inequalities. While race and class inequalities may be conceived of separately for analytic purposes, they are intricately linked. The two are interwoven in a complex and multidimensional system of stratification that manifests and generates inequality; they "work simultaneously and each can magnify or mitigate the effects of the other."[50] While scholars have argued the primacy of each over the other,[51] this debate is irrelevant for the purposes of this book. Rather than obscuring the connectedness of race and class, clarifying that connectedness—that interaction and dynamic—is more central to this project.[52] Although most sociologists agree that both race and class are social constructions, they also agree that the consequences of these constructions have had—and continue to have—very real consequences. Those consequences, rather than the constructs themselves, are the subject of scrutiny here.

If we accept that race and class are social constructions, then we must accept that we—either intentionally or by default—contribute to the maintenance of such constructions. Their impact on us is very real, as are the consequences of our participation in them; as the Thomas theorem says, "if we define our situations as real they are real in their consequences."[53] Understanding how people actively shape the perpetuation of inequalities is imperative to understanding not only those inequalities themselves, but the persistence, evolution, and potential dissolution of them. If we are to move forward in our understanding of social reproduction and social change, we must come to terms with the roles *we* play in perpetuating and changing the social problems we are concerned about. We must come to terms with the fact that the dilemmas that we face, the predicaments we are in, the quandaries that trouble us as individuals and in families— these, when taken together in sum totals of millions, are often much more patterned socially than they are distinctive to us personally. In order to come to terms with these issues, we must first identify and clarify them. American sociologist C. Wright Mills highlighted this goal as the special mandate of sociology: to further our understanding of the contrast between social-structural public issues and idiosyncratic private troubles.[54] It is too simplistic to say that individuals are solely responsible for their own decisions, or that social forces determine our lives despite our personal decisions.[55] The challenge for us is to pinpoint where structures and daily life intersect.[56]

Looking for Answers

Two sets of interviews were conducted to collect the data that is the heart of this book.[57] The first set came out of a large research project that I worked on with sociologist Thomas Shapiro while I was a doctoral student. These interviews were conducted over an eighteen-month period from January 1998 through June 1999. The participants were parents of school-age children from three metropolitan areas: Boston, Los Angeles, and St. Louis. One hundred eighty-two families (232 individuals) were included in the first phase of interviews, which consisted of approximately one-half black and one-half white families. The majority of the families were from the middle-class, though poor, working-class, and upper-middle-class families were also interviewed.

The first phase of interviews involved in-depth discussions with families concerning their assets, income, and decision-making processes regarding where they lived and sent their children to school. Participants were asked to discuss a host of topics including their family background, their parents' level of occupational and educational achievement, their life trajectories, their educational experiences, and their occupational history. Extensive and detailed questions were asked about income and assets, including questions about all forms of wealth and financial investments. The interviews included a series of questions about asset acquisition, and participants were asked to describe all assets they had ever received, given, or may expect in the future. They discussed at length their own senses of financial security (or lack thereof) and their plans for the future. Participants were asked about where they live and why. They were asked about where they send (or would be sending) their children to school and why. They gave detailed histories of why they chose to live in their neighborhoods and how they chose their children's schools.

The scope of information regarding families' wealth portfolios and their school decision-making was enormous. As I began to analyze the data, it quickly became clear to me that a significant and unexpected pattern was emerging: although the American Dream was not a focus of the project and participants were not asked about it, the families explicitly brought it up and evoked the idea of it in their conversations, stories, and accounts. They repeatedly used the American Dream as a major framework through which they explained their perspectives, used it to justify their own experiences, and relied upon it in their explanations for how things work in American society. This was true for families across the board. Especially striking was how interview participants used the notion of meritocracy to explain their worldviews and incorporated it into their decision-making processes—particularly in terms of education and where they were sending their children to school. The American Dream thus became a consistent theme of the research project—by the interview participants' own doing.

In examining parents' use of the American Dream ideology in the first set of interviews, a subset of those interviews emerged as particularly interesting to me: affluent parents who had received extensive intergenerational transfers and were now in the process of passing along the privileges of family wealth to their own children. These families commonly expressed their beliefs in meritocracy, incorporating it into their explanations for their financial success and upper-class social positioning, despite the fact that much of their relative social status and much of what they owned had not been earned by them individually. This was remarkable to me, especially because these families who had received the most unearned advantages—while acknowledging the generosity of their extended families—consistently and adamantly used their belief in meritocracy to justify their social positioning as individually earned and deserved. I wanted to know more about these families who had received considerable ascribed advantages, yet explained their own life trajectories as examples of individual hard work and American Dream success stories.

During the summer of 2003, I conducted a second phase of interviews to specifically target wealthy families and to focus discussion explicitly around the theme of the American Dream. While the first phase of interviews had not asked any of the families to explain their perspectives on wealth inequality or meritocracy, the second phase aimed to do just that. Furthermore, I wanted to confront families directly with this paradox—the contradiction between their inherited privilege of private family wealth and their belief in meritocracy. My goal was to find out how they reconciled this inconsistency in their own minds and made sense of it given their direct experiences.[58]

The second phase of interviewing took place from June through August of 2003. These interviews were with wealthy families from the metropolitan areas of Washington, D.C. and New York City. Twenty families (twenty-eight individuals) were included in this second phase, and the vast majority of them were white. Families were asked questions similar to those in the first phase, as well as a host of additional questions. They were asked about their perspectives on wealth and income, the acquisition and uses of family wealth, the intergenerational transfer of assets, and their philosophies on inherited money. They were asked about their perspectives on the financial help that they had received—financial help that they were in the process of passing along to their own children. They were also asked to discuss their perspectives on the American Dream; how it related to raising their children, as well as to the broader social contexts of education, wealth inequality, perceptions of social positioning, and so on. These interviews directly raised the contradiction between unearned wealth advantage and notions of meritocracy and equal opportunity, and families were asked how they understood this contradiction.

In both phases, families were identified through a structured "snowball" sampling method. They were interviewed by either myself or trained interviewers (students in sociology and social work from area universities) who were under my close supervision. Interviews took place in the families' homes, or if they preferred, the participants selected another place of their choosing for the interview. Some chose to meet in restaurants or cafés, and a few interviews were conducted in child-care centers, churches, or offices. If the family included two parents in the household, couples were interviewed together whenever possible so that the perspectives of both parents could be elicited. All of the interviews were semistructured, in-depth conversations that lasted between one and three hours each. Each was recorded and transcribed.

The five major U.S. cities were not chosen to be representative of any particular subset of the population, and the sample, while it is quite large for qualitative research of this kind, cannot be claimed to be generally applicable to the larger American population as a whole. Still, by focusing on a small piece of a much bigger picture I hope to shed light on mechanisms and processes in which we all participate and which have ramifications for each of us. One would hope that somewhere in the book, at least one of these families' stories will resemble that which a reader has known at some point in his or her life. Some of the families included are severely impoverished, living on assisted-living programs in low-income housing, while other families are interviewed at their exquisite vacation homes on the New Jersey shore. There are working-class families with children in severely underfunded St. Louis urban public schools, as well as families with children who attend some of the most exclusive private preparatory schools in Washington, D.C. There are middle-class families from the Boston suburbs, and families of exceptional wealth who own multiple properties around the country. Given the sensitive and relatively controversial nature of the topics involved, it is also noteworthy that parents were quite forthcoming in their perspectives on wealth, inequality, education, and the American Dream. Given the diversity of the families' socioeconomic situations, and the remarkably candid tone of their interviews, most of us would probably be hard-pressed to not come across just one that seems familiar. In fact, I suspect that we will recognize our friends, neighbors, colleagues, and even ourselves in the words spoken by the people interviewed here.

Enduring Patterns

The perspectives and experiences of the families interviewed will—I believe—resonate with many of us. I have purposefully avoided giving a lot of descriptive detail about the families whose quotations appear in these pages. I do this not so much to hide their identities, but because I do not think it is necessary; the quotations were selected because I thought they were the most representative, not because they reveal anything exceptional about the individuals who articulated them.[59] They could have come from any of the interviews with families like them, or they could have come from just about anyone you or I might know in similar circumstances. My hope is that rather than seeing them as unusual we will recognize them as quite usual—and that this, in itself, will help call into question aspects of our collective experience and our collective action (and inaction) that normally go unquestioned.

The ways in which wealth is accumulated, used, and passed along in families is a subject we know relatively little about. While the study of wealth has recently begun to witness an explosion of attention in the research literature most of this work has focused on understanding the landscape of wealth inequality. The sociology of wealth has mapped out this terrain, but has not yet approached it from the inside out. In addition, the vast majority of the scholarship on wealth has focused on those at the disadvantaged end of the wealth gap. Few have sought to answer questions about *how* wealth actually works inside families who have it, and none have made an attempt to understand how these families think about their inherited privilege. What this requires is to get inside the heads of people and attempt to understand the inner workings of a very private part of their lives in order to see things from their perspectives. In addition, we have to get inside the logic of the system to see how it is actually operating from day to day. These are important objectives because they have the potential to shed light on the mechanisms that are involved in the persistence of the wealth gap over time.

This book examines the extent to which parents—black and white, wealthy, middle-class, and poor—believe in the ideology of meritocracy, while at the same time understanding and acknowledging the advantages that private wealth can confer to children and families. On one hand, the families interviewed recognize and acknowledge how significant structured wealth inequality is in shaping family trajectories and children's educational opportunities. On the other hand, they claim their social positions have been earned and deserved through hard work and individual achievement, or lack thereof. Wealthy families are particularly provocative to examine because their stories so clearly contradict the notion of meritocracy. The more privileged parents interviewed acknowledge the advantages they have received through family wealth, and acknowledge the advantageous educational opportunities they are now able to pass along to their children because of them. What is really intriguing, however, is that at the same time, these same families hold close to their hearts the idea that they have earned and deserved what they have, and they argue vehemently that their privileged positions have resulted from their individual hard work, efforts, and achievements.

Since family wealth is such a private matter, and normally so unspoken of, it is often largely invisible. Thus, families with wealth often take its privileges for granted as a "normal" part of life, and families without it are not always cognizant of what they are up against when they try to compare themselves to others. While families with wealth acknowledge their privilege and claim their positions are self-earned, the reverse is true as well: families who could not possibly compete with peers who are reaping the benefits of wealth legacies nonetheless blame themselves for coming up short. The families with which we spoke both believe in the ideology and acknowledge structured inequality at the same time. They uphold the contradiction between the American Dream and the power of wealth.

Throughout the book we hear perspectives of American families and we see patterns emerge. But these families tell us more than just interesting stories; their perspectives paint a picture of the sociological dynamics among race, wealth, education, and ideology in our society today. Their accounts reveal some of the processes through which inequality and ideology are being passed along. The interviews show not just differences but profound similarities among people from different race and class backgrounds. And they show the impact of these backgrounds on their children's school experiences and life trajectories. When taken together, these families' perspectives and experiences shed new light on the enduring patterns we have received and raise important questions about the legacies our own children will inherit.

2

Meritocracy and "Good" Schools

Interviewer: When you hear the phrase *the American Dream*, what do you think of? What does that mean to you?

Connor: I think it means opportunity. The chance to make something of your life and be successful and move up in the economic class system, or whatever you want to call it.

Interviewer: How realistic do you think the American Dream is in today's society?

Connor: I think it's still pretty attainable. I think it's still real.

Interviewer: Okay, what role does wealth or class play in someone's ability to attain that dream in this country today?

Connor: I think it plays a very small role. If an individual wants to overcome either their class or some other drawback, they can.

—Connor Spence, pharmacy industry corporate
executive, white, Washington, D.C.

Most of us do not recall the first time we heard of the American Dream. Few of us probably remember being taught what it is. It is hard to trace back our understanding of it, hard to know how we know it. Yet we do know it, we recognize what it is, we seem to have learned it along the way. The American Dream encapsulates deeply held tenets of dominant merican culture and while all Americans may not feel compelled by it, many do. In the Post–Civil Rights Era, the beliefs in individualism and equal opportunity at the heart of the American Dream are also in the hearts of many of us.

More than anything else, our discussions with families pointed to this reality. The prominence of the American Dream in framing their perspectives, decisions, and experiences was profound—especially in regard to their children's educations. Regardless of whether the inter-viewer initiated it, parents evoked the American Dream throughout their interviews; they stressed its importance to their understanding of their children's life chances, and, when asked what the American Dream meant to them, parents responded in remarkably similar ways.

The American Dream of Meritocracy

The American Dream has been continually reinvented over time so that for each generation of Americans it has held different meanings.[1] And since "the American Dream" could mean different things to each of us, it might be more accurate to say "the American Dreams." At its core, however, some aspects of the Dream (or Dreams) are consistently fundamental. Simply, the American Dream explains the logic of our country's social system. It is a way (or perhaps *the* way) we understand how American society operates. It is how we make sense of our particular social structure. The American Dream rests on the idea that with hard work and personal determination any-one—regardless of background—has equal opportunity to achieve his or her aspirations. The American Dream promises that our sys-tem functions as a *meritocracy*. Within a meritocracy people get ahead or behind based on what they earn and deserve rather than what circumstances they were born into. This notion is central to the American Dream and is the central logic of how our system is supposed to operate. The American Dream, in many ways, defines us and sets our system apart from others.

Given the importance of the American Dream to our national identity, and the enormity of it in shaping our core ideologies, it is curi-ous how little attention the idea has received in academe, especially in the social sciences. Until relatively recently, no one had traced the his-tory of its origins, meanings, or cultural impacts. In the past decade, however, groundbreaking scholarship on the American Dream has yielded important understandings.[2] We know, for example, that the principles of the American Dream were promoted by even the very first settlers to arrive from Britain. Later, the American Dream was central to the charter of the United States when the Declaration of Independence was created. And, although the phrase "the American

Dream" does not appear to have been coined until around 1931, it has quickly become recognizable the world over.[3] The American Dream is, for better or for worse, the central creed of our nation.[4]

As a creed, the American Dream represents a basic belief in the power and capacity of the individual.[5] Deeply embedded in this belief is a particular notion of individual agency—the idea that over the course of our own lives we are each accountable for whatever position in which we find ourselves.[6] Full collective potential for this agency, though, depends on exactly that which the dream promises: A system of opportunity, so that regardless of background each individual has an equal chance to prosper. The American Dream promises that an egalitarian system will allow individuals to advance based on their own merits. This promise resonates throughout contemporary American society telling us—through multiple variations on a theme, through school assignments and television advertisements, through song lyrics and newspaper stories—that in a meritocratic process we rise or fall self-reliantly. So, despite differences across generations and regardless of the fact we each have unique hopes and dreams, we share the American Dream of meritocracy in common—that is, we are each subject, in one way or another, to our nationalist ideology of meritocracy.

Meritocracy explains not only how our society works but how inequality exists. The idea is that what we reap—good or bad—is merited; whatever we have, whatever our status, whatever our place in the social world, we earn. A system of meritocracy does not assert equality per se—within any social hierarchy some individuals will inevitably be positioned higher and some lower; rather, it justifies inequality of social positioning by the meritocratic process itself. Inequality of outcomes is justified and legitimized by equality of opportunity. This meritocratic idea has roots dating back to the British colonialists' aspirations for a society founded in a "natural aristocracy." In their vision, upward mobility and prominence would be merited and achieved rather than ascribed. For those first families settling from Europe, this vision was a defiant rebellion from other forms of social structure where social rank was inherited based on such distinctions as family lineage, royalty, and caste. Although they never precisely defined how merit should be measured, it was always clear how it should *not* be: achievement based on individual merit is *not* unearned advantage; it is *not* inherited privilege.[7] A meritocratic system is contingent upon a societal commitment to fair competition so that no individual or group is advantaged or disadvantaged by the positions or predicaments of their ancestors.

The American Dream of meritocracy is at once a simple idea and a complex national ethos. For some people the dream may simply be owning a home, while for others it might be striking it rich. Although those may be part of what the American Dream means for many people, as a foundational ideology it is about more than material abundance or a place with streets paved with gold. It is about opportunity—not just *an* opportunity, but equal opportunity. It is about not just *a* chance, but equal chances. In her landmark book *Facing Up to the American Dream: Race, Class, and the Soul of a Nation*, political scientist Jennifer Hochschild explicates the American Dream and identifies its main tenets. She distinguishes key premises that interlock to form its philosophical foundation. These premises include meritocracy—the notion that in our social system upward and downward mobility is based on personal achievement so that people get ahead or behind based on merit; equal opportunity—the notion that all members of society are given equal opportunity for social mobility; individualism—the notion that each individual makes it on his or her own; and the open society—the notion that the United States is a free country, the melting pot of the world, the land of opportunity for all people.[8] As Hochschild outlines, the American Dream is a set of deeply held beliefs, a particular mind-set. It is a particular way of viewing the world, and it is a particular way in which we want the world to view us. For many Americans, the American Dream is a great source of pride.[9] But even many who question it as an accurate portrayal of social life believe strongly in the egalitarian and inclusive principles for which it stands.

As a dominant ideology, the American Dream echoes throughout our nation; it carries on through generations and can crystallize in our hearts and minds.[10] But it can also be easily taken for granted, for as central the American Dream is to our national identity, we don't consciously reflect on it often. As historian Jim Cullen has noted, the American Dream is "an idea that seems to envelop us as unmistakably as the air we breathe."[11] We can be reminded of it, without even being aware, every time we are told that we will achieve if we work hard enough, or that we could have achieved if we had only worked harder. The American Dream can inspire great aspirations and explain great achievements, and it can depress us as we ponder our regrets. It is malleable enough to fit in almost any social situation. We can use it to justify our accomplishments: I earned it on my own. This is the result of my hard work. I deserve this. And we can feel the sting of it as we question ourselves: Should I have worked harder? Could I have gone further? Why am I not where he is? And, we can use it to question others' social standing: Why doesn't she try harder? Doesn't he want more? Why don't they make better choices? The American Dream is all around us, and, in many ways it is in us.

Ultimately, the American Dream is an explanation for the hierarchical ordering of our class positions in our social world. It explains our relative rank as the result of solely our own doing, not as the result of social forces or the circumstances we find ourselves in. It is not surprising, then, that Americans might genuinely believe that they independently earn and deserve their class positions—the dominant ideology of our culture tells them so. This internalized sense of class positioning has been the subject of scholarly research, especially in regard to working-class and poor families. In Richard Sennett and Jonathan Cobb's pivotal book *The Hidden Injuries of Class,* for example, they discuss the "hidden injury" of the internal class conflict experienced among working-class men. They write, "Every question of identity as an image of social place in a hierarchy is also a question of social value.... This is the context in which all questions of personal and social legitimacy occur."[12] The American Dream helps to sustain these "hidden injuries" by bombarding people with the message that their social place—and their social value, their self-worth—is directly and exclusively the result of their own actions.

In their interviews for this book, people spoke in depth and at length about the American Dream, despite the fact that in the first 182 interviews the families were not even asked about it. These parents were told that the project was to study assets and inequality, and during the interviews they were asked to speak about the communities in which they lived, their children's schools, and their families' financial histories. Repeatedly, however, the focus of the interviews turned to beliefs in meritocracy as families consistently brought up the subject and wove it into the conversations. I must admit that I myself was surprised with the extent to which the interview findings were so ideological in nature. And I was even more surprised when interviews—including those interviews from the second phase that *did* directly ask people about their thoughts on the American Dream—revealed the depths of people's commitment to, and belief in, meritocracy as a real and valid explanation for how contemporary American society operates. People from all walks of life spoke forthrightly of their belief in meritocracy not just as rhetoric, but as an accurate explanation of our social system.

Trying to confirm these findings has been frustrating due to the lack of qualitative studies that have asked people in depth about their perspectives on the American Dream. Curiously, even in terms of quantitative studies, surprisingly few public opinion polls have been conducted on the subject of the American Dream. However, related social survey data that do exist reflect that Americans overwhelmingly believe that their country operates as a meritocracy.[13] Indeed, after his review of such data, political scientist Everett Carll Ladd concluded that survey research "shows Americans holding tenaciously and distinctively to the central elements of their founding ideology." He found Americans' belief in the American Dream to be more intense, pervasive, and firmly entrenched than is generally recognized.[14] Very recent qualitative research on Post–Civil Rights Era views also finds that in in-depth interviews people are remarkably insistent in their beliefs that the playing field is level, that meritocracy is real.[15] While these findings are definitely in line with my own, perhaps the most compelling affirmation for me has been to discover that other sociologists doing in-depth interviewing on subjects *not explicitly focused* on the American Dream are finding, as I have, that respondents consistently evoke the American Dream—specifically the notion of meritocracy—as their own theme in interviews.[16] In the two hundred interviews conducted for this study, what families said—about their views, their decisions, and their experiences—was explicitly framed by their belief in meritocracy. These families' perspectives give a vivid account of the place and significance of the American Dream in contemporary life.

Parents' Beliefs in the American Dream

Interviewer: When you hear the phrase *the American Dream*, what do you think of?

Suzanne: My initial reaction is, just know that we live in a country that's democratic and that anybody—given hard work—regardless of their economic background, has an opportunity. It's not dictated for them. And they can make it if they just have the right values and they have the drive, that they can do it.

Drew: I guess it depends what class you're from. You might have a different goal or dream. And from the group that we grew up with, probably the most common dream was having a house, family, and all that. It's all yours—but you *earn* it.

Suzanne: That's right, it's whatever you are, everybody is gonna have a different goal. But I think again it has a lot to do with knowing you have opportunities where a lot of other countries don't offer you that.

Interviewer: Okay. In your own opinion, how realistic is the American Dream in today's society?

Suzanne: I think it's realistic. Totally realistic. I think that kids—like, in the projects—it's not really clear to them that they're capable of doing that. With just a little bit of hard work and some aspiration you *can* pull yourself out of this. You don't *have* to continue the cycle. You *can* break it! ... They're *totally* capable. And they *totally* have opportunities.... They have opportunity here. They're not in Iraq where they're sheltered and they have no opportunities and it's not democratic!

Sitting on a plush leather couch in their living room, sipping ice water, Suzanne and Drew talked about the American Dream. A white, professional couple in their early thirties, the Wrights were each very accomplished and came from affluent family backgrounds. At the time of their interview, Suzanne was working for a small high-tech company of which she was part owner with her father. Drew was a very successful high-tech recruiter. Their condominium in an exclusive development in the metropolitan New York City area was beautifully appointed; they dressed meticulously, traveled frequently, and their lifestyle appeared to be more than comfortable. In their elevated status and social class positioning, the Wrights were somewhat exceptional in our sample, but in their perspectives on the American Dream, they were not.

The Wrights and other families repeatedly articulated a similar view: that the American Dream is a realistic explanation for how our social system operates and that it provides a sound justification for where an individual stands in the hierarchy of social class positioning. While they did not use the word *meritocracy* to describe it, meritocracy was, in effect, what was discussed most often. Families were consistent in their explanations that in the United States social class positions are earned, deserved, and merited based on individual achievement or lack thereof. Broaching the topics of wealth and inequality inevitably generated discussions of individualism and equal opportunity. In these discussions, people's perspectives were clear. Essentially, they believed that with hard work and aspirations, people's chances are equal regardless of their backgrounds. As we will see in later chapters, these same families contradicted these sentiments by also claiming that some individuals are advantaged and disadvantaged by their access to family wealth. However, their first claim—and truly, a seemingly genuine one on their parts—was always that meritocracy is real. This was not just a rhetorical stance; families from across the race and class spectrum used notions of meritocracy to explain that their own social positions and the positions of others were legitimately the result of their own doing. Just as Suzanne and Drew had articulated a strong meritocratic stance, Anjillette, a black single mother from the Los Angeles area who was working as a vocational nurse, was explicit about the same themes.

> Anjillette: You know, I just say it's a matter of time, and just really buckling down and getting it done.

> Interviewer: You mentioned, Anjillette, that you know people who have two or three jobs, and they're just not making it. What do you think causes that? Or why do you think that's happening?

> Anjillette: You know, I really won't say. Because I think those are people that *choose* to do that.

Parents evoked, as Anjillette did, the American Dream's core credo of meritocracy to explain why people rise and fall. The underlying—or, in Anjillette's case, overt—presumption was that people independently *choose* their relative class circumstances. Regardless of their own social class positioning, and despite their vastly differing life experiences, the parents interviewed asserted that individual hard work is the main determinant of upward and downward social mobility. Lodged within this logic was a profound optimism about an individual's life chances. As one father from a wealthy white family in the New York City area insisted, "Hard work can go a long way toward overcoming most any obstacle!" But this adamant meritocratic belief had a flip side too: just as "success" was perceived as one's personal achievement, "failure," too, was seen as the direct result of one's own doing. In an interview with the Gordons, a well-off white couple from the Washington, D.C. area, James, a public relations director for a major D.C. media firm, was asked "What is 'the American Dream,' in your own opinion?" He responded, "The American Dream for me is equal opportunity. Second, no discrimination. Third, you have the right to be what you want to be. And the only other thing—which I feel—is you could do it if you want."

Those who were interviewed had a clear understanding of what the American Dream was, they used its basic notions in their explanations of contemporary social life, and they claimed to believe in it as a valid descriptor of the United States' social system. In the second phase of interviews, after having given their own definitions (such as James's, above), families were then given a clear-cut definition of the American Dream and asked what they thought of it. Remarkably, all twenty families responded by saying that they wholeheartedly agreed with it.

> Interviewer: Research has said that the American Dream is the idea that with hard work and desire, individual potential is unconstrained. They say that the American Dream promises that everyone, regardless of background, succeeds through their own actions. It's the idea that we get ahead through individual achievement alone. That our family backgrounds don't matter. What do you think of this definition?
>
> Lily: I think it's quite accurate. I do believe in that.
>
> Interviewer: Any part of it that you disagree with or you would alter?
>
> Lily: No. I don't disagree with it at all.

Given the heavily individualistic focus of the definition that was presented, I would have thought that at least some of the people interviewed would have found it questionable. However, none did.

Public opinion polls on Americans' values and beliefs generally confirm these findings. Although only a small number have been conducted, polls related to the American Dream show that Americans consider it to be an accurate description of how their country operates. One study found that when asked, "Do you believe in the American Dream?" at least three-fourths of the population replied that they did.[17] In another poll of over eight hundred parents, 98 percent of them said that they thought "equal opportunity for people regardless of their race, religion or sex" was an important or absolutely essential American value; 84 percent said that they believed the United States is "a unique country that stands for something special in the world"; and 99 percent agreed with the statement that "with hard work, people have a chance to move up and prosper."[18] In a similar vein, related social surveys also confirm the use of the notion of meritocracy in Americans' individualistic explanations for racial inequality. In their beliefs about the black-white inequality gap, Howard Schuman and Maria Krysan found, for example, that "most whites tend to place responsibility mainly on blacks themselves, with the primary emphasis on a presumed lack of motivation on the part of blacks."[19] Also, a Gallup Poll conducted in 2003 found that, in terms of education, 97 percent of Americans believe that individual factors (such as home life and upbringing)—not social factors—are to blame for differences in black and white students' achievement. In the same poll, 95 percent of the respondents thought that individual students' interest or disinterest in education was the cause for inequalities in student outcomes.[20]

A looming question in the research literature is to what extent Americans' beliefs in the American Dream of meritocracy cut across race and class groups. While the interviews for this book found that black and white families from various socioeconomic backgrounds seemed to hold equally deep beliefs in the legitimacy of the American Dream, previous studies show more mixed results. In her book *Facing Up to the American Dream*, Hochschild's analysis suggests that in the era since the 1970s Americans do pervasively believe in the American Dream as an accurate prescription for society, and almost equally as a description of their own lives. She finds, however, that upwardly mobile middle-class blacks' beliefs in the American Dream have been slightly declining. She also found that while poor and working-class blacks' circumstances have stagnated or worsened, their belief in the American Dream has remained persistent. Overall, Hochschild's research shows that the American Dream is "deeply embedded in most Americans' image of themselves and their society," but that blacks are becoming more discouraged about whether the American Dream applies to them as whites become considerably *more* convinced that it applies to blacks.[21] The oft-cited research in *The Hidden Injuries of Class* by Richard Sennett and Jonathan Cobb also observed that working-class people clung fiercely to the idea of the American Dream.[22]

At the same time, Jay McLeod's famous research with seriously disadvantaged urban teenagers found that the black youth he studied believed more strongly in the American Dream than did the similarly situated white youth in his sample. McLeod found the white teenagers disillusioned with the legitimacy of basic principles of meritocracy, while the black teenagers continually claimed that there was "no one to blame but me."[23] Also, Carl Husemoller Nightengale's ethnographic work documents how severely impoverished young black children have increasingly been "buying into" the American Dream over the past thirty-five years.[24] Finally, new research on post–civil rights attitudes and beliefs seems to confirm an increasingly literal interpretation of the American Dream in recent decades. Burgeoning literature in this field suggests that in the contemporary United States people hold very strong beliefs in the reality of equal opportunity in the wake of 1960s and '70s social movements.[25]

In the interviews conducted for this book, all parents were equally insistent on the reality of the American Dream of meritocracy. They used it not only to explain their current circumstances and the circumstances of others, but—notably—to fuel their faith in the boundless possibilities for the future. They invested their hopes for the next generation in it. This was one of the most salient features of the interview data: parents—regardless of background—relied heavily on the American Dream to understand the possibilities for children, especially their own children. Daniel, a white corporate executive from the D.C. area, explained as follows; his wife Karen, a homemaker, nodded in enthusiastic agreement while he spoke.

> Daniel: Defining what the American Dream is for each person is different for each individual.
>
> Interviewer: What would it be for you?
>
> Daniel: For me it is to see my children have a decent, honorable job. They earn a living, enjoy their life. That's what is important to me. Some say the American Dream is to get rich or to become a senator or whatever. No. I don't look at it that way. For me, the American Dream is to have the success if you work for it. To be free to live the way you want to.

The American Dream was entwined with parents' deep-seated hope in their children's futures so that the two seemed inseparable in their minds. And parents in dire circumstances were no less hopeful about their children's life chances than were parents in privileged positions. This hopefulness was so fierce that it eclipsed doubt and overshadowed even the most extreme disadvantages facing families. For example, Sandra Breslin, an unemployed black mother in Boston, was full of hope for her children, despite the fact that she desperately struggled to make ends meet. Coming from a family with a long history of poverty and struggle, she confessed that no one she knew had been able to "break out of poverty," but she professed nothing but pure hopefulness for her daughter and her son to do so:[26] "My daughter says she wants to be a nurse or a doctor. My son says he wants to be a lawyer or a fireman. And my daughter tells me she's going to take care of me when she gets older. So she, she's like a little doctor to me, 'cause she has this little doctor kit, and she works on it, and she plays like she's a doctor. So I think she already knows what she wants to be."

For the families interviewed, hope for their children's futures was, in large part, what believing in the American Dream was all about. Parents believed that their children's futures were bright and wanted the best for them. Their hope was anchored in their ability to see beyond the boundaries of their current circumstances, whatever those may be. Hope is "natural to the human heart," says Andrew Delbanco,[27] and this is especially true, I would argue, when it comes to parents' hopes for their children. The American Dream of meritocracy serves to justify parents' hopefulness, regardless of what they may have seen or experienced in the world around them. Molly and Paul Stone, a white homemaker and physician, respectively, from the New York City area and both from privileged family backgrounds, expressed the same general themes as did the other parents. While their social status and financial situation contrasted greatly with that of others such as Sandra Breslin, the Stones' optimistic outlook and hopeful meritocratic beliefs were quite similar to Sandra's and the other parents.

> Interviewer: When you hear the phrase *the American Dream*, what do you think of? What does that mean to you?

> Paul: Well it means, I guess, economic success and being able to live in a nice neighborhood.... And being able to support your family and being able to put your kids through good schools.

> Interviewer: In your own opinion how realistic is the American Dream in today's society?

> Paul: I think it is achievable. Whatever one's dreams are, I think they are realistic. And there's no reason why you can't achieve them.

> Molly: That's absolutely right. Absolutely.

The Great Equalizer and the Key to the Dream

If the American Dream of meritocracy is our country's promise, public education is what ensures that promise to all children. Education—more than any other institution—is the system's way of making certain that achievement is independently earned, not tied to one's background. Parents emphasized that it was because of this that they saw their hopes for their children as not just a dream, but truly possible. Joyce and Eliston Meador, a black couple, both social workers, who lived in inner-city St. Louis, exemplified this emphasis in their interview. Eliston explained, "One of the things that helps a person move from poverty to financial independence, or at least having a decent income ... you can live off of, is education. I mean that's the level that everybody can ascend to regardless of race, creed or color. If you're poor, I don't care if you're white, black, red, yellow—doesn't make any difference. If you don't have an education, you are not going to be upwardly mobile. So everybody has an opportunity to move up from poverty."

The American Dream does not guarantee that everyone will make it in America, but it presumes that despite inequalities in their circumstances each individual will have a fair chance, an equal opportunity, and no one will be unfairly advantaged or disadvantaged. Given that we are born into different families with very different backgrounds, the system must provide some way to balance out opportunities. A major role of the institution of education is to do just that; it is supposed to level out what is an initially uneven playing field. The parents interviewed clung to this idea. The interview with the Phillips, a white family from the suburbs of Washington D.C., provides just one example. Tallie, a homemaker, was quite outspoken about her opinions on the matter, and her husband Marcus, a financial advisor, wholeheartedly agreed.

> Interviewer: Do you think that every child that works hard in school has the same chances at success in life or are there other things involved?
>
> Tallie: I think they have the same chances.
>
> Interviewer: So you think regardless of the neighborhood or the type of school, you think as long as someone applies himself or herself that chances are equal?
>
> Tallie: I do think so, yes.
>
> Marcus: Yes.

While later we will see that parents also did question its legitimacy, they repeatedly asserted the notion that education is the Great Equalizer. The idea of the Great Equalizer is that no matter whom you are, no matter what financial or social background you come from, no matter what your family situation is, the school system diminishes inequalities of circumstance and provides opportunities to get ahead. In this way, the Great Equalizer is central to the proper functioning of the whole system: the institution of education is supposed to be where meritocracy is operationalized, actualized, and realized. It is supposed to ensure that regardless of background—regardless of whatever contexts of advantage or disadvantage we might be born into—our own positions in society are ultimately earned, deserved, and achieved by us and us alone. The families—including the Mitchels, an affluent white family with handsome homes in downtown Washington, D.C. and in rural Virginia—were consistent on this point. When asked how essential they thought education is to one's success in this country, Jacob responded right away: "I think that education is the Great Leveler. That's what sets me and my family apart is our education, advanced education. And everyone in my family has at least a master's or a double master's. And I think everyone has done well because of their education. We didn't start out with much. My father didn't have much. But I think the children, through education, ended up doing very well."

Education was viewed as the Great Equalizer making the American Dream real, and also as *the key* to the dream. Education provides, at least in theory, a clear route to follow: if you work hard enough in school then you can be anything, do anything, rise up to any level you choose. In the minds of the parents, however, this was more than just theory—as Jacob's quote above illustrates, parents saw it as real. Whether it had been so in their own experience or not, parents seemed to genuinely believe in education as the key to their children's future success. As such, it held paramount importance in the raising of their children; they understood their role as parents to include—as an important part—navigating the education system for their kids. Kimberly Harmon, a black single mother who was working as a receptionist in a downtown Boston office, explained her perspective regarding her son:

> Kimberly: Hopefully he can get a good education, 'cause that's the most important thing.
>
> Interviewer: Why is it so important? Why do you think a good education is so important?
>
> Kimberly: A good education is good because without education what are you going to be? You need your education. Everybody should know that!

For the parents with whom we spoke, education was of the utmost importance. When asked, "Why do you think education is so important?" parents responded quickly and matter-of-factly. Their tones implied that—as Kimberly Harmon had said outright—"Everybody should know that!" Education was so important because, as Melissa Desmond, a white, unemployed mother from Boston explained, it was perceived as determining life chances for a child.

Interviewer: Why do you think education is so important?

Melissa: Because if you don't know anything, you won't go nowhere. You won't. And I want my son to do something with his life. I don't want him to—I mean, I know, it's his choice which road he chooses, but if I can try and like show him, you know what I mean? That there's, you know, that he can *make* it by going the right way.

And, as Tonya Weymouth, a black military supply clerk from Boston explained, it was perceived as a child's ticket to success: "I want her to do better than I did. I want her to further her education. Because without it there's nothing out there. So your dream, if you want to be a doctor, something like that, you have to go to school for the education. And you can do anything you pretty much want to do, as long as you have the education. So, I'm all for that."

Previous studies of families from across race and class spectra confirm that since education is seen by people as the "principal means to economic advancement" in our current system, it thus becomes the focus of much parental energy.[28] Parents, such as the Wards, a black, working-class family from Boston, spoke passionately about their views regarding the role of education in the shaping of their children's future life trajectories. Eleanor, a homemaker, and Anthony, a carpenter, were interviewed at their small home in a black working-class neighborhood of Boston. Eleanor did most of the talking and was passionate about her children's education. While Anthony had a more quiet personality, he agreed with his wife on the importance of their children's education.

Eleanor: We all know those are minimum wage jobs—McDonald's, Burger King, all those places. But, if you feel you don't want to work those places, go to school! Go to school! Get an education! In a field that will interest you, whether it's day care, kitchen work, whatever. Go to school! Don't just sit on your behind just because you can't find a job that you want to pay you more. You're not going to get paid no more than what your experience will cover. So don't go out there thinking you're going to get a twelve-dollar-an-hour job knowing you don't have a high school diploma.... You should never go through life doing nothing, or depending on other people....

Without education you're not going to be anywhere. This is what you're going to have to do: you have to go to school whether you like it or not! And let it go at that!

Eleanor's and other parents' intense focus on the importance of their children's schooling is understandable when one considers how much they perceived was riding on it. In their views, their children's success was in large part hinging on education. Schooling was not just seen as an opportunity, but as the primary pathway to success in the social system. And, for many parents who were hoping for their children to surpass their own social class position (many poor and working-class parents especially, both black and white), education was seen as the avenue to that upward mobility.

Steven: My priority thing is school for the kids.... Their school, their education, it's important.

Interviewer: Why is that important?

Steven: Because society demands it and not anything else. They want to have a good job? They want to have some kind of a career when they get big?—They need to have a good education! ... Just that's going to be the thing that's going to divide poor and the rich.

For these parents, as *the* key to the American Dream, much was riding on education. As one parent, Elaine, explained, "We're all constantly thinking about schools, and constantly thinking about your kid's education all the time, and what you can do about it.... I believe it's *sooo* important, it's the most important thing for any kid. Because at least then you've got a choice.... If you've never had a decent education, you're stuck, you're trapped." And so much was at stake; as another parent, Lisa, explained, "Knowledge is power. Without education, you'd have nothing. With education, you can do and say whatever you want, but you need to understand this society out here. That's the bottom line. Have knowledge... definitely, definitely. Without that education, that's the struggle. Unfortunately, I wasn't able to go to college and increase my knowledge, but I do the best I can for my children. I count my blessings. For them I want better."

Parents of all race and class backgrounds heavily valued education and expressed intense commitment to their children's schooling. However, working-class and poor parents, who were disproportionately black, conveyed a particular depth and urgency to their commitment.

This was rooted in their hopes for their children to do better than themselves and in their beliefs that schooling was, really, the only answer. Karen and Billy Jones, a black, working-class couple from Los Angeles, were adamant in their view. As Karen explained, "Education is—it's the only way the kids are going to make it. That's it. Without that they will end up with the same exact life that my mother and I had. We can't have that! Anything to prevent my children from walking down that path. That's why an education is so important."

Not only did they want their children to be happy in their futures—as all parents did—but these parents consistently articulated that they "wanted better" for their children, that they "wanted them to go above" where they themselves had gone, that they did not want them to follow in their footsteps, or end up in situations like their own.

> Ana: Right now I'm just trying to provide as a mother, as a parent.... It is important to have an education. So that's a priority. That's my focus right now. I'm in working-class poor. There is no doubt about it. So I'm always—I'm always going to be the working-class poor. I'm never going to be above and I'm never going to be below, and that's why I'm focusing a lot of my money on my children's education. Because I want them to go above. Not that stuck in the middle where I am.

> Interviewer: Do you think education is going to provide them with that?

> Ana: Yeah, because I don't have as much education as they will have.... Yeah, it's going to make a big difference. I'm going to make sure of it. It's a priority.

Reflecting on their own experiences, parents who were struggling repeatedly blamed their situations on themselves, and specifically on their own lack of educational achievement. They understood their roles to be, at least in part, to foster their children's upward mobility. They wanted their kids to be better educated than themselves, and they wanted them to value education more than they had while growing up. As one parent, Kim, noted, "I know now that an education is the most valuable thing that you can have. And in order to survive in this world, you have to have an education. And the reason I say that is because I've had such a struggle to survive because I don't have the education. So that would be my primary goal.... You know, 'cause one of my most—the biggest thing in my mind is to get my children an education."

Although this was most evident in interviews with relatively less affluent and disproportionately black families, even very wealthy and/or accomplished parents—the most upper-class and the most educationally, occupationally, and financially high-achieving that we interviewed—expressed hope for their children to do even better than they themselves had. So, while they had different life experiences, and while they were speaking from very different vantage points, parents shared their focus on their children's education. As one white father, a surgeon from the Washington D.C. area, said, "I think everybody in the world wants a better life for their children." And as another parent, a black mother and a customer service representative from the Los Angeles area, said, "I see a lot of different types of families at her school. All of them, I think, are dedicated to their children's education."

"It's Not Necessarily Fair, and It's Not Necessarily Right"

Now it's not necessarily fair and it's not necessarily right, but I think certain neighborhoods *are* better, certain schools *are* better, and your children *will* have a better childhood and better educational background because of where they go. But it's not right. I don't think it's necessarily right, but I think everyone should have the same opportunities my children do, but they don't.

—Lori Olsen, homemaker, white, St. Louis

Since education is so crucial to the American Dream, this is—at least in part—why Americans care so deeply about their schools.[29] The families interviewed were intent on making sure their own children got the best education possible but were concerned about the state of America's education system. Despite their faith in the American Dream and their claims that education was the Great Equalizer, they were also up-front about their perspectives that different schools provided vastly different opportunities for kids; for, as much as the families interviewed believed in the egalitarian principles of meritocracy, they were also faced with the reality of drastically disparate school systems. As Sarah Otis, a white freelance journalist from Boston, reflected on this reality, "I mean, it's just obvious to me that there's a severe problem in the United States with education right now. And it makes me so sad, though, that, you know, all kids—I mean, I just look at my daughter's class, you know? They're all bright, wonderful little kids, you know? They should all have an opportunity to receive a decent education. And, you know, it's just so profoundly unfair."

Of the 260 parents interviewed, not one of them claimed that schools in America are actually equal. One middle-class black father summed up their collective view when he said, "The more money you have, the better the neighborhood you live in. The better neighborhood, the more taxes, the better the school. Your kid goes where you live." Parents regularly brought up how they thought it unfair that some children had to attend poor-quality schools while others could attend excellent ones. They emphasized this inequality and criticized it. They were concerned about their own children and voiced concern for all children. The Paynes, a white family from St. Louis, were just one of those interviewed who talked at length about this. Debbie, a child care worker, and Bill, a painter, had two children who were ages nine and six at the time of their interview. As Debbie noted,

> In a lot of city schools it's very dangerous, and I feel sorry for the parents of some of the kids that are forced to send their kids to these schools. They don't have the money to send them to private schools and it's a shame that they can't be taken care of better. I mean, I don't understand why. You know? I just don't understand it. I mean, I just don't understand why they can't make their schools a safer place, because everybody—I don't care whether you're black or white, rich or poor—wants their children to be able to go to a safe school and learn. You know? I mean, I just feel that way. I work with black, white, Mexican, and it doesn't make any difference what religion and race you are. Everybody that has children would like their children—they would like to know that their children are going to a safe school, or being in a safe environment.... Like I said, we all want the same things for our kids and our family.

In regard to schools, the parents we interviewed all basically wanted the same things: they wanted their children to be safe and to have the best chances for promising futures. While perhaps some parents may be indifferent, for the parents with whom we spoke, providing the best education possible was at the center of this parental commitment. When asked, "What do you believe is the underlying reason parents try to give the best education to their children?" Carter Martin, a white father from a wealthy family background and an attorney in a high-powered Washington, D.C., law firm, responded genuinely by saying simply, "I think they want their children to succeed and have a happy life. It's a matter of love; it's a matter of feeling that that's the right thing to do."

To understand the depth of their commitment to their children's education, it is important to understand that—for these parents—it came down to trying to do the right thing for their children. Simply, providing their kids with a good education was a critical part of what it meant to them to be a *good* parent. It was intrinsic to good child rearing. "You want your children to have a good life," noted Emily, another parent. "Good parents want their child to be comfortable and to be happy and successful. So we try to give our children the best that we can and we also try to give them what we didn't have.... I think it is, I want my children to be the best person they can be with whatever they've gotten, whatever their god-given abilities are.... And I want to give them some push towards succeeding."

A parent's love for a child is a force to be reckoned with, and for the parents interviewed part of that love was lived out in wanting to provide the best for their kids that they could. Education was an important component of that. With education seen as the key to the American Dream, a lot was on the line, and children's education took on paramount importance for parents. But, while our country prides itself on the creed that all children deserve an education that gives them equal chances to succeed, these families knew—from their own experiences and observations—that schools were fundamentally and drastically unequal in terms of the opportunities that they provide to their students. So, for the families interviewed, the challenge was not simply to provide *an* education for their children—it was to try to ensure *the best possible* education for them. As Joyce Meador put it,

> I guess the way I look at it is I'm a taxpaying citizen. I pay taxes down here in the city of St. Louis, just like the people that do in Fenton, in the Rockwood district. And I don't feel that they or their children should have a better opportunity to get education, a free education, than my children are. If we are both paying taxes for education, then why, you know, why is it that if they don't go to school out there, they don't get a chance to do anything with computers, or do any French, and any of that kind of stuff, because they live in the city?... My main objective is their education. I think they deserve to get a good education.... Most people, when they find out, you know, we live in the heart of the city, and your kids go to that school [a suburban school], they're like, "How do they get

out there?" It's a voluntary deseg [desegregation] program. And, of course that district is gaining something from me signing up for the program, because they do get additional money from the government for that. But, by the same token, I still think that my kids have a better chance of an education, a better education from being in that school district.

In regard to school decisions for their children, the parents' struggle was to navigate as best they could a severely unequal educational arena. While they often expressed that they did not believe it to be fair, they were forthright in their view that not all schools are high quality schools. With only a finite number of "good" schools, only some children will get to attend them. And this invariably meant that other children, as one father, Daniel Graham said, will have to "stay behind"—not by a parent's choice necessarily, but because this is the reality of unequal schooling:

Every parent, no matter what, they want the best for their children.... I think that comes with being a parent. I mean it is, I guess, in parents' blood that you want to give the best for your children. No specific reason. It just comes from the heart, from blood. I don't know ... that's just—you want the best for your kids. At least from my point of view, it's not that I want to have somebody else being in a disadvantaged position. It's just you want to do or give the best to your children. It comes from the blood. That's one reason. It's not that you want to have some other person stay behind. It's just you want the best for your children.

"Wanting the best for their children" clearly came from the heart for Daniel and the other parents interviewed. What also seemed to come from the heart were these parents' claims that although inequity was inevitably the end result, they did not necessarily want other children to be hindered; they just wanted to make sure *their own children* were getting the best schooling they could. As Vivian Windrow, a middle-class black mother of an eight-year-old daughter in Los Angeles, commented, "We want her in a good school. I was afraid of what I've heard about the L.A. public schools, you know? And her dad felt the same way, because she's an only child. So we agreed that we would do whatever we could to make sure that she gets a good education.... I would do all that I can to find the best school for her. You know, 'cause I believe education is very important. You've got to have a good education or you're not going to be able to do anything for yourself down the road."

Vivian articulated precisely the sentiments that parent after parent had stressed: that, given their emphasis on education, they "would do whatever they could to make sure their children get a good education." This meant they had to get their children into a good school. First and foremost, however, parents had to figure out which schools were the "good" schools.

A "Good" School

What was considered to be a "good" school? Parents said that good schools had updated facilities and equipment, stimulating atmospheres, and high-quality educational programs. They said that they were safe, had teachers who were dedicated, small class sizes, computers, healthy environments, and successful graduates who went on to excel academically and occupationally. However, as much as parents described in detail the types of educational resources characteristic of "good" schools, rarely had they actually explored the availability of these traits when considering schools for their kids. Similarly, parents often emphasized the importance of a school's rankings or standardized test scores and were quick to point them out if they knew them—but they rarely did. A divergence between what these families said was important in considering schools and what actually had been determining factors in their decisions was transparent in the interviews.[30] What they overwhelmingly *had* relied upon in determining whether or not a school was "good" was one thing: simply, if it was located in a "good" neighborhood. For example, in an interview with the Smiths, a middle-class black family from Los Angeles, Leslie Smith, a realtor, kept referring to certain schools as "good schools." When asked directly, "What is a 'good' school?" she replied,

> It depends on the school, and where the school is *located*. I think the Fairburne School is a very good school. Comparing it to private schools, I would say it ranks just as high as some of the private schools. If I sent [my son] to our neighborhood school, which is South Street Elementary, I would say private schools are a lot better. So, just, I think it depends on where you are in the city. How much money gets filtered into the school. And, for me, what I've seen—I have friends that are teachers. They're good teachers, but they're in bad situations, down in South Central L.A., where they have forty kids in their class.... And I don't think those kids get a good education.

"Good" schools and "bad" schools were defined—first and foremost—by their location. Molisa Parks, a working-class, black single mother from St. Louis, put it bluntly: "I mean, we all know that kids in the county get a better education than kids in the city—as far as the atmosphere, the equipment they have to work with, the change of attitude of the kids. It's just class sizes, anything and everything, computer equipment!"

Even when parents mentioned specifics such as safety, class size, or equipment, they usually spoke of them in the context of location. Rarely did parents use any information other than its location to substantively inform their judgment of a school.

That parents judged schools by their location was not surprising since previous research has identified a strong link between school reputation and location.[31] What was remarkable was that parents' perspectives on what makes a school's location a good one were so incredibly consistent. They all seemed to dictate the same basic formula: a good school is in a good neighborhood, and a good neighborhood is a wealthier and whiter neighborhood.

Race and class framed parents' thinking regarding the schools they wanted for their children to attend. This was true for white parents—who were often quite explicit about their desires to avoid schools with racially diverse populations. It was also true for black parents—who despite a desire for racial diversity in their children's schools, wanted the best quality schooling, which they generally presumed to be whiter and less diverse. And, for all of the parents, the more wealthy and affluent the area in which a school was located, the better the school was considered to be.

Elsewhere, Thomas Shapiro and I have argued that for the parents we interviewed, race was a defining factor, if not *the* factor, in determining a "good" school. In our interviews, parents tied a school's reputation directly to the race and class composition of its students. While claiming to be concerned about such things as safety and class size, the families we spoke with were ultimately seeking whiter—and, in their view, inextricably wealthier—school districts for their children, regardless of any other of the school's characteristics. Because we have focused on it previously, this social construction of school reputation and the race and class dynamics of school decisions are not major focal points here.[32] I would be remiss, however, to not at least mention the enormous extent to which families' perspectives were explicitly framed by race and class, and by racism and classism.

Race played a significant role in parents' logic where schools for their children were concerned. Their views, decisions, actions, and experiences were informed and structured by race and racism, and,

presumably, race and racism help to contribute to their maintenance.[33] Indeed, the interviews provide evidence that, as sociologist
Eduardo Bonilla-Silva argues, the contemporary United States is "a
racialized social system."[34] The families we studied were operating
within a racial structure, where, as Bonilla-Silva discusses, racially
motivated—or even racist—behavior such as choosing whiter schools
is rational.[35] Race and racism, however, were often conflated with
class and classism in complex ways.

Class rigidly structured school reputation, as parents consistently asserted that the "good" schools were located in wealthier,
more affluent areas. While I suspect that the frequently used phrase
"more money" was often code for "whiter," parents clearly believed
that better-funded schools were simply better schools. Class dynamics—as separate from, and as entwined with, race dynamics—helped
to frame families' views, decisions, actions, and experiences.[36]

Since schools are funded in large part by local property taxes,
the schools that were located in more affluent areas were presumed
by parents to have better funding and thus be better schools. This
was true regardless of whether or not a parent had gathered actual
information about a school or visited it.

> Eliston: The schools where they have more money per child—
> guess what they have in there? They have carpets, swimming
> pools and air conditioning! You know what I'm saying? But
> in the inner-city schools—these people, *our children*—have
> to go to school in the heat.
>
> Joyce: Baking!
>
> Eliston: Baking! With concrete slab floors, with no paint on
> the wall.
>
> Joyce: Most of the windows don't open, you know, because
> the school was supposed to be set up for air conditioning but
> you got a system where somebody doesn't do what they're
> supposed to do.
>
> Eliston: You got bars on the windows, screens on the win-
> dows, so that limits the flow of air coming into your room.
> It's like you're in a war zone.

Unlike most of the middle- and upper-class families interviewed,
Eliston and Joyce Meador (the black social workers from St. Louis

quoted previously in this chapter) had spent time in the inner-city schools to which they referred. They both grew up in the city of St. Louis, and as adults had done extensive community service work in the local urban public schools. However, many parents who spoke of the "nightmare" of urban schools or the "terrible conditions" in poorer school districts had never even visited the schools to which they referred. Whether they had done extensive research or none at all, the comparisons were repeatedly made between schools in wealthier areas (generally more suburban, and more white), and those in more impoverished ones (generally more urban, and more racially diverse). It did not matter whether schools in "better" locations were actually better schools—if a school's location was perceived as relatively wealthy (and/or white) then the school was automatically perceived to be of relatively higher quality.

Deborah Curley, a black mother and licensed social worker from Los Angeles, noted, "In the schools when you have, uh—areas that are more affluent—the parents and the businesses in the community, they all, they have more money, more income to put into the schools. And it makes a big difference for those schools and the, you know, and the parks and the other services in the area. You know, when you have corporations that are making big donations there's so much more that, that you can get for your child." Here, Deborah expressed a viewpoint that lined up squarely with that of other parents: that schools and school districts vary dramatically because more money translates into better schooling for a child. Sometimes the difference between a good and bad education in their minds simply meant the difference between schools in the suburbs versus schools in the city, or even a school's location on one side or another of a particular street. Families also spoke of specific sections of cities or of certain towns or neighborhoods that they perceived as having good or bad schools. But the comparison made most often was the one between schools in wealthier residential areas and those in poorer ones. Jen Doucette articulated this clearly in her interview. She and her husband Sam, a financially well-off, white couple both from upper-middle-class families, were interviewed in their exquisite home in Los Angeles where they lived with their young daughter. In summing up her perspective, Jen explained, "While I hate to say it, I think it's the truth: any school that has money will definitely be able to offer more to the students.... They have the money to do that, and they have the parent involvement, which also brings in money. Let's face it! The schools that are the most successful are in the more affluent areas: Santa Monica, Pacific Palisades, or Westwood. So when the families have the money to back the schools, they do better.

Separate and Unequal

Since American education has historically been structured around neighborhood schools, and since schools have traditionally been funded largely by local property taxes, schools and communities are inextricably linked. Just as parents considered schools to be "good" if they were in "good" neighborhoods, they considered neighborhoods to be "good" if they had "good" schools.

As Suzanne Wright noted, "We could have lived in Basking Ridge for $300,000 for a *townhouse,* or there's Battle Brook—or Frank Lloyd Township for that matter [*turning to her husband*], which would have been right around the corner from your office—and gotten a *huge* house for $300,000. But we didn't. Because why? Because of the schools... Why do people typically want to move into a town? Because of the schools. I mean it's sad, but that's true, right?"

With financial support from their families, Suzanne and Drew Wright were able to buy their first home soon after they got married. Although they could have bought a "huge house" for the same price in another area, they opted for a small townhouse because it was all they could afford in the specific town where they wanted to live in the New York City metropolitan area. Although other locations would have meant shorter commutes to work, a much lower cost of living, and, as they put it, "far more house for their money," the Wrights explained that they wanted to live where the best schools were located. For the families we interviewed, this was the norm. They most often cited schools as their primary consideration in deciding where to live. Figures from the U.S. Department of Education show this as the pattern nationally: at least one out of four families nationwide chose their neighborhood specifically for the schools there.[37]

At least in terms of the public school system, where we live determines where we go to school. And, since perhaps more than any other variables race and class segregation characterize our residential living patterns, significant schooling differences go hand in hand. If all of us—from all walks of life, from all racial and ethnic backgrounds, and representing every point on the socioeconomic spectrum—were spread out evenly in the country's cities and neighborhoods, then perhaps school funding and student populations would be generally equivalent. If that were the case, then perhaps localized school systems might result in more or less equal education—which might correspondingly go a long way toward making neighborhoods more uniformly desirable (or undesirable, as some would argue). However, we are not spread out evenly throughout the neighborhoods of America. Residential segregation is a major linchpin in educational inequality.

Patterns of residential segregation in post–civil rights America have been well documented by scholars across disciplines.[38] Data from the past two decades, for example, show that while residential racial segregation declined slightly through the 1980s,[39] that decline has since reversed and segregation is again on the rise.[40] In *American Apartheid,* sociologists Douglas Massey and Nancy Denton detailed the contours of race and class segregation and described the contemporary United States as categorized by "persistent" and "severe" segregation. Their work showed how racial groups—most acutely, African Americans—are intensely "hypersegregated": isolated from other groups, clustered in contiguous areas, concentrated in small areas, and centralized within urban areas.[41] Other data—for example, a 2002 report from the U.S. Census Bureau—confirm that blacks are still the most residentially segregated of any racial or ethnic group.[42]

Due to the ways that race and class are linked (through, for example, the historic racial wealth gap[43]), racial segregation is also, of course, inexorably class segregation. The resulting social inequalities are extreme, causing segregation scholars to conclude, as Massey and Denton did, that "racial residential segregation is the principal structural feature of American society responsible for the perpetuation of urban poverty and represents a primary cause of racial inequality in the United States."[44] Others have noted the ways in which residential segregation has molded our society into "a country of strangers,"[45] and how we are, for all intents and purposes, living as "two nations" with great divides between racial and class groups.[46] In Mary Jackman's words, residential segregation "achieves an unprecedented physical separation of the groups—it maximizes the spatial distance between the groups and it radiates over many domains of social life as separate schools, shopping, places of employment, and recreational facilities effortlessly form the existence of separate neighborhoods. Spatial segregation in neighborhoods thus spills over into all walks of life, creating de facto physical separation of the groups throughout social life."[47]

One of segregation's greatest fault lines lies in the fact that the nation's younger generations are perpetually educated in separate and unequal schools. A 2003 U.S. Department of Education report showed that 70 percent of white students attend schools that are at least 75 percent white. The same report revealed that 32 percent of black elementary and secondary school students are enrolled in schools located in large cities, compared to only 6 percent of white students.[48] Other studies' results are even more acute: Gary Orfield and John Yun's examination of school segregation shows that, in industrial states, over half of all black children attend schools that are of over 90 percent minority students; in large urban areas, over 90 percent of black children attend schools that are predominantly non-white.[49] In 2004, 70 percent of black students were eligible for free or reduced school lunches, compared to 23 percent of white students. Of those children who qualified, 76 percent of the black students lived in central cities, compared to 24 percent of the qualifying white students. In center-city schools, 61 percent of black students attended schools where over 75 percent of the students qualified for free or reduced-price lunches.[50]

Rather than being a Great Equalizer, separate and unequal schooling presents a direct contradiction to the American Dream of meritocracy. If schools are segregated and unequal, then a major avenue of ensuring equal opportunity is blocked. Efforts to reconcile this issue have been part of social justice agendas and education reform goals for decades. The U.S. Supreme Court's 1954 ruling in *Brown v. Board of Education* that "separate educational facilities are inherently unequal" is probably the most large-scale and well-known example. Fifty years have passed since the famous *Brown* opinion was declared, and while desegregation did achieve some very real gains in the school systems, substantive desegregation efforts have been more or less stalled for the past 25 years,[51] levels of school segregation have been worsening since the early 1990s,[52] and both integrated and equal education remain, for the most part, unrealized.[53]

The result of what Jennifer Hochschild refers to as "deeply embedded patterns of inequality" is that, as she puts it, "the worst-off students and schools have a completely different educational experience from the best-off students, with predictably different outcomes."[54] Wealthier schools spend on average 56 percent more per student than do poorer schools.[55] Seventy percent of teachers in schools located in low-income areas say they lack the books, supplies, and other materials necessary for them to successfully teach their students.[56] Children from poor families disproportionately attend weaker schools and are at greater risk for serious academic failure.[57] They are much more likely to drop out of their schools, attain fewer years of education, and earn less income later in life than children from more well-off families.[58]

Essentially, the research literature supports what the parents we interviewed believed. The schools that were perceived as "good" and "bad" were indeed probably better and worse in terms of the resources they offered, the educational opportunities they provided, and the chances and outcomes of their students. While there are always exceptions, the funding, resources, opportunities, and student outcomes of poorer, more urban, disproportionately black public schools are generally weaker relative to the "whiter, wealthier," more suburban schools that the parents so often compared them to.[59]

"Running with Fast Horses"

Interviewer: Do you think that coming from Walt Whitman High School, with a diploma from there, and recommendations, et cetera, put them at an advantage more than if you were at a less-prominent school in this area?

Carter: [*Long sigh.*] Probably. All things being equal, if you run with fast horses, you run fast, too. And they were running with fast horses when they were at Walt Whitman. I think the better the reputation of the school, the better the students there, the better the opportunities—in my opinion. That doesn't mean to say that there aren't plenty of successful people who went to smaller, unknown schools. There are. Really, at the end of the day, it depends on the individual. But having said that, there are networking advantages where the—it's the number of students at these different schools, the Ivy League schools, for instance. Duke, while it's not an Ivy League school, it's similar in many respects. The people you know, they become business associates later on in life if you're in a business environment. Of course, if you're going to be a doctor, it doesn't make any difference. But it depends on what field of endeavor. If you're going to be in the top echelon of certain professions, then it's very helpful.... Again, it comes back to that saying I said once before: You run with fast horses, you run fast, too.

—Carter Martin, attorney, white, Washington, D.C.

In regard to school inequality, it was not only differences in funding, resources, opportunities, and student outcomes that concerned parents. Parents were highly cognizant of what they perceived as enormous differences in schools in terms of the social status of the students who attended them. While they were clearly concerned with making sure their children received a high-quality education, they were exorbitantly *more* concerned with the caliber, social standing, and family backgrounds of their children's potential classmates. From their perspectives, enrolling their children in school meant providing them with reading, writing, and arithmetic skills, but it also meant choosing their social environment, determining who their classmates and friends may be, and selecting their peers.

Parents wanted their children to, as Carter Martin put it, "run with fast horses" so that they would "run fast, too." They emphasized the importance of a school's social environment in determining the prospects for student achievement—achievement educationally, and achievement in life. They talked about wanting their children to be "exposed to" and "surrounded by" kids who were "smart"; "striving to achieve"; "well-behaved"; and would "do well in life." As one father said, "The person's ability is one factor. But a good portion of the deal is that, as they say, 'It's not what you know, it's *who* you know.'"

Parents wanted their kids to attend schools with peers who would positively influence their work habits, social lives, and life chances. They were also quite clear regarding those with whom they did *not* want their children to attend school. As Deborah Curley explained her logic, "I was just really concerned about the kinds of children that my child would be exposed to. I definitely didn't want her exposed to a lot of the kids that are in the population that I work with. So that's a consideration too, you know? So the more that you spend on a school, then you guarantee that that's not going to happen. You know that your children won't be exposed to, uh, kids that have been abused or neglected. You know, that kind of thing."

Impressions of student populations and perceptions of school reputations, whether grounded in direct experience (as was the case with Deborah), or based purely on ungrounded speculation (as was the case with the majority of parents we spoke with—especially white and middle-class parents),[60] often had deep race and class undertones. Often, of utmost importance in parents' minds (and often undoubtedly tied to race and class stereotypes) were questions about the "character" or "values" of the student population: Are the school's students "good kids," "from good families," with "the right values," and "bright futures?" Or are they not? The subtle—and not so subtle—subtext of such reasoning on the part of parents involved their questioning the race and class composition of schools. An excellent example comes from an interview with Mary Masterson, a middle-class, white mother from St. Louis:

Mary: It's like, I look at the grunge factor or I look at the, the, state of the place, I look at the parents, you know.

Interviewer: What do you look for? I mean, in the parents or—

Mary: Oh, this is going to sound so snobby of me: I was raised white collar and not blue collar, it's true.

Interviewer: Okay, so you're looking for—?

Mary: Um, I'm looking for a mixture. And … Kirkwood is … University City was not quite a good mixture because really the schools were about 85 to 88 percent black.... But, uh, here at Kirkwood, there's probably only 25 percent black, some of them are bussed in from the city, and I don't think they integrate very well. So .... It's the economics and, and the way that people talk, you know?... And, uh, they say, 'Ahm gohna aks hum' instead of 'I'm gonna ask him'—well, then, they go down a notch in my esteem, you know? It's the kind of thing where if my daughter is going to spend the night at somebody's house I want to meet the parents. And I won't make a judgment, I won't say, 'No, you can't stay there,' but I'll tuck away in my head kind of where I think this parent falls. You know, they may be economically down on their luck these years and I can see that, like, a just-divorced couple and my daughter spends the night with her girlfriend when she's at her dad's house, and that's a real small, ticky-tacky little house because they haven't been divorced long and the dad is not, I want to say, back on his feet yet. Um, and that all goes into my consideration of, of the evaluation.

Often having never visited the schools they were judging, nor directly observed any of the students at them, parents' perceptions about their children's potential peers were based almost entirely on word-of-mouth or blatant presumptions. Thus, school reputations were constructed almost entirely around parents' subjective impressions of who attended the school. Results from other recent research show similar findings. For example, in a study by education researcher Jennifer Jellison Holme, parents of high socioeconomic status in California were found to know virtually nothing firsthand about the schools to which they chose to send their children. Parents' school decisions had been based solely on the subjective reputations of area schools. These reputations, as it turned out, were founded almost exclusively within parents' own social networks, and were based almost entirely on the race and class characteristics of the families whose children were attending the schools.[61]

Research studies have documented that the social environment of a school does indeed significantly impact student achievement and student outcomes. The greater the proportion of wealthy students who attend a school, the higher the likelihood of that school's students completing high school, and the higher the chances for their successful educational outcomes.[62] Jennifer Hochschild and Nathan Scovronick's extensive review of the literature on this subject has concluded, "One of the few things we know for certain about schooling is that the class background of a student's classmates has a dramatic effect on that student's level of success.... This finding has been documented over and over in various countries and schools and with different methodologies and sets of data."[63]

Some may wonder if the schools themselves really make such a large difference at all, if we can even be certain that education is central to achievement or, ultimately, to an individual's social positioning later in life. Indeed, some experts have argued that schooling does not matter nearly as much as it is presumed to matter, that life chance outcomes would be similar regardless of educational experiences.[64] For example, some claim that the supposedly poor parenting skills of black families and the supposed cultural deficits of poor families are actually the significant agents in negative outcomes of black students and the long-term intergenerational transmission of poverty.[65] Surely family background and many factors besides schools and outside of the education system matter greatly to individuals' life chances, and variables well beyond school quality affect children's trajectories and chances for success.[66] Schools can not be isolated as the sole distributors of opportunity or even as the primary influence on a person's life course. However, ultimately it seems that not just the families we interviewed, but also most researchers and policy makers tend to agree that, as social welfare scholar Mark Rank puts it, "A quality education is one of the most vital assets that an individual can acquire."[67] It would be naive to think that school experiences and school quality do not have at least a significant effect, if not profound effects, on a child's path in life.

As Rank argues, "It is blatantly wrong that some American children, simply by virtue of their parents' economic standing, must settle for a substandard educational experience, while others receive a well-rounded education."[68] As he discusses in his book *One Nation, Underprivileged*, due to the fact that the public schools are funded primarily through their local tax bases (mostly property taxes), school districts in wealthier areas generally have more ample funding (for things such as teachers' salaries, smaller class sizes, purchasing books, supplies, equipment, and technological resources, etc.) and thus, can offer higher quality education to their populations. The sorts of things that wealthier school districts can afford for their students correspond directly to the key school quality benchmarks identified as positively influencing student learning and performance. A report by the U.S. Department of Education pointed to indicators such as a school's academic environment, teacher academic skills, and pedagogy, technology, and class size as characterizing high quality educational environments.[69] Indeed, in their research, education scholars Jeannie Oakes and Marisa Saunders found that such things as textbooks, technology, and curriculum materials are "educationally important," and the consequences of not having such things (or having inadequate levels of them) on student learning and student outcomes are "particularly harsh." They also found that schools serving low-income students are the schools that are most affected by shortages of such resources.[70] In the end, most of us would be hard-pressed to claim that differences in schools do not matter when, as Linda Darling-Hammond and Laura Post report, in the United States the wealthiest 10 percent of school districts spends ten times the amount on educating their students than the poorest 10 percent, where poor and minority students are concentrated, spends.[71] Certainly none of the parents we interviewed made the claim that school inequalities did not matter. In fact, they claimed the opposite: they believed that the differences between "good" schools and "bad" schools mattered greatly to their children's experiences. And, as we will see, they attempted to act on that belief.

Regardless of the reasons why, and regardless of whether they thought it was "fair or right," the parents we interviewed believed that some children were advantaged and some were disadvantaged based on where they could go to school. Schools, in their view, were profoundly important; schools were seen as the ticket to the American Dream, the route to success in the meritocracy. So, for them, getting their children into "good" ones was critically important.[72] While they believed in the American Dream and defended the education system as the Great Equalizer, parents at the same time emphasized the uneven landscape of school inequalities. With all of them intent upon sending their children to a "good" school, the question logically follows: Who gets to go where?

3

Buying In and Opting Out

Yvette: If we were talking about the neighborhood that I *really* wanted to move in, it would probably be further north, in Maryland Heights. Those are some really nice homes and I think that's the Parkway School District, which probably is a better school district. I'm not sure. I'm not sure if it's Parkway or one of the other school districts. But I'm sure it's a pretty good school district, because they have really, really nice homes!

Interviewer: You just assume the schools are better because the homes are better?

Yvette: Probably so. The more money in the neighborhood, the better the schools are.... It's all about money in America. If you're poor, and you live in a poor neighborhood, you can bet the neighborhood schools are poor, too. Just like Parkway School District. Parkway School District is West [St. Louis] County. They have the best school district in the county.

Interviewer: Really?

Yvette: Yeah. I mean, it's West County! Everybody out there is rich. My doctor's kids go there. And I know he's got money! He's a specialist. He's on the board of several different—you know? So I know he's got plenty of money. My husband used to work at Parkway School District. Kids pulled up in Mercedes and Porsches, all kind of stuff. Stuff *I* can't even drive, the kids are driving…. Unfortunately, if you're poor, you don't get the best. You only get the staples…. So a lot of times you might spend a little extra money to be in a neighborhood that will get them in the school district that you want to get them in. And as we got older and as we got more used to having children, we did start researching school districts; you know, talking to people, looking into the different services and things that they provide. So we kind of have an idea of where we want to be. And, unfortunately, that requires that we spend more money. And the correlation is, the more money you have, the better school district you're going to be in; because the more money that's going to be in that school district…. So, you know, it's just a matter of where you can afford to live…. And as far as the racial thing, the white kids have more access to the better schools. A lot of them can afford to send them to private school. That gives them an advantage.

—**Yvette Medina, insurance claims adjuster,**
black, St. Louis

In their desire to ensure the best possible chances for their children's futures, the parents interviewed placed an enormous emphasis on education. In the midst of each of their own attempts to access "good" schools, and in the context of a culture that stresses the primacy of individual merit and self-reliance, these parents could hardly be expected to see the larger patterns of their decisions. But when taken together as a whole, the accounts of even just two hundred families reveal distinct social patterns in how parents made the decisions that they did regarding their kids' educations and how children wound up in the schools they were attending.

From the parents' perspectives, "the more money in the neighborhood, the better the schools are." However, the problem for many families was their lack of the financial resources necessary to access the schools they wanted for their children to attend. While some families were very happy with the schools they had chosen, others explained in great detail how their children were not attending the schools that they wished they were able to choose for them. In a family's ability to access "good" schools, parents *believed* that money mattered, and money *had* mattered greatly in their own decisions and experiences. The interviews revealed not simply the role of money in school decisions, but specifically, *the power of wealth*. Wealth gave families the capacity to act on their beliefs effectively, to attain the educational opportunities that they wanted for their children, to ensure the best possible chances for them. The power of wealth was an important—although normally quite invisible—way in which wealth-holding families were able to choose what they viewed as the best schools.

Buying In: "To Get the Best Schools"

Interviewer: How did you make the decision to send him to the school that he is attending?

Jacki: Well, I just looked for the school district that seemed to be the best one in the St. Louis area.

When her son Michael got close to starting first grade, Jacki Frohmer, a social worker, began inquiring about St. Louis area schools. It didn't take long for her to decide on the Ladue School District for her son. Jacki found that, among the people with whom she talked (her family, friends, and acquaintances she encountered day to day), the schools in Ladue were regarded as the best in the area. Being white and middle-class herself, Jacki admitted that most of the people she had talked with were also white and middle-class. Nonetheless, the suburb of Ladue seemed to have a reputation for an excellent public school system. According to Jacki, the Ladue schools consistently rank high on standardized testing, and most of the students graduated to four-year colleges. Most important to her was that the kids attending Ladue schools were, in Jacki's opinion, "good kids." But, as she explained, the houses in Ladue are expensive so accessing the schools there is "not easy to do!"

As a divorced, single mother with an annual income of $32,000, it was hard for Jacki to imagine how she could buy a house in Ladue. She stressed throughout her interview that she needed every cent of her income just to make ends meet for herself and Michael. Savings were, she said, simply "out of the question." Jacki figured out that while she could probably handle the monthly mortgage payments, a down payment on a house in Ladue seemed impossible. She also explained that there was virtually no rental property in the area as it was comprised mainly of condominiums and single-family homes. Nonetheless, she said that "no matter what" she was determined to get Michael into the best schools she possibly could. And that—in her mind—meant "buying into" the Ladue schools. Jacki seemed proud of her story during her interview, repeatedly emphasizing her maternal tenacity and her resolve to do the very best for her son educationally.

Jacki felt tremendous pressure to move out of their home in St. Louis City and into a better area—preferably Ladue—before

Michael began first grade. Her view of the St. Louis city schools was dismal; she described them as "buildings crumbling down, and not enough books, and no computers, and parents that don't care." For Jacki, getting Michael out of there and into Ladue became her top priority. She bluntly gave her perspective: "If I wanted my child to get out of elementary school able to read and write, we had to move there."

> Interviewer: Did you look in other communities besides Ladue?
>
> Jacki: Um, no, not really. The focus was on getting moved into Ladue School District.... The only one that could be even remotely satisfactory was Ladue.

Jacki's story was straightforward at first: She said that she "just *had* to move," so she did. She emphasized that it "wasn't easy," and that she had to make sacrifices, but that in the end it was worth it for Michael. Michael was nine when the interview took place, and Jacki felt he was getting a great education. On the surface, Jacki's story is just the kind people seem to like to hear: motherly resolve; parental self-sacrifice; good, solid educational values; and persevering against the odds. This is where the story would have ended for her if she hadn't been asked for further information in her interview; if she hadn't been asked in depth about the intricacies of how this move to Ladue had been made possible; if she hadn't been asked how she had done it financially. We don't usually talk about money matters in normal conversation—nor, for that matter, in social science interviews. At first Jacki was quite unresponsive, simply reiterating what she had already said: "And so I thought, 'Well, we gotta get into Ladue School District somehow,' and that's how we moved into the first condo." Eventually, however, when asked directly, another layer of the story began to unfold:

> Interviewer: When you moved to your new apartment or condo, was it difficult to come up with down payment? Or—
>
> Jacki: No.

It was at that point in the interview that we began to see how private family wealth had played a critical role in how Jacki and Michael's experiences had played out. The power of wealth—although not normally prominent in how stories and experiences were initially portrayed—was, upon deeper analysis, quite heavily folded into the relatively wealthy families' perspectives, decisions, actions, and experiences.

In Jacki's case it would have been unfeasible to buy a home in the Ladue School District with her income alone. So she swallowed her pride and pulled out all the stops: ultimately, the move was made possible by significant help with a down payment from her family and her ex-husband's family. She explained that, like her, they all wanted to ensure every possible opportunity for Michael. In addition to help with the down payment from her parents, grandparents, and in-laws, Jacki was relying regularly on family members to help her and Michael out when she was in a financial pinch. From time to time, she had received help paying large bills—for example, her parents had recently paid for her to have expensive dental work done that she otherwise would not have been able to afford.

As we delved deeper into Jacki's experiences, the role of wealth could be traced back as powerful throughout her life: she had been fortunate to have a secure financial start in life, her parents had paid for her college education allowing her to start adulthood debt free, and she had received gifts of money all along the way for her graduations, her wedding, the birth of her son, and so on. In Jacki's view these gifts had been, for the most part, insignificant. In fact, she hadn't even considered them to be "help." They were, in her mind, just "things families do." She emphasized that they had not been large amounts of money: $500 here and $1,000 there, she explained. Although these gifts were small in her mind, through the lens of wealth we can imagine how such help, while perhaps slight, would have been nonetheless advantageous to Jacki along the way. Jacki listed other gifts that she and her son had received from her family as well: presents received at holidays and birthdays, vacations and excursions that her parents had paid for, and lots and lots of toys, clothes, and other things that had been purchased for Michael by his grandparents and his aunts over the years. As the details unfolded, it was clear that what Jacki had initially portrayed as unremarkable had, over time, added up to be quite significant. Ultimately, the generosity and financial safety net of Jacki's middle-class family had helped solidify her own middle-class social positioning. The perpetuation of that class standing—and all the benefits that it affords—was also unfolding for the next generation, as Jacki and her family were passing it along to Michael.

Jacki's plan to access "the best" for her son involved moving to an affluent suburban school district in an exclusive, predominantly white, residential area. Two hours into the interview, she openly said that part of what made Ladue "the best" in her mind was that it was an expensive and almost entirely white neighborhood. These things, she explained, were indicators to her of a good neighborhood and a good school district. Jacki's openness about her race and class biases may seem surprising; however, as it turned out, many white middle-class families expressed similar sentiments quite overtly.[1] They openly discussed the roles that race and class had played, and were playing, in their decisions about where to live and send their children to school. Just one of many examples of this comes from an interview with the Olsen family in St. Louis. Lori, a homemaker, and Dan, a corporate manager, were typical of white middle-class families interviewed.

> Lori: I don't think it's right that my children get to go to a private school and get to wear Adidas and, and there are other children living in the city who aren't even fed breakfast, who wear raggy, holey clothes, who have teachers who don't want to be there, and they get no educational benefits whatsoever.

> Interviewer: Do you feel like race has played a role in any of the decisions that you all have made?

> Lori: I have to be honest and … I'm probably wrong for even saying it, but truthfully, it's in the back of my mind, yes.… But I do want to clarify one thing. If there was a nice black family who my husband worked with at Clearwater [the company where her husband works] and they bought the house next door to us and had the same values and the same desires and goals that we had, I would have nothing [against them], and I wouldn't be afraid to have my children carpool or sit by them. I guess I am racist deep down inside, and I feel guilty for admitting that, but those poor inner-city kids whose parents are on crack and who don't care about them and don't feed them and have drugs and guns lying around for them to bring to school, I'm afraid of them. I am afraid of them. And maybe I want to shelter my kids until they're older and they can handle it better. When they're young, I don't want them to be exposed to that type of situation.… Well, I shouldn't say that they have to work at Clearwater; they don't have to work at Clearwater, but they have to work and have to save and have to strive and try to better themselves. But if they're out selling drugs on the corner, I don't want my kids to be around that. And I don't want my kids being shipped into a

school like that.... I feel guilty because I'm not doing anything to make their life better or try to help them. I'm hiding
out here in my little nice neighborhood and my little private
school and I'm like sticking my head in the sand and pretend-
ing like these problems don't exist. So I do have a sense of
guilt over it.

For the families interviewed who had the financial leverage to
move there (a disproportionate number of which were white families), buying into Ladue and places like it often became the goal for
precisely these reasons. Survey research confirms that white families
often purposefully and conscientiously avoid residential areas with
integrated or minority-populated schools.[2] Our interviews indicate
that this is not always because these parents actively wanted to avoid
diversity or racial integration (although some certainly did), but
because they (or because they also) genuinely saw whiter neighborhoods as offering better schools for their children.

Race clearly impacted the decisions of black families, also. This
was especially true for middle- and upper-middle-class black parents
who could potentially afford houses in expensive white neighborhoods but felt hesitant. Given the racism expressed on the part of
many white families interviewed, it is hardly a surprise that many
black parents expressed concern regarding moving to white neighborhoods. They were understandably wary about placing their children
in all-white or predominantly white schools where they might be one
of the only black students—if not *the* only black student—there, and
where, as one father said, "they would probably have no black teachers, no black friends, and no black mentors." Unlike most of the white
families who actually preferred white environments and had sought
them out, black families felt conflicted and sometimes expressed dis-
tress about placing their child in an all-white school (whereas only
two of the white parents interviewed expressed similar sentiments).

Ultimately, regardless of whatever was or was not motivating
them, the school decisions of the families who had "bought in" were,
as they described them, relatively simple: figure out where the best
schools are and move there. As we dug deeper into their stories however, the white middle- and upper-middle-class parents recounted the
financial support, help, and generosity that they had received from
their families along the way. Although family wealth had been passed
along throughout their life experiences and was usually perceived by
them as quite unremarkable, in the final analysis, it was what had
ultimately made their "buying in" possible. Although not usually
part of their stories at first, transfers of wealth within families added

up over time and often made a big difference in school possibilities for the youngest generation. It did not take many interviews for the pattern to become clear: in how families chose the schools they did, family wealth mattered.

Jacki Frohmer's story epitomizes many of the other white, middle-class and upper-middle-class parents interviewed: they wanted their kids to get the best education possible; they asked around and found out which schools were generally considered the best, and—when they could afford to (which, with the help of family members, they often could)—they bought in. Melanie and Troy Haynes told a similar story, although this white family had access to significantly more financial resources than had Jacki. Melanie explained their family's choice of schools:

> Melanie: We were relocating to Los Angeles, and I called a friend of mine who's a teacher down here ... and I said, "Where do we go to get the best schools?" I did not want to pay for private school. And she said, "Manhattan Beach or Hermosa Beach—don't go to Los Angeles—these are the independent school districts right here in South Bay." ... So, it's where I decided to look, looked at homes here, looked at the schools and decided this was pretty good.

> Interviewer: So, you didn't go on any other areas of consideration?

> Melanie: No, I did not want to be in L.A. Unified School District, it was more what I *didn't* want to do. So what were my options?

> Interviewer: And what, in particular, were you looking for in terms of schools?

> Melanie: Um, you know, smaller classrooms, ah, a lot of parent involvement in the schools, I think that makes a big difference in the quality of education, the staff, the look and feel of the campuses, what kind of um, you know, what extracurricular things they have in the classroom. Computers, music, P.E., the things that I would consider basic that had been cut from public education in the last twenty years. That's what I was looking for....

> Interviewer: Why were you hesitant to go to L.A. Unified?

Melanie: Oh my God, where do I begin? Read the newspapers! There is no way I would let my kids go, I would've home schooled them if there was no other option before I got involved with L.A. Unified School District system—being that it has no business being the bureaucracy that it is and that they screw it up right and left! ... Yeah, that's a good way to sum it up!

In the process of relocating for Troy's job, the Hayneses made the decision early on that Hermosa Beach was the place for them. They explain their decision as having been based entirely on wanting their kids to go to school there. With an annual income of $70,000, the family was financially comfortable, but their income did not afford for them to buy in to one of the relatively affluent neighborhoods that make up Hermosa Beach. At the time of their interview, it was not unusual for homes in the area to run well over a million dollars, and it was hard to find a house on the market for less than $300,000–400,000. In a detailed discussion of their financial situation, Troy and Melanie explained that their income was quickly consumed by the day-to-day expenses of life with three kids. To come up with the sizable down payment required to purchase a home in Hermosa Beach was impossible. They did, however, move there.

In telling their story, the Hayneses breezed over the pragmatics of their move and focused instead on extensively discussing the area's excellent education system. Later in the interview they were asked how they had come to own their Hermosa Beach home. It was then that Melanie explained how, in fact, the move had been set in motion by her father. He knew how important it was to Melanie for her family to live there, he wanted his grandchildren in the right schools, and he knew Melanie and Troy could not do it on their own. By putting a sizable down payment on their house for them, and signing the mortgage in his name (with the agreement that Melanie and Troy would pay the monthly mortgage payments), Melanie's father's help allowed the Haynes family to "buy in."

Discussion of the details of their home purchase was short-lived, as Melanie and Troy again seemed to want to highlight instead the exceptionally high quality of the schools their children were attending as a result of their move. They were, they explained, "just thrilled" with their decision to move to Hermosa Beach. As Melanie commented, "Our youngest is going into the fourth grade at his school about two or three blocks away. It is a Blue Ribbon School, which is a national honor, the highest. It's a California Distinguished School. It's one of

America's ten best elementary schools, according to the Duke University Survey of Elementary Schools. It's just really, really exceptional."

The Hayneses' two older children attend the local high school, which they were proud to note is "also a National Blue Ribbon School and a California Distinguished School."

> Troy: According to *Newsweek* it's pretty much the nicest high school in the United States.

> Melanie: Yeah, it also ranked nationally for high schools. So, we're pretty pleased with the education they're getting.

As the interview went on it became clear that while the Hayneses' capacity to buy into Hermosa Beach had been made possible by Melanie's father, their overall upper-middle-class social positioning— their family's residential community; their children's schools and future education potential; their social circles; their lifestyle; their general life chances—was at least in part the result of a whole series of intergenerational transfers of family wealth over the years. These intergenerational transfers hadn't just materialized in the form of the house down payment, but also in an abundance of other gifts, loans, and financial assistance from Melanie and Troy's extended families over the years. This flow of financial resources, and the support and security it had given them along the way, ultimately put the Haynes in a socioeconomic bracket quite higher than they would otherwise be if relying only on their earned income.

> Interviewer: Have you ever received presents from family— presents in terms of large amounts of money from family members?

> Melanie: How large is "large"?

> Interviewer: Over five hundred dollars?

> Troy [*to Melanie*]: Yeah, from your mother a few years ago.

> Melanie: Yeah. Family members helped out on occasion.

> Interviewer: Can you give me an idea of one or two?

> Melanie: My grandmother gave some money about, what ten years ago?

Troy: Yes.

Melanie [*to Troy*]: She's asking for specifics. She gave us twenty thousand dollars about ten years ago that we put into home improvement.

Melanie and Troy went on to explain that they had received money from other family members at times too, and that they expected inheritances from both sides of the family in the future when relatives pass away.

The Haynes family presents an example of what was generally found in the interviews with white middle- and upper-class families. For these families, help with down payments, financial gifts and loans, and intergenerational transfers of wealth—in relatively small or large amounts over time—were commonplace. Indeed, these were so commonplace that often the families themselves did not consider them to be remarkable or noteworthy; in many cases, they listed such things as part of their financial histories only when directly asked about them. Families in such positions explained that this was "just what families do," that this was "that parent thing," and that it was "only natural to want to help out your kids and grandkids." They consistently regarded the passing along of wealth as "a really nice thing," "given out of love," and, as one father explained, "just the way it is in a family—you help each other out, you know?" For those who had received them—even in small amounts—financial assets, support, and transfers of wealth had accumulated over time and throughout the life course to have big impacts on the life trajectories of their families. School decisions were one such point of impact. The interviews revealed that, when traced back, family wealth resources were often *the* reason that parents were eventually able to choose the schools they wanted for their kids. And it was clear that many of the families benefiting from the receipt of intergenerational transfers would not otherwise have been able to send their kids to such "good" schools.

If they could, parents had chosen to buy into what they considered to be the best schools for their children. This is not surprising given what they had told us about their hopes and dreams for their children, their beliefs about education, and their concerns about unequal schools. However, in order to buy into the "best" school districts, these families had also bought into very exclusive neighborhoods. The Schwartz family, an upper-middle-class family from the St. Louis area, for example, had bought into one such area. As Maryann Schwartz explained, "Our neighbors, of course—as you can see it's an upper-class neighborhood. Um, it's, doctors, a lot of doctors and business people. And I think the main reason people live in this neighborhood—there are some people that use private schools, a few, but most people use the school district which is supposedly the best. So that's the reason I moved here.... Uh, I, I don't think, I don't think there is a better school district!"

With the help of considerable family wealth, Maryann and her husband Joseph had been able to buy into the Clayton School District. At the time of their interview, the Schwartzes were living in a $425,000 house in one of the most exclusive suburban neighborhoods of St. Louis. While Joseph's $185,000 annual income as a physician and academic had contributed significantly to their upper-middle-class lifestyle, their move to the Clayton School District was nonetheless testimony to the power of wealth in their experience. Maryann put it this way: "Both my parents and his parents were very generous." When asked to explain, she complained that it would take too long to list all the financial support they had received. "I don't know!" she said, "It would take about a half hour! They were *extremely* generous!" As we got into the details, the Schwartzes gave some examples of what they had received from their families over the years. Joseph's father had paid for his medical school education (tuition and living expenses in excess of $260,000); Maryann's grandmother had left them an inheritance when she died ($10,000); Maryann's parents had bought them cars and had given them significant amounts of cash at various points (two examples were that they had received $40,000 on one occasion, and had for several years received rental revenues from properties that Maryann's parents owned).

With Joseph's income this family would most likely be quite well off no matter what. However, his income *combined* with the privileges of family wealth has resulted in the Schwartzes' capacity to make choices over time that they otherwise would not have been able to make. The most relevant of those choices to the focus here is the Schwartzes' choice of schools for their children: help from both sides of the family had made buying into their chosen school district possible. And, along with the schools they chose, the Schwartzes were also able to choose a neighborhood and home with which they were very happy.

Their interview took place in their home and, looking out of a living room window, Maryann was proud to point out her neighbors' houses and talk about the affluence of the families who lived there and the exclusiveness of the neighborhood. Their own house, Maryann explained, had "I don't know, about eighteen or nineteen rooms, including five bedrooms." She continued, "Yeah, and we ... just got a letter from somebody that's—I mean, this is a really sought-after neighborhood, apparently. And somebody just sent us a letter that said, you know, 'We want to buy a house in here if there's anyone that's willing to sell a house.' And I thought, Wow! I've never gotten this kind of letter before! But it's, it's a really great location. It's just, a lot of people are tired of commuting. And it's, it has really good public schools."

In the Schwartz interview (and in many other families'—particularly white families'—interviews), much of the race and class dynamics at play in what they articulated—in the framing of their worldviews and perspectives, and in their actions and experiences—transcend the scope of this book.[3] It seems, for instance, that for many of the white middle- and upper-middle-class parents interviewed, their children's schooling may be acting as a culturally supported way for them to justify their own establishment in exclusive communities, legitimize the homogeneity of their family's social networks and environments, and—in some cases—help to solidify the parents' own class positioning and sense of class identity. Even further, some interviews pointed to the possibility that parents were using their children's education as a proxy for what actually seemed to be a sort of jockeying for social status on the part of parents themselves. It was clear that many parents took great pride in the educations they were providing to their children; but, in some cases, it almost seemed as if the point was more about how children's educations reflected positively on the parents' own achievements, social standings, and good parenting skills than it was about the children themselves. While such conjectures cannot be fully supported by the interview data at hand, they raise important questions for future research.

Regardless of the possible disjunction between the reasons that parents *claimed* they had done what they did and the reasons they might *actually* have done so, the interviews exposed clear patterns on the topic of family wealth divisions and the perpetuation of class status. One of the central themes from the interviews was that intergenerational wealth had given families such as the Schwartzes, the Hayneses, and Jacki Fohmer the capacity to act on their choices. Despite whatever their decisions may or may not have been rooted in, no matter what their rhetoric or actual beliefs were, they defended their choices as being in the best interest of their children's futures. And intergenerational transfers of wealth over time had ultimately translated into these families' abilities to act on their decisions. Although at first not transparent (not necessarily even to themselves), in the experiences of families with some wealth to pass along, wealth was folded into their decisions so that parents could *act*. Wealth can be leveraged—and was leveraged by those families interviewed who had access to it—to provide opportunity for the next generation. Wealth hadn't simply accumulated, it had been *used*. And, regarding education, wealth *was* used for very specific purposes within the families who had it. It was used to choose schools.

For Maryann and Joseph Schwartz, the key to accessing the schools of their choice had been having the financial leverage to do so. Interview after interview with middle- and upper-middle-class white families outlined the same story: the financial assets these families ultimately relied upon to buy into the schools of their choice had at least partly originated in private wealth passed down in families. Depending on the circumstances and the extent of wealth resources available in a family, it sometimes "took some finagling" (as one person said), and it sometimes was "not difficult at all!" (said another), but choosing schools they felt good having their children attend was, indeed, possible.

The power of wealth allowed these families to choose what they viewed as the "best" schools, and, moreover, it allowed for them to *avoid* what they viewed as "bad" schools. When asked why they chose the suburban public school that they did, one parent said bluntly, "Because I did not want them to attend a regular St. Louis city public school! I think they're horrible, horrible, horrible!" In their rejection of urban public schools, many families had moved out of city school districts and into suburban neighborhoods just before their children reached school age or at other crucial times during their kids' education such as at the time of transition from elementary school to middle school or from middle school to high school. But again, in virtually every family who had moved to access certain schools (or to avoid certain others), some sort of flow of financial resources over the years had helped to put them in the position to be able make such a choice and act on it.

In *The Hidden Cost of Being African American: How Wealth Perpetuates Inequality*, Thomas Shapiro analyzes the same interviews regarding these families' community choices and the role that help with down payments played in their abilities to attain homeownership. He discusses familial help with down payments as an example of "transformative assets" that give families the ability to transform their own lives and the lives of their children. He argues that wealth is used at important milestones over the life course to maximize opportunities and secure advantage. This "family inheritance" is crucial in areas such as homeownership, Shapiro explains, where unearned wealth can lift a family beyond their achievement or earned income.[4] Such was also the case in parents' choosing of schools for their children: private family wealth was not only essential in their ability to act on their choices, but for the families who had it, private family wealth was often used as a "transformative asset."

Of the parents interviewed, those who had been successful at "buying into" the schools of their choice were overwhelmingly those who were white and whose experiences had included some degree of intergenerational transfers of wealth within their families. In interviews with these parents, they discussed school decisions from the perspective of it being a matter of true choices. Their choices were indeed numerous and their race and class positioning allowed them to navigate the process in a way that accounted for that. A white, middle-class father from Boston summed it up nicely; in explaining his decision to buy into the school district he had chosen for his son, Mark Campbell said simply, "We wanted him to have the best he can have." For Mark and other parents in similar circumstances, settling for anything but the best was simply out of the question—and it could be. With numerous options, these families were in positions to be able to make decisions and then act on those decisions. They bought into neighborhoods with great schools—more often than not relying on family wealth, at least in part, to do so—and felt good that the choices they were making were in the best interest of their children's futures. They framed their choices and experiences as part of what they were doing to be good parents. While some of the more wealth-privileged families had chosen to buy into "the best," for others the best choice had been to opt out of the public school system altogether.

Opting Out: "Private School Is Best"

I went and did all my research when my first son was starting school, and I went right down the street here to the Curly School and was very upset at what I saw. I mean, the classrooms are dirty, the teachers are just yelling, and then there was some kid—brought a knife into school! And on some other kid they found a gun. And [in the district school placement process], I got the Curly. So I went private. I'm paying tuition. My children are at the St. Mary's in Brookline. It costs a lot of money.... And my other issue is middle school. There are no good, safe, middle schools, um, in this area, that I would feel comfortable even allowing my child in. So, we're private.

—**Anne Carroll, substitute teacher, white, Boston**

From the perspective of Anne Carroll and her husband John (a master carpenter), there were no good public school options whatsoever.

For them and for some of the other families who could afford it, private schooling was a way to opt out of the public system entirely and choose what they considered to be a better educational route for their children. Those who had chosen private schools consistently repeated three sentiments: that private schools were the best schools; that private schools offered exclusivity and a specific kind of social environment that appealed to them, and that public schools were not good enough or safe enough for their kids.

> Maria: I want her to get a good education, so ... I never even thought about sending her to public school. It wasn't an option at all.

> Interviewer: You didn't go to visit them or anything?

> Maria: No.... No. Wasn't an option.... Because I don't think the teachers feel the same in private school as they do in public school. I think a lot of the teachers in public schools have given up, you know what I mean?... It's just not an option for me, not at all.

As with the families who had bought into what they saw as the best school systems, the families who had chosen private schools emphasized that they had done so simply because it was the right thing to do for their children's educations and futures. Regarding how they were managing their decisions financially, the families' explanations were usually simply that they were willing and able to pay the yearly fees for private schooling. This was framed as a parental commitment to education, or as a sacrifice on their part to do what was best for their kids. But, when the families' financial portfolios were divulged and their histories tracked, the interviews elicited details that would not otherwise have been clear. Although not obvious at first, the ability to opt out was surprisingly often traced back to private family wealth. As it turned out, often extended family members (usually grandparents) were paying for part, or all, of private school tuitions, or they had contributed in other ways that had ultimately made the choice of private school possible.

An illustrative example is that of the Bezdells, a white, middle-class family from Boston. In their interview Nancy said right away why they had chosen private school for their daughter Moira:

> Well, she's a very good student and she had to go on to middle school this year—Boston public. And there's kind of general

consensus that there is only one good middle school. It's very difficult to get into and she didn't get in. She got into what people consider the second best middle school. And we went to visit it and we were appalled at—not issues of safety or anything like that—but the level of boredom that she would have experienced... We were so unimpressed. We were only there an hour and our kid would die of boredom. It was driving me crazy to be there.

Nancy proceeded to explain that they had decided early on that if Moira did not get into the "one good middle school" they were going to pay for her to attend private school. When she did not get in, their visit to the "second best middle school" just served to confirm their decision to opt out. At first glance it appeared that they had made the decision, were paying the tuition, and that there was nothing more to it than that. But later in the interview the Bezdells were asked to explain *how* they had chosen private school—financially, and Nancy answered, "I think that for me, knowing that with my mother I might have access to— [*silent pause*]. There is a certain sense of security for the future that I have. I'm crossing my fingers on it a whole lot, but I think it might be there."

They explained that they felt they could risk putting a big chunk of their income each year toward school tuition because they were not concerned about their long-term financial situation: They had no major debt and felt confident that they could rely on their families in a pinch; their parents had paid for college, so they had no student loans to pay off; their parents had contributed significantly to their house down payment, so they had an affordable mortgage; and they expected to inherit at least $300,000 upon the death of Nancy's mother, so they had that to look forward to down the road. Although they were not building any savings and did not themselves have a financial buffer (at least no buffer independent of knowing they could rely upon their extended families if need be), the Bezdells' household income of $62,600 had allowed for them to be able to pay their daughter's private school tuition fairly comfortably. In discussing their financial situation in depth it became clear that the Bezdells' decision to choose private school for Moira was possible in large part because of family wealth. The financial security that family wealth had provided for them allowed the Bezdells to take more risks with their money than they would have felt comfortable with otherwise.

While the Bezdells said they had chosen private school to prevent their daughter's boredom, most of the families who had opted out of public schooling spoke explicitly of their desire to provide their children with the kind of sheltered environment they believed private schools offered. One St. Louis mother (whose parents were funding her children's—their grandchildren's—private school tuitions) stated this perspective succinctly. When asked why she had chosen private schooling, Gina said, "Maybe it will shield them." Many parents who had been able to choose private schools felt similarly; they liked the idea that private schools offered exclusivity and a specific kind of social environment.

As another mother, Glenda, put it, "Instead of kids loud, jumping off the wall and everything, there's a totally different atmosphere, totally different. And you can just—you just feel a sense of security. And anyway, you have to pay for your kid to go there, so the classroom setting is much smaller, you know, not as many kids, and not many people are going to pay to send their kid to school when they can send them free to public school."

While Glenda and many other parents perceived private and public schools' atmospheres as "totally different" from each other, very few parents who had opted out had ever actually visited the local public schools they were avoiding. Glenda, for example, who had characterized public school as "kids loud, jumping off the wall and everything," later confessed that she had never "really considered"— let alone seen firsthand—the public school options. Like most of the other white, middle-class parents we spoke with who had opted out, Glenda's perceptions of the public schools' reputations were enough for her to have ruled out public school altogether. Julie, another white, middle-class parent who chose private schooling for her children, is another case in point.

Julie: Our neighborhood school is not an option.

Interviewer: Why not?

Julie: I guess it's just things I've heard. I have not gone to check it out, I have to admit. But we've been in the area a long time, we've seen some kids that go there and what they have come out of there knowing. And it's not impressive.

For families who opted out, the bottom line was that, in their minds, private schools provided a better education and social environment than public schools—and they had acted on that. Whether parochial, arts, or elite country day schools, private schools were considered to be the best schools by those parents who chose them.

Judith: In fact, to be honest with you, I had a book in here that talked about—it rated schools, public and private schools.

Interviewer: In St. Louis?

Judith: In St. Louis.... A report called "A Report Card on Schools.".... So I found the best school because academically he [her son] qualified. I mean, he tested very well. I sought Country Day because it was supposed to be the best.... Private school is best for him because it is small. Private school is best for him because as a consumer we have the opportunity to receive the type of services we need, the personal services that we need in order to—that happen to influence his behavior and his academic influence. Private school is—this particular private school is—best for him because he feels that he has a social network. This particular private school is best for him because it is one of the best in the metropolitan area.

As with the families who had bought in, families who had opted out were proud of their level of commitment to high-quality education. Choosing private schooling was, for them, part of how they understood their role as good parents. In choosing what they viewed as "the best," these parents felt they were parenting as best they could. Abraham Keenan, an architect from the Washington, D.C. area who had himself grown up in a wealthy white family and attended private schools, articulated this perspective:

Abraham: Well, my wife and I strongly believe in the best education we can give to our children. So from the very beginning we tried—at least we did our best—to put all our children in the best available school. So they were all going to private schools. And so far, I think it's paid off.

Interviewer: What kind of kids went to these schools?

Abraham: In the high school—I would say my son went to a school that I could tell they were all better than upper society, I would say. And the majority were almost all of them white. I know were a couple mixed races here and there that I guess you would find everywhere. But the majority were well-to-do families and white.

National data support Abraham's observation that "the majority" of private school students are from "well-to-do families and white." The families of students in private schools own on average $20,000 net financial assets versus $7,000 for families whose children have only attended public schools.[5] One out of every 10 white children versus one out of every 25 black children attends private schools;[6] and 78 percent of all students attending private parochial schools are white, versus 10 percent who are black.[7] And, since nearly 80 percent of all private school students live in urban areas, it appears that private schools draw students heavily from urban white families (families in which parents' decisions were based largely on wanting to—as they expressed in our interviews—"escape" or "avoid" their local urban public school systems).[8]

Generally the private schools chosen by the families interviewed were very exclusive in terms of race and class composition. For white families, especially, this was often one of the aspects (if not *the* aspect) that parents liked most. While black families often expressed feeling concerned about the more homogeneous schooling environments of private schools, most white families openly talked about how this was a private school characteristic that appealed to them. Rarely did white parents mention lack of racial diversity or predominant affluence in the student populations of the private schools they had chosen as concerns for them. But even those—including black families—who did see race and class homogeneity as negative dimensions of their kids' school environments, explained that making what they saw as the right educational choices for their children had ultimately outweighed the disconcerting lack of diversity that seemed to come with those choices. Linea Doherty, a white mother from Boston, explained how she conceptualized the lack of diversity in her children's private school as a "problem"; however, she still felt she and her husband had made the right decision for their family. As she explained,

> Regardless of all the sorts of problems of the diversity and economic differences, the place is amazingly beautifully equipped. They have amazing resources. I'm sure, excellent teachers. Excellent facilities. You know? There's nothing to want, you know? They have this beautiful theater. The music, I mean, not just music, but beautiful music rooms, with excellent music programs. You know? All those arts are really incorporated. So, all those things that sort of just get by within the public system, you have tremendous resources in that particular private school. And it's a beautiful grounds. You know, it's sort of like, "Wow!" To be in a big, bright,

beautiful building all day? It's a different feeling than being in the city.

Another white, middle-class parent, Mark Kiefer from Los Angeles, explained, "I grew up in public school, attended public school all my life, and [*turns to his wife*] you too, Valerie. I guess when I became an adult I thought the people who enrolled their kids in private schools were rich, stuffy, arrogant people. I thought, 'Why do you think you are too good for the public school system?' That was my take. And I was pretty reactionary toward private school. Then we had kids! And what might be acceptable for you might not be acceptable for your kids. You start coming up with a new standard for your child."

Whether they had "come up with a new standard" for their children, or whether opting out had been "the only option" all along, parents who chose private schooling were able to do so only because they could afford to, financially. When traced back, it had been a particular kind of financial resource that had ultimately made the difference for these families; while income was helpful (and might at first glance appear to be the obvious explanation for how opting out was possible), in fact, *family wealth* had played a substantial role in their decisions. And the family wealth relied upon to opt out had almost always originated from having been passed along in their families. The interviews show how *significant* wealth does not necessarily have to mean *large amounts* of wealth. Wealth moving through families—over time, and even in small amounts—had a very real impact on the educational trajectories of the next generation.

Surely not all white families, but nonetheless most of them and definitely a large proportion relative to black families, had received college educations, wedding gifts, help with first-home down payments, help with the purchase of cars or major appliances, gifts, loans, cash, help paying for private school tuition, inheritances, and all kinds of financial support from their parents during their lifetimes. Sometimes these were in small amounts and sometimes they were in large amounts, but the ability to rely upon them along the way had been helpful and, at least when it came to school decisions, consequential. Intergenerational transfers were sometimes made at major milestones—such as to help buy a house in order to access certain schools—but this was not the only way that family wealth was of consequence. In a thousand little ways it had added up over time so that a decision such as "opting out" could eventually be acted upon. As one parent who had decided to put his son in private school said, wealth "gives you an alternative." He elaborated, "We don't *have* to send him to the public schools if we don't feel that will benefit our children. We can—and have the assets and income to—send him to private schools."

Family Wealth and Intergenerational Transfers

There's nothing like inheriting wealth. It gives you opportunities that you don't otherwise have. Wealth is wonderful—if you can get it.

—Eva Rice, homemaker, white, Washington, D.C.

Strongly held beliefs of equal opportunity, meritocracy, and individualism are at the core of the American Dream. Parents we spoke with told us that they believed in the American Dream and genuinely thought of individuals' relative positions in the social system as having been earned. Yet the inheritance of private family wealth flies in the face of what these values stand for. When traced back, the family wealth relied upon by the parents who had bought in and opted out had rarely originated through individual effort, but instead had been received from family.

Family wealth is a historical legacy passed down through generations. And, because of the roots of the racial wealth gap, family wealth categorically and systematically advantages some groups—specifically, white families, especially white families with backgrounds of family wealth—over others. Parents from all backgrounds were navigating school decisions for their children. But family wealth had made it relatively easier for some parents—disproportionately white parents—to choose the schools they wanted, the schools they thought were best, the schools that they felt good about. Of those interviewed, the families who were buying in and opting out were not *necessarily* the ones with the highest incomes (although many of them did indeed have relatively high incomes); rather, they tended to be white families who could combine their income with the power of wealth. These families had benefited from intergenerational transfers and from a sense of security that the financial safety net of family wealth had provided them. While income paid for their families' regular expenses and supported their lifestyles, wealth had been used by the families who had it to *go beyond* that. Parents had relied upon family wealth to leverage what they viewed as advantageous educational opportunities for their children. Family wealth, as Eva Rice said, provides "opportunities that you don't otherwise have." "Wealth is," as she said, "wonderful." That is, "if you can get it."

Among the two hundred families interviewed, wealth was something they had been able to "get"—at least originally, and definitely

most often—through intergenerational transfers. Larger-scale studies confirm this to be true. Despite the fact that social science has
traditionally "ignored or downplayed the inheritance factor,"[9] recent
research reveals that wealth accumulation for most households relies
heavily on the transfer of assets across generations within families. A
hefty portion of total wealth holdings in the United States originally
comes from such transfers: at least one half, and, depending on the
study estimates, perhaps as much as 81 percent.[10] As families have
passed wealth along in each consecutive generation, the advantages
that come with it have continued to be conferred, and the wealth gap
has only widened. And, as the baby boom generation begins to pass
their assets along to their children and grandchildren, economists pre-
dict that in the coming years these intergenerational transfers will be
even more significant than they have been in the past.[11] The intergen-
eration transmission of wealth in families has huge ramifications for
each generation that receives it; as sociologist Lisa Keister notes, "the
transfer of wealth from one generation to the next may be the single
most important determinant of who owns what, how they got it, and
what effects it has on both individual- and system-level outcomes."[12]

   Research and policy literature suggest that asset ownership and
growing up in a wealth-holding family does indeed render positive
outcomes and positive lifelong effects for children,[13] leading to "succeeding generations."[14] As the experiences of the families who were
buying in and opting out highlight, one result of the intergenerational
transfer of wealth is that parents with family wealth were able to
place their children on educational trajectories that they believed
to be advantageous. They chose the schools they did because they
believed they would have real, positive impacts on their children's
life chances. As already discussed briefly in chapter 2, these "good"
schools in fact probably were having significant positive effects.

   In addition to those studies previously discussed, other research
shows that children from wealthier families generally perform better, achieve higher, and go further educationally than those from
families with less or no wealth. We know, for instance, that children
of parents with greater net equity in their homes and higher amounts
of liquid assets complete more years of schooling.[15] We also know
that a family's wealth affects children's academic achievement even
when a family's income is held constant, and because white students'
families have substantially more wealth than black families, the
related variables account for at least part of the patterns we continue to see in regard to white students' higher test scores than black
students' on average.[16] White students consistently score higher in
reading and math than do black students when tested at ages nine,

thirteen, and seventeen; white students graduate from high school in greater numbers; and white students go on to college in greater numbers.[17] High quality educational experiences surely have at least some part to play in this.[18] The payoffs for students down the road are significant; education plays a major role in determining the educational and life course trajectories of children as they grow into adulthood—including their occupational mobility. The average income of working-age men who complete high school is $28,878, while the average for college graduates is approximately $50,000.[19]

In terms of the specific schools themselves—the schools the families we interviewed believed were "good" and "bad"—curiously little empirical research examines actual educational disparities or differences in school quality.[20] However, some data does exist; Kati Haycock, director of the Education Trust, finds in her analysis of the results of numerous research studies that better teachers, for example, matter. Teachers who can achieve more effective teaching have immediate and cumulative impacts on student achievement.[21] This is an important point when we consider the inequities in schools' abilities to procure the better teachers. For instance, in a study by Linda Darling-Hammond, inequalities in children's access to qualified teachers were documented. She found a disproportionate number of untrained and uncredentialed teachers assigned to schools serving high-minority, low-income populations of students, and she found powerful negative effects of such large concentrations of unqualified teachers on both students' opportunities to learn and overall student achievement.[22]

These examples from the literature point to the same conclusion that the families we interviewed drew: specific indicators of higher quality schools translate into better educational and long-term outcomes for children. Also important is another body of literature that addresses other, more subtle aspects of the "hidden curriculum" such as cultural capital,[23] access to better college guidance counselors, and (at some of the more exclusive private schools, at least) access to social and occupational networks. While here we have seen how middle- and upper-middle-class parents used their own family wealth to choose advantageous schooling for their children. In her books, *Home Advantage* and *Unequal Childhoods,* Annette Lareau complements these data by shedding light on how such parents also use their social and cultural advantages to maximize those educational opportunities. In Lareau's analyses, she finds these families using their considerable nonmaterial resources to positively influence their children's school experiences and outcomes.

Lareau's research team went inside the schools these children attended, and their households, and found that parents were heavily involved in their children's educations through such things as their relationships and interactions with teachers and other school officials, participating in school and extracurricular activities, and being directly involved in their children's learning. An effect of this was that parents were able to use their own privileges, experiences, and their particular worldviews to successfully maneuver the school system and help access better educational resources for their children; they were, as Lareau put it, able to "concertedly cultivate" their children's successes. She contrasted this to working-class families who, without the same social and cultural advantages on which to draw, focus instead on their children's "natural growth."[24]

In another study, Peter Cookson and Caroline Hodges Persell examined the experiences and perspectives of children attending elite private schools. In their book *Preparing for Power*, Cookson and Persell report on their findings regarding wealthy families' use of elite education to reproduce their upper-class positioning for their children. They argue that "learning certain social roles and behaviors is the central—and perhaps the only—purpose of education." They go on to explain, "We know that where individuals go to school determines with whom they associate, and we also know that the social characteristics of schools' student bodies have powerful effects on a number of 'student outcomes.'" They conclude that schools not only shape a student's academic learning, but—perhaps even more important—schools shape students' lifestyles and life chances.[25]

The families with wealth used it—as distinct from income—to act on the beliefs that *all* of the parents had expressed: their beliefs about the importance of education to their children's future life chances, their beliefs about the importance of "good" schools. The families with wealth used it—as distinct from income—to access educational opportunities for their children that they believed would benefit them in the long run. Although it had neither altered their own decisions nor actions, the fact that other families had fewer options from which to choose was something of which the more wealth-privileged families were well aware. Within their acknowledgment of this reality, the parents who had bought in and opted out often expressed feeling "bad" or feeling "sorry" for other families who had fewer options. Sharon, a white, upper-middle-class mother from a suburb of New York City, talked at length about how she "really felt" for parents who did not have the same choices as had her family, noting, "I feel really glad that we have had this amount of freedom to make a great choice for our kids at Montessori. And I really feel for parents who because of financial restraints are really stuck with some programs that are completely inadequate. I just think it's just, what a shame!

And how hard it must be for some parents because they have no choice."

Despite their emphasis on how strongly they believed in the American Dream of meritocracy and despite their defense of education as "the Great Equalizer," when it came to school decisions parents had purposefully acted—within what they clearly viewed as a system of unequal schools—to secure advantage for their children. But the parents who bought in and opted out to secure the "best" schools were able to do so in large part because of the choices that family wealth had made possible for them. Their situations, perspectives, decisions, and experiences stood in sharp contrast to those of other parents trying to make do, or feeling stuck, with fewer options.

4

Making Do and Feeling Stuck

Alice: It all ties in together. The money you make determines just, in most cases, where you live.... And then the neighborhood you can afford to live in, of course, dictates the school district you're in. So it all interacts.

Interviewer: Do you feel like your son's going to get the best opportunity to go to the best schools?

Alice: No.

Interviewer: You don't? The schools you're looking at aren't the best that you would pick for him?

Alice: They're the best that I can *afford* to send him to. That's what I'm saying.

Interviewer: Okay.

Alice: No, he will *not* get the best education, not what most people would call the best education. He's going to get the best that we can afford to give him.

—Alice Bryant, office administrator, black, St. Louis

Unlike families who had relied upon private family wealth to help them buy in or opt out, those without such resources were restricted to their own income as they attempted to navigate decision making regarding schools for their children. This put wealth-holding families and families without in quite different situations regarding the schools they could choose.

Family wealth framed school decision making. While family wealth had opened up educational options for those families who had it, lack of family wealth had constrained those families without just as much. For the more wealthy families, intergenerational transfers over time and the security of a financial safety net had helped make it possible for parents to choose schools for their children that they felt good about. Those who did not have access to family wealth had to make do on their own, often felt stuck with subpar schools, and—as Alice Bryant expressed above—believed that their kids were "*not* getting the best education." Parents who were "making do" and "feeling stuck" valued education just as highly, if not more so, than any other parent. And they wanted good schools for their kids. But they were navigating the process of school decision-making within a very different set of circumstances.

Making Do: "The Best We Can Afford" and "Fudging It"

I just want him to have the best that's available, you know, that I can find. And that I can afford.

—Alice Bryant

Alice Bryant and her husband Bob (a professional musician) were typical of the middle- and working-class families we interviewed who did not have access to wealth. Many of these families had done well for themselves, had achieved high levels of education and occupational status, and were earning substantial incomes. And a disproportionate number of them were black. While from all outside appearances these families seemed the perfect model of the American Dream—upwardly mobile, self-reliant, rising up through the system on individual merit alone—what became clear through the interviews was that with only rare exceptions, these families could not outearn the power of wealth. Income, unless extraordinarily high, simply could not provide the leveraging of opportunity and the sense of security that family wealth had granted to those who had it.

The Bryants had university diplomas, had jobs that they enjoyed, and a combined annual income of $45,000. They were the first members of their families to attend college and own their own home. They described themselves as having always worked hard to save money for "down the road." They explained that schooling for their son Matthew was their "top priority." Unlike the families highlighted in chapter 3, however, the Bryants had not ever received financial help from their families, and could not expect to. In fact, with both sides of their extended family relying on them, the Bryants' intergenerational transfers flowed in reverse: Alice and Bob felt financially obligated to do what they could for their parents and other family members, and they regularly gave them money. This had made saving for the future tremendously challenging.

Although he was only four years old at the time, the interview with the Bryants revolved around their concerns about their son's future education. As self-proclaimed "planners," Alice and Bob planned far in advance by searching for a neighborhood with good schools before Matthew was even born. It had been difficult. Finding a home they could afford—let alone one in a good school district—was not easy, and they realized early on in the process that they simply were not going to be able to live in the kind of school district they hoped to. After much research and strategizing, they bought a house in what they believed to be the best school district that their "meager down payment" could afford. They considered the schools there "acceptable," though not what they would have chosen for Matthew if their choices had been less constrained, and reluctantly they moved there. The Bryants had thought a lot about private school, and had gone over the figures repeatedly, but they just could not realistically afford it anytime soon. In their interview, Alice and Bob were matter-of-fact about their limited options. "There are schools that probably will give a lot better education, but we can't afford to send him there," Alice explained. "And then if he doesn't go to private school, the school district that we live in is *not* the best—I mean, you're not going to get the best education out of the school."

Throughout the interview, Alice emphasized that she was neither hopeless nor depressed about the education situation, but that she was simply unwilling to sugarcoat it in her discussion of it. She and Bob planned to continue to do whatever they could for Matthew—to ensure that he had, at the very least, a "decent education"—but they felt self-consciously aware that their son's educational trajectory would be limited by their own financial limitations.

Interviewer: So, when you say you want him to have a decent education, what would be decent?

Alice: Decent to me is, where I send him to school, and I know he's being exposed to—how can I say this?—quality education. Where he's being exposed to things that are a challenge to him, that will make him think. So that I know he has good math skills, good science background or skills. You know what I'm saying? I'm going to do that, even if I have to get him a tutor on the side. I don't want him to just slide through, or barely make it, or just have enough education to where he's down in the lower level of the S.A.T., you know what I'm saying? I want him to break up there with the—I want him to come out of school, do whatever he wants to do. But I want him to have a degree, so that he can go out and be an engineer, an architect, a doctor, a lawyer. I want him to have a profession. I'm going to force it on him! That's what I call a decent—I want him to finish college and be able to make over fifty thousand dollars a year. That's a decent income. So he can marry, have a family, and take care of them. So that he knows, "This is your responsibility: go out there, get an education, you get a job.".... Everybody wants to drive a BMW, and a—what's the other thing?—a Benz, an Infiniti. But you need to know, to get these things, you need an education. There's nothing wrong with wanting those or having them, but don't think that you get them just getting C's in school, or going when you feel like it, or hanging out with the boys, or selling drugs, or what have you. You need to know, this is how you get there, this is the route you take. And that's my main interest, and that's what I'm going to push for. That's my main goal.

Alice and Bob obviously wanted a "quality education" for their son—they desperately wanted it. And it was a source of huge disappointment for them both that they were unable to secure this. Toward the end of the interview, Bob reached out supportively to touch Alice's shoulder as she confided her heartbreak that she was unable to provide the best educational opportunities for their child. She explained how she felt she was somehow failing at being a good mother. She explained her frustration with her and Bob's inability to buy a home in a school district she would have liked. She explained that she just could not understand how other parents seemed to be doing what she and Bob could not. Alice's voice quieted when she said, "I didn't have enough money to buy where I would really like to be." She went on, "There are schools that probably will give a lot better education, but we can't afford to send him there."

The Bryants' situation demonstrates circumstances that are similar to those of many of the families interviewed who did not have wealth in their extended families. Alice and Bob's situation resonated particularly strongly with other black, middle-class families who, often despite their own high-achieving status and good intentions, had not had family help to propel them along the way nor financial resources to rely upon in making school decisions. And, as with all the parents, the Bryants and others in similar circumstances believed strongly that the school decisions they were making were critical to the life trajectories and future chances of their children. The level of frustration on the part of these parents was almost palpable in their interviews. An interview with Amanda and Clifford Adams, a middle-class black couple from Boston, exemplified this.

> Amanda: I don't trust Boston public schools at this point with providing the kind of education I'd like for him.... If we can't get the money to put him into private school—that's why I said moving might be an option. Because, since I can't afford to pay for the private school, then I may think in terms of selling the house, and moving to a community that I think the school system would a little bit better.

> Interviewer: Westwood, you mentioned.

> Amanda: Yeah, that's my ultimate dream. But probably we would end up living in Framingham or Natick or some place like that.... I don't know, Westwood, well, it's predominantly, I'm sure, upper-upper-class white families. As a matter of fact, in the last three years they built a community of homes that were for 'low income.' Whatever they call "low income"! But you know, homes that were "affordable." So probably homes at $200,000 instead of $600,000. So, I think they know that they have a problem and they are trying to address it. But it's still not a community that I think we could afford to live in unless our income changes drastically in the next couple years.

That Amanda and Clifford Adams and Alice and Bob Bryant were unable to access the kinds of schools they wanted for their children was something of which they were keenly aware and spoke of explicitly. What was not so much on the surface, however, was the fact that the families they compared themselves to—the parents who got to choose the better schools that the Adams and the Bryants only dreamed of—were able to do so, at least in part, because they had benefited from a reliance on family wealth that relatively less privileged families could not. Hidden from view was the underlying reality (an unspoken, and, in fact, often *unknown* reality) that, without the help of family members and without a family financial safety net, the Adams and the Bryants were on their own in a way that others were not. These families were making do in a way that wealth-holding families simply were not. And, with intergenerational transfers very often flowing in reverse—from child-to-parent rather than from parent-to-child—there was limited potential for "making do" families to ever be able to catch up to their relatively wealthier and disproportionately white peers.

In their making do, a strong sense of discontent and frustration on the part of some parents had led them to strategize ways to subvert the system. As one father said, they were, as a last resort, "fudging it." Without being financially able to buy in or opt out, these parents (most of whom were white, non-wealth-holding families) had found ways to bend the rules, get around the rules, manipulate the system, or they were outright lying in order to get their children into better schools. Ellie Cromer, for example, confessed that she and her ex-husband resorted to using a false address to get their daughter into the school that they wanted. Although she lived with Ellie full-time, in all of their official documentation they had claimed that their daughter lived with her father. By using the false address, they succeeded at accessing a school in Santa Monica—the school they wanted.

> Ellie: She goes to school in Santa Monica, which is where I should be living. But what we did—because we're getting divorced, Ian got an apartment in Santa Monica so that she could go to school there.... You do anything to get your kid into a good school! Like, you'll pay somebody else's gas bill. I'm sure you know about things like that. The first on the list are the people who live there. And the next people on the list are the people who work there. And the next is day care there, and all that sort of thing. But I was desperate to get her into that school, 'cause that's the only school I wanted her to go to, you know, because it's such a good school. And so you do anything! Parents would do anything to do that, to get their kids into a good school, you know? And they do.
>
> Interviewer: So your ex-husband lives in—

Ellie: Santa Monica ... it wasn't in the divorce agreement. He just feels the same way as I do, in fact more importantly than I do, about her education. So he did that, you know? And he will stay there until she's finished that school. And then whatever happens after that, we'll do whatever it takes to get her into Santa Monica High School.

Another parent explained that using a false address was "the only way to get around it ... it just took a lot of ingenuity, and really out-and-out lies.... But it was clear it was the only way it was going to happen. And it was the only way that I wasn't going to get stuck." This notion—the idea of trying to not "get stuck"—was prevalent among the families who were making do. For them, making do meant doing the best they could with the constrained resources that they had and attempting to avert "truly disastrous schools." When false addresses, "out-and-out lies," or other creative (albeit sometimes illegal) solutions were seen as the only options, then parents sometimes implemented them in order to avoid the alternative—having their child stuck in a weak—or, even worse, a "horrible"—school.

In each interview with a family who admitted to be "fudging it," parents expressed their sense of inner conflict about the situation, and they especially emphasized how much they hated to teach their children to lie. One father said simply that "it didn't feel right." But, ultimately, in their view, it was worth it to know that their kids were in the best schools they could get for them—regardless of how they had gotten them there. The lengths to which some parents were willing to go (taking a job in a school cafeteria in order to get their child into that particular school, for example) and the creative strategies some described (renting a grandmother a small apartment in order to use the address to access the local school system, for example) were remarkable. But they also repeatedly emphasized that fudging it was stressful. The Staymans, a white family from the Los Angeles area, are a good example. They had managed to get their two children into the schools of their choice, but they had done it illegally by using a fabricated address.

Interviewer: What sort of things were you looking for in the schools?

Ginny: Good schools. I don't know. It's just like Santa Monica has a good name, and good schools.... And in order for her to go, I had to give some wrong address. And Matt was against it. He hated it. Because at first, you don't sleep good with it, you know? Like, Oh, what if they catch us?—whatever, you know? It puts pressure on my daughter, too. She can't really say where she lives on forms and stuff. But I just didn't care.

One of Ginny and Matt's biggest concerns was the impact that their fudging it was having on their kids. They talked about how their daughter could not have friends over or host slumber parties because other parents might then find out where she really lived. They told stories about the near misses and accidental slipups in conversations between their kids and their teachers. And they explained how they had to closely monitor what their children brought to school to be sure that no magazines or mailing labels that showed their home address would be revealed. The Staymans talked extensively about how risky it was, how they worried "all the time" about getting caught. But on the other hand, from the Staymans' perspective and from that of the other parents who were fudging it, the alternative risk—the risk of ending up in a terrible school—seemed worse. That risk was a constant theme in interviews with parents who were making do; they repeatedly insisted that they, "just could *not*" let their kids "get stuck in bad schools." As Matt noted, "The schools here would just, they would just kill. I mean, they would kill anybody who was trying to study. They would kill. I mean they would kill that ambition altogether." It was those schools that Matt described that parents who were making do were desperately trying to avoid. In interviews, these parents conveyed their sense that they were walking a thin line and trying hard not to slip. Whether they were making do with the best schools they could get and wishing for better, or fudging it to subvert the system, the pressure these parents felt was to stay afloat, to keep themselves held up, to do the best they could for their kids with whatever they had. The hardest part seemed to be their awareness that other kids had access to better educational opportunities than did their own children. The tension, frustration, and disappointment this created for parents who were making do were intense. Yet, the idea of being stuck with their child attending "a terrible school" seemed profoundly worse—simply, it seemed unbearable.

Feeling Stuck: "Stuck Some Place Where You Can Afford"

Of the two hundred families interviewed, about 33 percent (sixty-six families) were working-class or poor, with thirty-eight of those families living below the official income poverty line. These families generally had no savings, assets, or family wealth whatsoever. About one-third of the poor families were working poor and two-thirds were unemployed. Most of the working-class and poor parents interviewed had come from working-class or poor family backgrounds; members of their extended families and social networks were usually in financial situations very similar to their own. The dynamics in terms of how these parents made school decisions were acutely different than those of the families previously discussed.

Most important, from the perspective of these parents, school "decisions" were not really decisions per se. Their interviews were marked by their pervasive sense of "feeling stuck." It was evident that for these parents, choice making had been virtually nonexistent since from their perspectives, and in their experiences, there were very few, if any, good school options available for them at all. While other families were buying into the better districts, choosing private schools, or making do as best they could, many of the working-class parents and all of the poor parents we interviewed felt that they were stuck with nothing but bad options. One parent, who spoke for many, talked about feeling "trapped" with "nowhere to turn." Most expressed utter dissatisfaction with the schools their kids were attending. And all of them stressed that they would choose alternative—better—schools if they could. But, with extremely constrained resources, the "buying in" and "opting out" that we had seen play out with the more privileged families simply were not feasible here. And the "making do" that distinguished many other middle- and working-class interviews just did not characterize the experiences of the families who felt stuck. Given that they would not actively *choose* what they perceived as "bad" schools for their children, and given that they saw no good options available to them, these parents often found themselves caught in what they themselves viewed as worst-case scenarios.

Iris Panford's story provides an example that typifies many of the working-class and working-poor families interviewed. Iris was a black, thirty-eight-year-old, single mother of six-year-old twin girls, working in Los Angeles, and making about $32,000 a year as a paralegal. With rent, monthly bills, childcare, and her student loans, Iris could barely stay afloat financially. Her highest priority was to save enough money for a down payment on a house so that she could get her daughters "out of the city" and "into good schools." However, her savings were not accumulating swiftly enough, and at the time of her interview the dream of the house seemed, to Iris, just that—a dream. When asked about financial resources or help along the way, Iris talked about her parents and said, "They're great!" She went on to explain that her parents took the girls to the movies sometimes and that they helped her with buying school clothes for them when they could. She also explained how her mother and her sister sometimes helped out by babysitting for the twins when Iris had to work late at night. But, in reviewing her financial history, it was apparent that Iris had never received any significant financial help from her family or anyone else. Iris said that she knew her parents and most of her other family members were struggling themselves, and she worried about them. As much as it was hard for her to stretch her income to cover all of her expenses, Iris still had been trying to financially help her parents, sister, and close friends as much as possible. She had done so often.

At the time of the interview, Iris had been renting an apartment in Los Angeles, but it was not at all where she would have liked to be. She said she hated living there because of the schools.

Interviewer: Did you consider any other schools?

Iris: Yes, I tried to get them into Westwood Elementary. Why Westwood Elementary? Westwood Elementary has an outstanding computer department, a smaller ratio, student to teacher. Also, their test scores for the students that leave there and go on to higher education, their test scores for the students are way up there. I mean, way, *way* up there! I think it's because the teachers who have been at that school have taught there for years. They are grounded in that school, and they are making it the best school it can be. But they only take people who live in the neighborhood. And that was the neighborhood I initially tried to move into, but I couldn't afford that at all. That was way out of my league.

Interviewer: Was that the primary reason for wanting to move to Westwood?

Iris: That was *the* reason for moving to Westwood! And they have a radius they will show you on the map. You have to live between these streets, these streets, and these streets. If you live in that area, your child can automatically go there. If you don't live in the area, they do take people from outside of the area, but they only take nine students a year. They take a few people from outside the neighborhood. You have to apply to come from out of the neighborhood. They put everybody's name in a hat, and then they draw the names out of the hat.... So, if they draw your name you get in. If they don't then forget it.

Interviewer: Did you apply?

Iris: I applied, but we didn't get selected.

Interviewer: Did you ever consider private schools for the kids?

Iris: I couldn't afford it. I've considered it and thought about it, and there are a few, even at my church, they have a school, but I couldn't afford it. I'd have to work two full-time jobs to try to do that. As a single parent, some of those things are just not an option for me, like private school, private tutors, private dance lessons for her. Malika sings really, really well, and I would love to get her a coach so she could really learn how to sing. But it's just not in the budget. Not right now.

Interviewer: Is the only barrier money?

Iris: Yes.

Interviewer: How does that make you feel?

Iris: Sad. Sad. There are a lot of things that I would love to do for them that I just can't.

Interviewer: If you had the means, Iris, would you be in Westwood now? Would that have been your first choice?

Iris: That would have been my first choice.

Interviewer: For the school?

Iris: Yes, definitely.

Iris's interview ended with her talking at length of her plans to continue trying to move into Westwood, or at least someplace similar, as far as the schools were concerned. Despite the fact that her net financial assets totaled negative $5,000 (because of student loans she was still trying to pay off), and despite that she expected no financial assistance in the future, Iris was exuberantly hopeful about her daughters' futures. When the interview was over, the girls ran out from their bedroom to their mother, and Iris, obviously delighted with them, looked up and smiled. Locking eyes with her Iris gave a knowing look, as if to say, "See? How could I *not* be hopeful about these two girls?"

Halfway across the country in St. Louis, the Touran family was in similar circumstances. Ruby and Roland were in their mid-thirties and had four children, the oldest of which was in fourth grade. Ruby was working as a respiratory therapist and Roland as a meter reader for the electric company. They both had degrees from community colleges, and together their annual income was $30,000. They were renting an apartment in the city and were trying to save enough money to move outward and buy a house in "a good school district." Saving, though, was a struggle. Their income barely stretched from paycheck to paycheck. After fifteen years of marriage, their net financial assets totaled only $800 in savings. Both black, Ruby and Roland had grown up in poor black neighborhoods and most everyone they knew had struggled financially. As adults, now both sides of their families were relying on them for financial support. They consistently did whatever they could for their parents and other relatives, including helping to pay their rents, buying groceries, or lending out cash when someone was in a pinch. The Tourans said they "worried a lot" about what would happen as time went on. They anticipated that as their parents aged they would become more and more responsible for them financially.

The Tourans defined themselves as "proud people," and sitting in their home during the interview it was clear that they took great pride in what they had. So, it was not easy for them to talk about their financial situation and their frustrations with it.

Ruby: My son's in public school. For some reason, they have the lowest test scores in the district. That's been the big publicity thing all year. But he does, I mean, he does really well. He's an honors student. I wish I could send him to a private school.

Interviewer: How old is he?

Ruby: Nine. He's in fourth grade.

Interviewer: So if you could, you would send him to private?

Ruby: Yeah, if I could.... I just can't afford it.

Interviewer: So why are they going to the public schools?

Ruby: 'Cause that's where we live, and it's because we don't have money for a private school. Financial. It was totally financial.

As the interview continued, Ruby went on to express that she felt thwarted by their situation. In her view, their children were at an obvious disadvantage because of the schools they were attending, but she felt at an absolute loss about what to do.

Other families, especially black families, expressed feeling stuck in similar circumstances. Like the Tourans, most of them were working—in some cases working multiple jobs—yet they could not identify any avenue with which to get their children into the schools that they would like to choose for them. As one working-class white mother, Darlene, said, "If you have the money your child has an opportunity to go to school wherever they want to or wherever you want them to go. If you don't have the money, you've got to settle for a little less. If you have the money, you can buy wherever you want to buy. If you don't—regardless of what color you are—you're stuck someplace where you can afford. You don't have many choices."

It is true that, as Darlene alluded, race itself does not *overtly* determine where one lives. As she put it, "regardless of what color you are," without the financial resources to move elsewhere, "you're stuck someplace where you can afford." However, because of the historic and entrenched connection between race and the wealth gap, it is no coincidence that the black families we interviewed were more often than not challenged with the reality of being heavily constrained in regard to schooling options for their children.

Given how constrained they felt, and the depths of frustration they expressed, it was astonishing how hopeful families who felt stuck remained. Hearing story after story, it became hard not to wonder how these parents maintained their ability to hold out hope in the face of such bleak prospects. Knowing how deep-seated their beliefs were in the role of education to the American Dream, and knowing how heavy of an emphasis they had placed on the value of a *good* education, it was heartrending to hear the perspectives of parents from the most disenfranchised vantage points. Carl Booth, for example, a black father of two from Boston who was supporting his family with his minimum-wage earnings working construction jobs, frankly stated his perspective:

Interviewer: Can you tell me a few things that you find particularly good about the school she is going to now?

Carl: None.

Parents such as Carl told of the severely underfunded, under-resourced, and understaffed schools to which their children were

assigned. These were the places where none of the parents we interviewed wanted their kids to be, the schools that the parents who
could were avoiding. For the families who felt stuck with their children attending them, complaints about these schools were many, were
based on firsthand experience, and were substantial: overcrowding,
sometimes with thirty or forty students in a classroom; inadequate
staffing and burned-out teachers; lack of funding for basics such as
textbooks, paper, and chalk; no libraries, computers, or extracurricular activities; unacceptable facilities with leaking roofs, no heat,
or broken air conditioning—the lists went on and on. These parents
explained repeatedly that "the only reason" their kids were attending
these schools was because they saw "no other choice." An interview
with Regina and Arthur Boyles, a black, working-class couple from
Boston, was one such example.

Regina: I don't like Boston public schools.

Interviewer: Why not?

Regina: They don't get a good education there.... I just don't
think that they are getting an education in Boston public
schools.... I don't think they are learning enough. I just don't
like it.

Interviewer: Do you have a few good things to say about the
schools that they are going to right now?

Regina: No. I just don't like it. I'd rather them go to a different school. They are here at the school they're in now because
of where I live.... I just don't want them there.

Parents who felt stuck found themselves with their kids attending schools that they disapproved of, receiving educations that they
believed were truly inadequate, and wishing for better opportunities
for their children. These parents were no different from all of the others in that they had said they believed in meritocracy, and in schools as
"the Great Equalizer," yet at the same time also believed that schools
were unequal. The difference was that other parents had managed
to avoid the schools that the children of the parents who felt stuck
were attending. Parents feeling stuck believed that their children's
schools were not the "good" ones, nor the adequate ones—they felt
stuck with the worst ones. They dreamed of getting their kids out of
there, moving to better school districts, or enrolling them in private

schools. But for these families who felt stuck, no matter how much they were hoping, wanting, and wishing for better, their chances of actually attaining better seemed so far out of reach.

Wealth Poverty and Intergenerational Transfers in Reverse

That's the kind of thing that not having money makes you realize—that money empowers you, it empowers you. You're able to want something and attain it, not just want and wish.

—Moszela Tessler, professional care provider for disabled adults, black, Los Angeles

Parents from disadvantaged family backgrounds were attempting to navigate school decisions for their children, but they were navigating within highly constrained sets of choices, if they saw choices at all. Without family wealth to rely upon, parents who were making do and feeling stuck were on their own, and more often than not they found themselves "wanting and wishing" for better, but unable to act on that. They did not, in the words of Moszela Tessler, feel "empowered"; they were not "able to want something and attain it," they were only able to "want and wish." When it came to schools for their children, this translated into parents' inabilities to choose the schools they actually wanted. While wealth-holding families had generally been able to access schools that they felt good about, those with family histories of wealth poverty—no matter how much they would have liked to make the same decisions—usually felt constrained from being able to do so.

All of the parents had placed a major emphasis on the importance of good schools for their children, and most considered overseeing their children's educations as paramount in their role as parents. They felt responsible for getting their kids into the best possible schools and thought of this as a major key, if not the key, to a successful start in life. The parents who had managed to get their children into what they viewed as good schools were very proud of having made such good choices. And, in interview after interview, other families praised such parents for their good parenting and good values. By the same token, the parents of children who were in "bad" schools were blamed by other parents—especially, it seemed, by working- and middle-class white parents—for their "bad choices," and were criticized for their lack of educational values. Kimberly, a white, working-class mother from Boston, was just one of many who articulated such a stance. "I don't blame it on the children, I blame it on the parents," she commented. "If your parents are never around and they take no interest in your education, then neither will you!"

However, in talking with parents in depth, the evidence abounds that this "blame-the-parents" logic is simply incorrect. In spite of the ideology of meritocracy's claim to the contrary, when it came to school decision making, all parents were not equally comparable as self-sufficient, independent choice makers. All parents did not equally have the freedom to make whatever school decisions for their children they believed best. If they were in comparable circumstances, then perhaps we could rightly blame and praise each parent for the choices that they have made. However, as we have seen, it is not so straightforward: different sets of financial capacities allowed for different sets of educational options. And those financial capacities were—more often than not—shaped by family wealth.

Of those interviewed, the families who were making do and feeling stuck were not necessarily the ones with the lowest incomes (although several of them did indeed have very low incomes); rather, they were the families who could not combine their income with the power of wealth and could not rely on the security of family wealth. While income paid rents and mortgages and covered day-to-day living expenses, wealth had allowed families who had it to go *beyond that*. In regard to schooling, parents had used wealth to leverage educational opportunities and propel children forward—often well beyond what they would have been able to do with their income alone. For parents without that family wealth to rely upon, going *beyond* where they were was not possible. Rather, they were navigating school decisions with their earning power alone. While some were managing to make do, those parents in the most disadvantaged circumstances simply felt stuck.

Within a structure of unequal education, families' school "choices" (or lack thereof) were rigidly stratified along race and class lines so that the power of wealth became—at least in part—the power for the wealthier, disproportionately white families to make decisions and act on them. One way that the power of wealth played out for them was through their ability to create what they saw as advantageous educational opportunities for their children; their ability to do what they chose where schools for their kids were concerned; their ability to avoid getting stuck with nothing but bad options. Of course, not all white families are advantaged by wealth, and not all black families are disadvantaged; examples of families that are exceptions to these norms blur the lines as reminders that social life is neither uniform nor able to be perfectly mapped out. When looked at as a whole, however, the *patterns* are powerful and have powerful implications.

National data shed light on the context in which the interviews were situated and point to the broader implications of what the families shared with us. The median net worth for black families is about $14,500, compared to $61,500 for white families.[1] Half of all black families—compared to less than a quarter of all white families—have zero assets or are in debt.[2] And the link between family wealth and children's educational trajectories is undeniable: broad studies examining the relationship between parents' financial capacities and their children's educational performance conclude that "parents' economic resources appeared to matter at all levels of schooling."[3] As our interviews suggest, and larger-scale survey research confirms, one of the major consequences of growing up poor is the inability for poor children's parents to "purchase better learning environments for their children."[4] The result is that family wealth has a significant effect on academic outcomes such as the level of education achieved and the probability of dropping out.[5] Young children living in poverty test lower for cognitive and verbal abilities.[6] Poor children are two times more likely than nonpoor children to have to repeat a grade of school.[7] Poverty experienced during adolescence negatively affects teenagers' long-term educational attainment.[8] And children growing up in poor households are half as likely as nonpoor children to eventually earn bachelor's degrees.[9]

Educational researchers have argued, as Gary Orfield and Susan Eaton have, that the roots of these sorts of discrepancies are in "the systematically unequal educational opportunities offered to poor and minority children."[10] Our interviews point to the somber reality that in the context of a national education system of vastly unequal schools, family wealth was a key determining factor in sorting out which children got to go to which schools. Parents would all have chosen the best schools if they could, but they were "choosing" from within very different circumstances. Within these structural circumstances (circumstances that very often had long, multigenerational, entrenched family histories), parents' choice making (or lack thereof) was presumably having very real impacts on children's experiences. School selection greatly affects the environments children are socialized in, their perspectives on their futures, and their identities. Since education matters so much to mobility and achievement, kids born to families of different race and class groups have varying educational chances from the start. This stands in direct conflict with the core values of the American Dream.

Melvin Oliver and Thomas Shapiro, among other sociologists, have argued that the persistence of the wealth gap—specifically, the racial wealth gap—is due in large part to our country's long history of racism and discrimination, which originally prohibited black families from owning wealth and, still today, discourages asset accumulation through racially discriminatory policies and practices.[11] Over time these mechanisms have resulted in what Oliver and Shapiro refer to as the "sedimentation" of race-class inequality. "Because blacks bring virtually no assets forward from the previous generation," they note, "the wealth they amass pales in comparison to that of their white counterparts. No matter how high up the mobility ladder blacks climb, their asset accumulation remains capped at inconsequential levels, especially when compared to that of equally mobile whites."[12]

This conundrum—that wealth accumulation in black families "remains capped at inconsequential levels," "no matter how high up" they climb—is both a heavy legacy and a contemporary socioeconomic reality unfolding daily for families in such experiences as their school decision making. While it may not be transparent to them as such, with the racial wealth gap so deep from the start and with the system of schooling so substantially unequal, asset-poor families (disproportionately black families) are able to neither catch up nor keep up with their asset-wealthy (disproportionately white) peers. This, as well as the long history of structures and policies which have contributed to this debacle, are what have set the stage for what played out in the experiences of the two hundred families with whom we spoke.

Wealth inequality grows over time in large part because the wealth passed along in wealth-holding families continues to accumulate with each generation. This makes it difficult for non-wealth-holding families to set aside enough income to be equivalent with what wealthy families are inheriting (and virtually impossible for poor families—it is hard to justify savings when food and housing needs are not being met). Wealth amasses upon itself when it is invested—whether in savings accounts, stocks and bonds, homes and property, or in the next generation's education, experiences, and opportunities. Wealth begets wealth. Still, there has to be money to start this cycle, some chunk to begin accumulation for each family, and these initial assets had—at least for the participants interviewed for this project—most often originated from being passed along within their extended families. The family wealth parents had relied upon to access highly respected schools for their children was usually traced back to intergenerational transfers of wealth.

If, as is true among families nationally, at least half of total wealth holdings in the United States come from intergenerational transfers,[13] then successive generations in the families who cannot pass along intergenerational transfers are simply at a disadvantage. Families do accumulate some of their wealth by saving portions of earned income,[14] but wealth originating from income savings and wealth originating from intergenerational transfers are different—especially in a country that prides itself on meritocracy. Families who receive intergenerational transfers receive *unearned advantages* that directly benefit them. Families left to develop wealth from scratch must rely solely on their own earnings. Intergenerational transfers provide a head start that those without it do not have.

At least in our interviews, the relative lack of intergenerational transfers in asset-poor families was not a result of less closely knit families or of parents not wanting to help children—clearly these families were just as tight-knit and generous-minded as any of the others. Rather, within their family networks, wealth had not been built up or passed down over generations so that now financial resources were simply unavailable to trickle down in small ways over time—let alone to contribute in larger ways toward efforts such as the younger generations' mortgage down payments or grandchildren's private school tuitions. In fact, the parents we interviewed who were receiving the least intergenerational transfers were also the ones who were most likely to be financially supporting others in their extended families or social networks. In direct contrast to wealth-holding families, the younger generations of asset-poor families were often the ones being most heavily relied upon to financially support their parents, their siblings, and other family members. And again, because of the racial wealth gap, a disproportionate majority of these families were black.

In regard to middle- or upper-middle-class black families, intergenerational transfers in reverse were extremely common. High-achieving black parents interviewed described feeling immense pressure to financially assist relatives, friends, and their own parents. As opposed to white families interviewed at all class levels, who in general tended to receive money from their parents and others far into adulthood, black families tended to be giving to, not receiving from, the generations before them. The sharing of resources with extended families and communities was extremely common for black parents—in fact, the norm. As a result, their potential for such things as procuring advantages for their own children and saving money to develop wealth was in constant tension with the responsibility and obligation they felt to give money to friends and family. This was a heavy burden that white parents we spoke with rarely shouldered.

Intergenerational transfers in reverse were also common in the working-class and poor black families we interviewed. In her classic book, *All Our Kin,* Carol Stack noted the significance of this kind of resource sharing among poor, black families. Stack's study and her analysis are still directly relevant to the interview findings here. In addition to already having low levels of income, the pressures and obligations working-class and poor black families so often felt to help others meant that many of the black parents we spoke with had no reasonable way to save or establish wealth on their own. Stack also wrote about how the poor black families she studied—while sharing what little income they had—were unable to accumulate savings: "There is no way for those families poor enough to receive welfare to acquire any surplus cash which can be saved ... in contrast to the middle class, who are pressured to spend and save, the poor are not even permitted to establish an equity."[15]

Other scholars have also pointed to the significance of intergenerational transfers operating in asset-poor families in reverse. Ngina Chiteji and Derrick Hamilton's research found that almost 30 percent of the wealth gap between middle-class black and white families can be explained by the financial help black families are contributing to less-well-off relatives.[16] They found that "poverty among siblings and parents reduces the probability that their nonpoor relatives will own both bank accounts and stock" and that "assistance to poor relatives depresses overall wealth accumulation." Chiteji and Hamilton conclude that "poverty in the family constrains asset accumulation among the nonpoor" to such an extent that it "potentially explains why black families have less wealth than white families do, on average."[17] Intergenerational transfers in families over time are a major source of the wealth gap, but the dynamic of intergenerational transfers *in reverse* make its cleavages run even deeper. Since many black families often start with less to begin with, this flow of financial resources in reverse—while done from a sense of mutual reciprocity and an intention to help family and community—ironically cleaves the race-class divide even further. Given how important the strength of reciprocally shared resources has been to the resiliency of black kinship networks throughout American history, considering how to address this dynamic is especially complex and intrinsically problematic.[18]

Ultimately, without all the benefits of family wealth—the financial help and sense of security that generally came with it throughout the life course—families experiencing wealth poverty (not only in their immediate family, but families who have wealth poverty in their extended families as well) found themselves in very different circumstances than their wealth-holding peers. Their perspectives, decisions, and experiences were framed by these differences so that the interviews provide a rich tapestry of the history and legacy of the wealth gap playing itself out in contemporary American life. In regard to educational decisions for their children, parents were competing with each other for what they viewed as a finite number of spots in the better schools. Essentially, though, while it was not always apparent to them, it was an unfair competition. The difference between those who had reaped the benefits of family wealth and those who had not often meant the difference between buying in, opting out, making do, or feeling stuck.

Who ended up where was not a coincidence. Children did not simply wind up at the top or get stuck at the bottom of the educational hierarchy. And, despite their deep beliefs in the tenets of the American Dream, which parents' children ended up where was not based on a simple matter of merit. Neither was it a matter of who had tried harder or who cared most about their children's educations or futures. Family wealth was monumental in structuring school decisions within families. And family wealth was, for the generations receiving it, an unearned advantage.

5

Wealth Privilege

Some people have big advantages they were born with because of family and their family circumstances. And other people have big disadvantages for the same reasons. There's nothing that wealth doesn't make easier.

—Olivia Holden, university administrator, white, New York City

The American Dream tells us that where we end up is a result of our own doing. It assures us that regardless of the circumstances to which we are born, with hard work and determination we all have equal chances. At its core, the American Dream is about a fundamental belief that our country operates as a meritocracy, that those who rise upward in the system do so through their own individual achievements, and that the highest achieving are rewarded by positions at the top of the social, political, and occupational power structures. A merit-based system ensures that life chances are not determined by family of origin, that social positioning is rightly deserved. As our nation's credo, the American Dream of meritocracy promises that we are competing on a level playing field, and that the competition is fair. We have seen that the families interviewed believed in it.

The reality of wealth in America, though—the way it is acquired, distributed, and the way it is used—is a direct contradiction to these fundamental ideas. In interviews with American families we have seen a way in which that plays out. Examining school choice making (just one arena wherein families potentially experience the ramifications of wealth inequality), those parents from backgrounds of even moderate wealth had a significant advantage over parents with family histories of wealth poverty. Disproportionately white, wealth-holding parents used the financial assistance, intergenerational transfers, and security of their family wealth to help access schools for their own children that were viewed as advantageous by all of the parents. Meanwhile, parents without family wealth to rely upon, who were disproportionately black, were navigating the same arena unaided, with relatively limited resources and constrained capacities. A central incongruity surfaces when families' school decisions are considered in the context of the American Dream: the assets that the wealth-holding families had owned, relied upon, and utilized in choosing schools had most often originated from nonmerit sources. Inherited wealth and the security of family wealth were critical advantages being passed along to the next generation—advantages often unearned by the parents themselves, and always unearned by their children.

A foundational conflict exists between the meritocratic values of the American Dream and the structure of intergenerational wealth inequality. Simply, advantageous resources inherited and passed along in families are not attained through individual achievement. Although wealth can, of course, be earned by an individual entirely independently, in the case of the families we spoke with, it had not. This is the aspect of family wealth that concerns us here. Family wealth generates *unearned advantages* for those who have it. It is a form of *privilege*. In light of their beliefs in the American Dream, how do those families who present the most transparent contradiction to the idea of meritocracy—families with wealth privilege—understand their positioning and the unearned advantages they pass along to their children?

We could presume that, as with other forms of privilege (such as race privilege or gender privilege), wealth privilege would generally appear invisible and be taken for granted by those who have it.[1] However, one of the most striking aspects of the interviews was the acknowledgment of wealth privilege on the part of wealth-holding families. The parents who had benefited from family wealth acknowledged a structure of wealth inequality that grants privilege to some families and disadvantage to others, and they acknowledged the advantages they were passing along to the next generation through the schools that they chose.

Passing Along Advantage: The Schools We Choose

I went to Beverly Hills High School. I was very fortunate. And those people that live in Beverly Hills, they do anything for that school. The school needs something? Not a problem! Anything! It has the best facilities—the best of everything. And we had a planetarium in our school, to learn the stars. And telescopes to check them out. Come on! Indoor swimming pool? We learned to swim inside! That's not normal at a high school. I can understand that because I've experienced that.... It's sad, though—that that school is so much superior to some of the other schools.

—Iris Panford, paralegal, black, Los Angeles

Where schools for their children were concerned, parents who were making do and feeling stuck explained that they wanted and wished for better schools for their children. They were up front regarding their concerns about the schools their kids were attending and about the negative implications they perceived these schools as having for their children's future life chances. Parents who had bought in or opted out, however, stood at quite a different vantage point.

Parents who had bought in or opted out believed that the schools they had chosen were crucial to ensuring advantageous educational opportunities for their children. Many, like Iris Panford, had themselves gone to "superior" schools, or schools that were "some of the best" in the areas where they had lived while growing up. Now, in making decisions for their children's educations, these parents believed that these "best," "superior" schools created important advantages for their children, versus other children who did not attend them. How did these parents understand the advantages they were passing along?

> Interviewer: Do you think that the type of school that your kids have gone to puts them at an advantage over others? And, if so, what kind of advantages do they get from attending that elite school?
>
> Joel: It definitely had an advantage for them. First of all, they got a good education. Better, cleaner environment. With all the problems you hear in a lot of schools nowadays, they didn't come up with any problem of that nature. Yeah, it did help. In a way, you might think it was a kind of disadvantage, too—because they did not see a lot of things that maybe normal kids would see in public high schools.

Interviewer: Do you think that the advantages outweigh the disadvantages?

Joel: I would think so! Yeah! Definitely!

Interviewer: And you think they get a better education by going to those schools?

The Conrad family was one of the wealthiest interviewed. They had significant family wealth on both sides of the family that had been instrumental over the years in the development of their substantial financial portfolio. Joel owned a major national retail business (which his parents had originally helped to finance), the family held extensive investments, and each of their teenage children had trust funds in their names, which had been accruing since they were infants. Since they had been married, Grace had not worked outside the home. At the time of the interview, the Conrads were living in a large, elegant house in an affluent suburb of Washington, D.C.; Joel, Grace, and all three of their children drove very expensive cars; the family regularly enjoyed international vacations and a wide range of cultural events, hobbies, and experiences.

All three of the Conrad children had attended elite private schools throughout their lives, and all of them were fluent in a second language—French—by the time they were in fourth grade. At the time of the interview, Bridger, the Conrads' oldest son, was a Wharton Business School student; Devon was a sophomore at Rice University; and Taryn, like her brothers, was attending an exclusive private preparatory day school. Among her classmates were the children of Washington-area business owners and powerful politicians, lawyers, and lobbyists. The Conrads were also keen to report that Chelsea Clinton had attended the school. Taryn was planning to apply to colleges the following fall and hoped to be accepted by early decision to Princeton University.

Much of the Conrads' interview centered on their beliefs about education; the couple talked at length of their commitment to learning and about the success later in life that a good education can provide. For these reasons, they said, it was of the utmost importance that their children attend "the best schools." Although this has required significant resources (the private schools the Conrad children have attended since kindergarten charge annual tuitions ranging from about $10,000 to $25,000 per child), their financial portfolio had made it possible. As was evident in their interview, the Conrads believed these schools were paying off in the short- and long-term advantages they had provided for their children.

While the Conrads were an exceptionally well-off family, their perspectives on education and advantage were not at all exceptional. Joel's belief that "you definitely have better chances" if you can attend the better schools was typical of the wealth-holding families interviewed who had placed their children in what they perceived to be the "best" schools—whether those were private or public schools. They believed that the educations and social environments these schools provided were granting their children advantages that they would not have otherwise.

Not far from the Conrads' home, Faith and Carter Martin's interview took place in Carter's office overlooking one of the most high-powered streets of downtown Washington. Covering one of his office walls were framed photographs of his family—a vacation in Europe, a ski trip to Colorado, parents' weekend at summer camp, family social occasions. Sitting on leather couches and sipping iced tea, Carter pointed out his children in the photos as he spoke of them during the interview.

> Interviewer: Can you tell me a bit about each member of your family, as far as their age, if they're in school, what they do— your immediate family?
>
> Carter: I'm a lawyer.... I have five children.... My wife does not work. She takes care of our homes—we have three homes and she takes care of them and does a lot of charitable work as well.
>
> Interviewer: Could you tell me why you chose to live where you do?
>
> Carter: I moved to Bethesda about thirty-two years ago, and at the time I moved there, it was a new neighborhood, it was close to Washington, D.C. It had excellent schools—the *premier* high school in the Washington, D.C., metropolitan area. It had excellent elementary and junior highs.
>
> Interviewer: Okay. Do you think the ability of your kids to go to a great school like that—the premier school in the city— puts them at an advantage over others who may be living in less-affluent areas of the city?

Carter: I think it's a given that the better education you get, the better prepared you are for life. So, to the extent they went to an excellent high school, it got them off to a good start. That's not to say that there aren't other schools—it's not just the school, it's the students, it's the people you meet there, and it's also the teachers you have and how they motivate you as an individual. But all things being equal, it was a *significant advantage.* There are private schools in the area that are just as good, if not better. But they were happy to go there. At that time, it was considered the premier high school in the area and one of the top high schools in the country. They had a significant head start by going to Walt Whitman High School.

The Martins' interview stood out because Carter articulated so clearly a viewpoint that all of the families shared, but that the wealthier families had direct experience with: the idea that "it's a given that the better education you get, the better prepared you are for life," and that excellent schools confer to children a "significant advantage." Their interview also stood out because it was so conventional in regard to the experiences of the wealthy families interviewed. As just one example, the Martins' move to Bethesda (where houses regularly sell for over a million dollars) was facilitated by family wealth. The highly profitable sale of their first home, which had been bought with a down payment given to them as a wedding gift, had made the upgrade to the Bethesda School District possible. Throughout their lives, as was typical of members of wealth-holding families, Carter and Faith had benefited from intergenerational transfers, financial assistance, and the comfort of knowing there were resources to fall back on if need be. Also typical was that the Martins were passing along the same advantages they had received to their own children now as parents themselves. One such "significant advantage" they were conscientiously passing along was the highly reputable schooling they were ensuring for their children.

For those families who had been able to access them, the "good" schools they provided for their children were—in their minds—unequivocally worth the price. As Vivian Windrow from Los Angeles repeatedly emphasized, "money talks."

Vivian: It's unfortunate, but I think that money talks.

Interviewer: Money talks in what way?

Vivian: Well, money talks with regard to what kind of service you're going to get. When people pay more for schools, I mean, yeah, anybody can send their kid to public school. But the reality is, if I'm spending this kind of money on school, I expect my daughter to come back reading. You know? I expect this, I expect that. You know? Yeah, I expect it.... You know, that's the reality of it. The money makes me think that I deserve a little bit more.

Interviewer: Do you think that people who don't have as much money are somehow at a disadvantage?

Vivian: Oh, yes, I really do. I honestly do.

That Vivian and others who had successfully accessed the better schools believed that they "deserved a little bit more" is an important dimension of their use of, and thinking about, wealth privilege. In discussing their use of financial clout—the leveraging of their family wealth—these parents also unabashedly expressed a sense of entitlement for "better." Better education for their children, better opportunities for their children, better chances for their children. This—"better"—was exactly the advantage they were pursuing—and that which they believed they had established for the life courses of their children through the attainment of such "good" schools.

In these families' experiences, they had witnessed the power of wealth firsthand and had seen what it could provide where schools are concerned. They talked about the academic curriculums of the very "good" schools their children attended; the excellent teachers, resources, and facilities found at these schools; the positive social environments their children were experiencing; and, down the road, admission to top-notch colleges and universities, access to powerful social networks, and further advantageous opportunities. The parents saw the affirmative impact of these things on their own lives, and on their children's learning, worldviews, social skills, and life chances.

These parents also saw, on the other hand, that the "other," "not good schools" (as many referred to them) put those children who attended them at a disadvantage. Just as when asked if she thought that "people who don't have as much money are somehow at a disadvantage" Vivian had responded, "Oh, yes, I really do," other families expressed similar beliefs. An interview with the Prestons, a white family from the Washington, D.C. area, provides an example. Madeline, a CIA executive, and Karl, a government attorney, and both from wealthy family backgrounds, had two children. They candidly discussed their views on the subject at hand. Karl noted, "You gotta have a good primary and secondary education. That's available at a fair number of public schools in the U.S. But to most poor people, it is simply unavailable, period. The public schools of Washington are an excellent example. There are a few primary schools that are so-so. Most of them are absolutely deplorable. And most of the secondary schools are just horrible. People graduate from them regularly without being able to read, write, add, or subtract."

As Rorrie, another parent, explained (and here again we see an expression of a sense of entitlement on the part of the relatively more upper-class families in expecting better for their own children),

> Just reading some of the testing results in the *Times*—the *Los Angeles Times*—the majority of children are not on their grade level. They're below. Their reading scores are bad. Their math scores are bad. I think that the teachers are probably overwhelmed and not able to put the time in that the children probably need. That there's, you know, too many kids in the classroom. I feel like—and you know, this may sound snobby or whatever—but I feel that if a parent is willing to pay for their child to go to school, most likely they're supportive of their learning in the home. So maybe more of the parents at this school will be along the same lines of thinking that I am, maybe—value system. And that's not a slight to the other parents. I understand that, you know, in public schools there's a general population so you're generally with all kinds of people. But, for me personally, those are issues I just don't want to deal with. I just want to concentrate on her [Rorrie's daughter's] education right now. So that's why I chose to send her to private school.

In the minds of these parents, the schools that they chose not only gave their children important advantages that they felt they were entitled to, but also allowed them to avoid the "general population" or "all kinds of people" by encapsulating them in a social environment populated by others of similar—relatively privileged—race and class backgrounds. Important, however, is that while they casually (and proudly) referred to their decisions by saying, as Rorrie did, such things as "that's why I chose to send her to private school" they also openly acknowledged that not every parent can make such choices. Comparing children from different family backgrounds, parents were very much aware of a link between structured educational inequality and structured wealth inequality. Here Madeline Preston was asked to clarify her perspective, and she did.

Interviewer: If we were to take two kids in high school—one went to an inner city public high school in the D.C. area, the other one went to one of those prestigious private schools in the D.C. area. And they both apply themselves in school as much as they can. Do you see them as having the same opportunities in this country?

Madeline: No. And the things that matter other than that are the quality of the schools. Particularly the primary and secondary schools.... No, I don't think that they have the same opportunities. I think that certainly we have individual illustrations of the ability of somebody to come from a very deprived background and to do extraordinarily well. Colin Powell is kind of the showcase example of that these days. And I know some individuals who have done that as well that are friends. But I also know that they overcame a hell of a lot more than I did. And had to. And I'm quite sure that the route to success is just a lot rougher. You've gotta overcome a lot more obstacles.

Everyone can call up token examples, such as that of Colin Powell, or individual friends of theirs who have "come from a very deprived background" and "do extraordinarily well." All of the families interviewed tended to do that. However, families with wealth privilege, who were poised in relatively advantaged situations over such individuals, were also quite open in acknowledging their advantage. They understood that for those from relatively disadvantaged backgrounds "the route to success is just a lot rougher." Specifically, in regard to the schools they had chosen for their own children, they understood that other kids in less fortunate positions would have to "overcome a lot more." In acting on their school decisions these parents relied on their own wealth privilege to a large extent, and in doing so were able to pass along advantage to their own children. School decision making was an arena in which the intergenerational transmission of privilege played out for these families; they were aware of it and they acknowledged it.

How do families with wealth privilege understand their relative positioning in the social world? And how do families disadvantaged by lack of wealth understand their circumstances? Given the commitment they had expressed to the values of meritocracy, to what extent did the families acknowledge a structure of wealth inequality?

Acknowledging Advantage: A Structure of Wealth Inequality

Lily: Well, it definitely helps if you've got a lot of money. But it shouldn't keep you from achieving your dreams if you don't have it.

Interviewer: Do you believe that the American Dream is equally true for all people?

Lily: Well, it's hard to say. I imagine it's a little easier if you come from a wealthier background. It does help if you're wealthy. But it doesn't preclude you from achieving your dreams if you don't have money to begin with.

Interviewer: So, comparing two random individuals, one of which is from an upper-class family background and one of lower class, do you think they both have the same chance to make something of themselves?

Lily: Yes. But I also feel that one has a little bit of an advantage, the wealthier one [silent pause]. Okay, the other does have more obstacles, I suppose. But it shouldn't prevent him from achieving his dreams. There is no reason why they can't eventually realize their dreams. But I will have to admit that I think it is a little bit more difficult for them.

Interviewer: What about your own family?

Lily: Well, definitely wealth does help meet your ability to help your kids buy a home, for example. And also, you can have money put aside in trust for them so that they're able to be financially well off and be able to invest in whatever they want down the road too. So somebody that doesn't have any wealth has a disadvantage there.

Interviewer: Do you believe that your own position in society has or will provide some underlying advantages for your children or your grandchildren?

Lily: I think so. We've achieved a fairly decent amount of wealth, and I think that helps even the children and the grandchildren down the road too.

—Lily Boothe, piano teacher, white, New York City

Given the fact that these families had so vehemently expressed their beliefs in the legitimacy of the American Dream, it was startling to hear them so openly discuss the reality of structured wealth inequality in American society. Not only did parents talk openly about this, they expressed specific views concerning the advantages conferred by wealth. Wealth-holding families thought of wealth as a distinctive resource to be used in particular ways, and even asset-poor families had concrete opinions about how they would use wealth—as opposed to income—if they had it. Regardless of whether a family had a lot, a little, or none, wealth was thought of as a special form of money, different from income. Wealth was perceived as a vehicle to provide opportunities, experiences, and material things, as well as a source to provide other less tangible advantages that were harder to articulate but no less important (a sense of security, or confidence about the future, for example). As a whole, families' perspectives on the advantages of family wealth centered around two notions: wealth as a *push* and wealth as a *safety net*. While families across the board alluded to these ideas, they were especially prevalent among the wealthier families, who emphasized them repeatedly.

The first notion, of a "push"—or an "edge," as some referred to it—was used by parents to explain how family wealth put some people ahead of others right from the start and "paved the way" for them over time.

Interviewer: Do you believe that you would have achieved the same social and economic situation that you have today if you weren't given the same financial support from your parents?

James: I would say no, because I feel what it has given me is the edge today. But for us today—for what I am, where I work, my abilities as well as my level of education—I feel without that I don't think I would be where I am today. Because the son would not have been successful without his father doing this—

Pamela: Paving the way for him.

James: [*Nods.*] So, his father paved the way for him to start off and climb up the ladder to be what he is right now. Each kid has the potential, aspiration, a dream. And with wealth you can guide them, you can steer them that way. And you can help them, smooth the way for them, open up doors which they had never seen before.

Pamela and James Gordon, just as the other parents from backgrounds of family wealth, had experienced how that wealth had given them a push and believed it had made a positive difference in the trajectory of their life course. And they believed that this same push they were now giving their own children would also make a difference for them down the road.

Some of the wealth-holding families interviewed were more resistant than others to explicitly conceptualize that "push" they referred to, or those differences "down the road," as concrete "advantage." Joel, for example, asserted right away that wealth passed on to children is "not advantage." He did, however, believe that "it helps." While he described the wealth passed along in families as "a pushing factor," he was careful to not suggest that this translated into actual advantage.

Interviewer: Does the financial help in terms of wealth that some people receive from their families give them certain advantages?

Joel: Not advantage, but it helps. It will help.

Interviewer: Do you think it's significant?

Joel: Depends on what kind of financial help you're talking about.

Interviewer: I'm not talking about billionaires. I'm talking, like, giving a kid, after he graduates, a $45,000 car. Or giving him, like, $30,000 for his wedding gift.

Joel: That helps, yeah, that does help. Yeah, the normal help that the parents give to the children, that is a pushing factor. Just puts you ahead a little bit.

Interviewer: Do you believe those without stable economic situations have a harder time achieving success?

Joel: Yes, I do. That's the rule of life. I mean if you have the money you have peace of mind. So you probably can make better decisions. If you're under pressure for lack of money you could go wrong, you could make wrong decisions, definitely.

Here we see a tension between the ideology of meritocracy and the reality of structured wealth inequality in the nuances of how Joel Conrad talked about, perceived, and made sense of family wealth. While a few other parents expressed similar resistance to acknowledging that the "push" of family wealth was a form of privilege, most families did not.[2] Victoria and Abraham Keenan, for example, conceptualized what they were doing for their own children as "absolutely" giving them advantages. While they were careful to point out that they were not "multimillionaires" like other people they knew, they did fully believe, and acknowledge, that their family wealth was giving their children "a better chance of becoming successful." Implicit in the way they discussed the passing along of their wealth was their acknowledgment that by doing so they were passing along advantage.

Interviewer: Do you believe that your position in society will in the future provide advantages for your own children or your grandchildren?

Victoria: Children, maybe.... I see where you're going with that, though, because my best friend was raised by her grandparents and they were multimillionaires and that money just trickles down from one to another to another generation. We're not in that kind of position.

Interviewer: But even like the fact that your father helped you to start your business, or your parents helped to pay for your education, or that they helped pay off your loans. Do you think that will actually trickle down and provide more advantages?

Abraham: Absolutely, because we're gonna do the same things.

Victoria: I think that it will.

Abraham: We're gonna start saving money for our kids' college funds and we're gonna encourage them to go to college and everything and be successful. We'd definitely like to see that sort of thing.

Interviewer: And that will pay off in advantages down the road for them?

Victoria: Absolutely.

Abraham: Gives them a better chance of becoming successful.

Family wealth was believed to give children a push that, as Abraham said, "gives them a better chance of becoming successful." Some families, of course, can give bigger pushes than others, but even small pushes are clearly advantageous. Children who get the pushes of family wealth benefit from advantages they did nothing to individually earn. The acknowledgment of this on the part of the families who were passing advantages along is an important part of their perspectives on wealth privilege and an important insight to how they think about inequality.

The second major way that parents depicted the advantages of family wealth was in how it acted as a "safety net" for them in important decisions and throughout their lives. Parents from wealth-holding families repeatedly articulated their sense that family wealth was a safety net that gave them tremendous "peace of mind." The Barrys, a white couple whose families on both sides had given them significant financial assets over the years, described their wealth holdings and the family wealth they believed they could rely upon in the future as "a sense of economic security." When asked what that sense of security provides for them, Briggette answered, "Sleep at night. It's very nontangible things. Being able to give my children a sense of peace. Being able to live worry-free. It's really nontangible things. Knowing that I will probably never have the income that my parents had, but still being comfortable with that and being able to provide for my children what they need."

Another parent who explicitly described her family's wealth as a safety net, went on to explain, "Well, I think just having, um, the assets, just gives us a certain freedom.... You know? You're ... freer and more comfortable." The sense of security parents felt from the safety net of family wealth, their desire to reestablish that safety net for their own children, and their ability to rely on it and expand on it in investing in their children's futures cannot be overemphasized. This was a major way that individuals we interviewed—for example Cynthia and Paul Perkins, a white middle-class couple with three children in Boston—acknowledged the power of wealth and wealth's associated privileges. As Cynthia noted, "My parents are well off.... If I didn't have my parents and Paul's parents, I would feel very economically insecure and may have very well made different decisions. I look at my parents, I mean they put so much effort into building security for the future.... So, I think having them around makes me feel more secure than I would otherwise. You know? A cushion for the future."

When a safety net of wealth—or, "a cushion for the future"—could not be relied upon, families without it felt the insecurity of having nothing on which to fall back. This is where the difference between wealth and income is perhaps the clearest. As Lenore Meehan, a young black mother from Boston explained it, "You know, if you look on paper, I make a lot of money, but it doesn't feel like it.... I mean, I don't feel like I'm economically secure at all." While she was up front about the fact that she felt she made quite a lot of money working as a dispatcher for the police force, Lenore's income simply could not provide the sense of security that family wealth was granting to those parents who had it.

The families interviewed from all race and class backgrounds made a clear distinction between wealth and income and had concrete understandings of the kinds of advantages that family wealth can provide. Their conceptualization of the "push" and the "safety net" that wealth affords for families and children (and that lack-of-wealth prohibits) reveals their intrinsic awareness and understanding of the power of wealth. Their acknowledgment of the role of wealth in shaping opportunities, life trajectories, and future chances reveals their awareness and understanding of a structure of wealth inequality.

> Interviewer: Do you believe that you would have achieved the same social and economic situation that you have today if you weren't given the same financial support from your parents growing up?
>
> Abigail: Probably not.
>
> Interviewer: So you think that was an essential ingredient?
>
> Abigail: For someone like me, yes.

As Abigail Connor said, "for someone like her"—someone from a wealthy white family with accumulated, historically rooted race and class advantages—intergenerational transfers of wealth along the way had created a real form of contemporary privilege: family wealth advantage that is not earned entirely independently but that makes opportunities relatively easier to attain, aspirations relatively more achievable, and life chances relatively more optimistic. When asked to reflect on the way this had played out in their own lives, Abigail and others "like her" were quite aware of the essential role that their family wealth had played in their lives. As Emily Mitchel explains,

> Interviewer: Do you believe that you would have achieved the same social and economic situation that you have today if you weren't given the same financial support from your parents growing up?
>
> Emily: No.
>
> Interviewer: [*Silent pause.*] How essential, if at all, do you believe family wealth is in attaining success?
>
> Emily: I think it certainly helps. I think more people who have money tend to excel than people who have no money. It gives you the education, it gives you the contacts, it gives you the clothes, the way of talking. The things that make life easier. Can you do it without it? Yes. Is it as easy? I don't think so.... I think early in our history hard work was really important. But I think money—you can work really hard and be the best foreman on a construction job, but it's not gonna get you a villa in France or a villa in Tuscany. It's just gonna get you whatever kind of advance you want, and a place to live. So I really think that wealth or family money is one of the essential ingredients.

Parents who had benefited from the advantages of family wealth consistently expressed their beliefs that they would not have achieved their same level of success without the financial support that they had received. Of the families who had benefited from family wealth, in only two cases did a parent insist without any compromise that they would have ended up in exactly the same position without any of the financial support that they had received from their family. And, in the two exceptions it is possible, of course, that they are correct. It is also the case that we have no way to really know.

In addition to talking about how it had impacted them, parents with family wealth also discussed how they were using that wealth to shape their own children's lives. They were consciously aware that their own relatively privileged positions were enabling them to pass advantage along to the next generation.

Interviewer: What role does wealth play in someone's ability to attain their dreams?

Molly: Well, it makes it a lot easier!

Interviewer: As far as what you said about your family, you guys are in a great situation compared to some other families.

Molly: Most.

Interviewer: Do you believe that your position in society has or will provide some underlying advantages for your children or grandchildren?

Molly: Oh, it has. I have three children, with five degrees, plus a CPA. And obviously we were able to afford that. They had no college loans, so it provides them with advantages. We've always helped them along the way when they needed money and we could do something. But we're not wealth spenders. We come out of middle-class backgrounds. We lived in the same house for thirty-five years, we don't have a million-dollar house. But without economic stability, it limits your choices. Any time you have more money, you have more choices.... I mean, if what's passed down, if your family owns the company, and you become president of the company when your father retires, maybe there's a little closer connection or nexus between family wealth and achievement. On the other hand, if your family has provided your education, well, you're certainly better off than those for whom the education has not been provided.

From these parents' perspectives, family wealth provided specific advantages such as educational opportunities that without it, their children would not have had. As Elizabeth Cummings, a white mother from a wealthy St. Louis family, explained,

No question about it! I mean, if my parents hadn't had the money to send my kids to the Hills School, we couldn't have considered it. We would have had to really do belt tightening, and financial aid, and many more loans, more mortgages. It would have been very difficult and a real strain on us, especially with two. And we probably would have felt like we just couldn't swing it as a family. So, I don't know, I would have had to have gone out and gotten a job that would pay enough to justify two kids in private school. With that, it would have meant not being able to mother them as much myself. Or my husband having to change work, and all the soul searching that would have meant for him. It's unimaginable. I can't envision a path that we would have been able to so comfortably just sail on over to the Hills School.

Alice, from a similar class background, expressed similar sentiments.

Alice: We wouldn't be in this house if it wasn't for my parents. But we would probably be in more debt!

Interviewer: Do you feel like where you choose to live is a really important factor in determining your kids' access to quality education?

Alice: Yeah, yeah, I think there's a huge difference in schools. A huge difference!

Finally, a white father summed it up by stating, "I think, unfortunately, you have to have it to get it. It makes it a lot easier. If you can pay for education for your kids, that means they can go wherever their abilities will take them."

Parents' awareness of a structure of wealth inequality among families, and its real-life impact on individuals—especially children—was pronounced. While they did not use the words that a social scientist might (they did not, for example, talk about "differential 'life chances' as an important aspect of social class stratification" as a sociologist would), they expressed ideas about social structure, the perpetuation of social inequality, and class stratification. One mother from Boston, for example, put it quite bluntly: "I think the more money or the more assets that you have, maybe the better education you receive. I think wealthier people have always had better chances at better schools, better programs, better communities."

The idea that "you have to have wealth to get it" (or, at least, that having wealth makes it *relatively* easier to get more) and the idea that "wealthier people have better life chances" (or, at least, that wealth confers *relatively* better chances for success), stood at the heart of these interviews. And these concepts stand at the heart of the matter here: if family wealth makes the next generation's wealth relatively easier to acquire, and if wealth makes success (however defined) relatively easier to attain, then people born into families with wealth are born with a distinct, unearned advantage. They are born with privilege that others do not have. The families interviewed saw this, expressed concrete understanding of it, and believed it was true that "family wealth has a *great deal* to do with success."

Interviewer: What role does family wealth play in someone's ability to succeed in America?

Carter: Well, having the wealth—capital—is a very important ingredient in success. If you have a business idea and you have the capital, you have a much better chance of succeeding. So family wealth has a *great deal* to do with success. In fact, it's one of the most important—brains and wealth are the two most important factors. I think that some people have a better chance than others. But everybody has a chance. For instance—like you asked the question about wealth—if you come from a wealthy family, you have a better chance. There is no such thing as equality, even in the American Dream! [*Laughs.*] If you're John D. Rockefeller's grandson, you're going to be more successful than most other people. That's the way it is.

Interviewer: Do you think your own position in society has provided, or will provide, some underlying advantages for your children or grandchildren?

Carter: I think so, yeah.

Interviewer: How so?

Carter: Well, they have the availability of more opportunities, they can travel, they can get better educated, and they can enjoy the better things in life. They get opportunities to do things that other kids never dream of being able to do.

A structure of wealth inequality is a reality that all of the families interviewed were observing and experiencing in their lives and the lives of others. What is remarkable was the extent to which—and the frankness with which—the families expressed and acknowledged it given its juxtaposition to the values of meritocracy they held so dear.

Perhaps those meritocratic values explain why so often families with wealth privilege went out of their way to assert that, while they acknowledged the advantages that family wealth had given them, they did not think it was fair. They often expressed their concern that their views might be portrayed as them thinking the situation was just and wanted to make clear that they did not. They emphasized how badly they felt about families who did not have the same advantages. As Lori put it, "I feel really glad that we have had this amount of freedom to make a great choice for our kids at Pacifica. And I really feel for parents who—because of financial restraints—are really stuck with some programs that are completely inadequate.... I just think it's just, what a shame, and how hard it must be for some parents because they have no choice."

Another parent said, "Life's not fair. We appreciate that we're fortunate, but it is certainly not fair." And another said, "I think that as you have more assets you have more choices but that, um, it is, it is wrong to leave out people who don't have assets. I ... I think there's raw potential that you need to look at. It would be a shame to pass it by."

In these families' experiences, wealth had often originated from intergenerational transfers, and affluent parents acknowledged that these assets had given them a real advantage—and they were clear that this was an advantage *over* others. While again, the specific term *wealth privilege* was never used by the interviewees, they clearly understood and articulated the unearned advantages of family wealth. They were candid in expressing their perspectives, not only in discussing the impact of the structure of wealth on their own lives, but also in discussing its impact on the lives of others. Examples from the interviews summarize first how wealth-holding families acknowledged the impact of the structure of wealth on their own lives.

> Interviewer: Do you see the way advantages are passed down through family wealth? How could you explain that?

> Karl: Well, I'll give you an example. My wife's family accumulated some wealth. That has served them very well and given them wonderful advantages. My wife's salary was okay as a senior government employee but she was able, for instance, to send both of her daughters to really, really good schools. And her nieces to really, really good schools and very

expensive schools. And when one of her nieces decided that she wanted to be a violin soloist, she spent $1.25 million on a Stradavarius. It's hard to buy a Stradavarius without wealth, income won't do it. And sending your kids—one went to Ivy League schools through med school. The other went to all Ivy League schools through law school. Sending your kids through those kinds of very, very expensive college educations, you *might* be able to do it on a senior civil servant salary, but it's a *whole lot easier* to do it with some wealth in addition to that! We have no mortgage. It's nice. People with wealth just don't have to think quite as hard about it. I think everybody would like to feel like they've done it all on their own. And anybody who has achieved success by any standard certainly must have done a fair amount on their own because there are people born with golden spoons in their mouths all the time who manage to break their teeth on the spoon and throw it away in no time. So there's always gonna be some degree of truth to the *I did it on my own*. But it's a pretty rare case when it's absolutely true. And so I think it's highly unlikely that there's anybody who can say absolutely they did on their own. And most of us who succeed had lots of help.

And second, wealth-holding families acknowledged the impact of structure of wealth on the lives of others.

Suzanne: We have some friends who are very high up. Let's say in finance. He's there because he had the opportunity at Princeton and when he came out his parents knew people and he was able to get the position. And I'm sure he's very, very good at what he does, but to disregard the fact that perhaps what he came from had anything to do with it would be wrong. I think people our age want to think they got everywhere they got on their own. But I don't think that's necessarily always the case. You know where I'm going with that?

Interviewer: So there's that example of your friend who went to Princeton and got a great job. And you can see how in his life he had certain advantages?

Suzanne: He had *total* advantages!

Drew: The money that his parents had certainly gave him this opportunity. No problem for them to pay for him to go to Princeton. Yet they didn't give him a lot. Like, he didn't have his own car.

Suzanne: But hold on a second! He grew up in the same town we did and they didn't even send him to our school, the top-ranked public school in the state; they sent him to Exeter, which is *ridiculous* because our school's *good*. So here's someone who was sent away to private school because they knew that that would give him certain advantages down the road. And that got him, plus his hard work, into Princeton. And then graduating from Princeton clearly helped him. But then his dad has connections, so that probably helped him, too. I think this guy's a very hard worker. I don't have any doubt in that respect at all. But I think in that instance if he would be one of those people that would say that—for *him* to say that [is] how *he* grew up!?—I think there definitely are people that where they are is because of— *not* hard work. I'm not saying *this* person, but *let's face it!* There are people in this country who are where they are because it was *handed to them.*

Interviewer: Okay. How essential, if at all, do you believe family wealth is in attaining success?

Drew: Chances are greater of somebody being financially successful if they come from a financially stable home....

Suzanne: I think it's cyclical.... I think that more times than not people are in the range they are because that's where they started and that's where their parents started and that's where their grandparents started.

Wealth Privilege As a Private, Public Power

Within a structure of wealth inequality, family wealth or lack of it grants unearned advantages to some individuals and disadvantages to others, depending on the families to which they were born. This was acknowledged by the parents interviewed as they expressed their beliefs that wealth gives families who have it advantages that they did not merit through individual achievement. In examining one

site where this can potentially play out—school decisio
parents believed wealth made a significant difference i
capacity to choose the schools that they thought woul
efit their children. And their direct experiences made pl:
was, indeed, the case. Their collective action was pattern___ _ _____
with wealth privilege used it to actively choose good schools (schools
that were the most reputable, and also that tended to be populated
by children from predominantly white, relatively wealthy families),
while families with histories of relative wealth poverty, who were
disproportionately black, were constrained from acting on what they
believed in and wanted for their children—good schools. Wealth was
a very private power that was used in a very public domain to access
advantageous education for children.

Given the landscape of vastly disparate schools, a structure of
wealth inequality is a powerful way in which opportunity for children is unequally distributed. Wealth can enable a family to access
resources and advantages for the next generation that they would not
be able to provide otherwise. And family wealth is usually, at least
to some extent, unearned. There are always exceptions—individuals who truly start from nothing and manage to create fortunes in a
lifetime; people who win the lottery and are suddenly millionaires;
families who save pennies and amass assets without any assistance
whatsoever. Most of us know at least one such example. However,
as we have seen, even in the only two hundred families we interviewed,
the patterns were very clear—most families do not amass wealth
from nothing; most families do not strike it rich by sheer luck; and
most families do not accumulate their wealth from savings alone.
These interviews provide a rare glimpse into the inner workings
of wealth within families, and into those families' perspectives on
wealth inequality—rare because wealth, like most aspects of money
and social class, is not something we usually talk about, especially
not in the United States.

We learn from an early age that it is inappropriate, improper,
even rude to ask questions about other people's money. We may talk
around it, complain about it, or flaunt it, but social class and specifics
of money wrapped up in it most often go ignored—at least overtly, at
least publicly. Social class is, as bell hooks writes, "a taboo topic" in
our society.[3] Wealth is part of the taboo. The fact that wealth is not
talked about is important because it means that how families acquire
wealth, the intergenerational transmission of it, and the purposeful
use of it are normally hidden from public view. In this way, wealth

remains a "taboo"—or, what Katherine Newman refers to as a "hidden dimension"—of our society.[4]

There is a code of secrecy that surrounds wealth in our society. We normally do not ask such things as how much someone has saved in the bank; what was inherited when a relative died; how much cash was received on a wedding day; what portion of a down payment was contributed by family; how much of children's education is financed by grandparents; what value a family's furniture or jewelry holds; or how much interest was accrued on this quarter's investments. Family wealth might be discussed with financial advisors, but usually not with neighbors or coworkers, and often not even with close friends or family. The story of family wealth is almost never told, and when it is, the details are often vague. A family's wealth portfolio, let alone how much of it originated from family sources and how it is used to propel advantage, can easily fly under the radar despite its power in shaping that family's experiences and worldviews. But surely if the two hundred families interviewed here are any indicator at all, among middle- and upper-class families, and disproportionately white families, intergenerational transfers are significant and occurring regularly. In these families, wealth was being passed along, amassed, and used in a myriad of ways throughout the life course. The power of wealth is *private*. But it creates opportunities, provides experiences, and opens doors that very often are in the *public* domain.

The private, public power of wealth has big implications, especially when the undercurrent of the American Dream runs so strong. Wealth can easily go unnoticed, and we are often left to assume that it is not an important variable in a life trajectory or that only a very small group of people benefit from family wealth in any significant way. Meanwhile, as we have seen, it was an important variable in a life trajectory, and many more families than we might have imagined were benefiting from it. Wealth privilege is like a buoy, helping to keep those who have it ahead and afloat, pushing them upward, and there to rely upon if the waters get choppy.

Most of the white families interviewed had experienced—to some extent—the privileges, or the buoying effects, of family wealth. In comparison to black parents of all socioeconomic backgrounds, white parents much *less* often were supporting their own parents and extended families and had much *more* often reaped the benefits of the financial assistance and support associated with family wealth over time: intergenerational transfers and inheritances passed down to them in small or large amounts; the "push" and the "safety net" of their families' relative class positioning; their college educations at least partially paid for by their own parents; help with first-home down payments and other major purchases; gifts; loans; assistance in funding investments and business ventures; new or used furniture, appliances, cars, and the like passed along—a steady stream of "big" or "tiny" things that made a difference. These were sometimes passed along at major milestones during the life of a family, or they might have been given routinely, perhaps even daily.

Others studying wealth have implicitly and explicitly argued that while income is received and used from day to day to support daily living, wealth is received and used in families at important milestones in life to create opportunities and leverage advantages for the next generation.[5] While wealth was certainly received at major milestones in the wealth-holding families interviewed here, its accumulated receipt in the more mundane experiences of these families was just as important to its acquisition, development, use, and far-reaching impact. Not only did wealth appear to take on a "cumulative effect" as it was passed along at major milestones and continued to amass,[6] but the interviews also brought to light the more day-to-day, commonplace receipt and privileges of family wealth—the *accumulative advantage* of family wealth over time, the relatively minor, "invisible," taken-for-granted privileges for people from wealthy backgrounds that together add up, that matter. The transfer of wealth within families can happen in momentous moments, but it can also be more fluid: buoying, securing, and orienting those individuals who have it in thousands of subtle ways.

Others have discussed the accumulation of advantage and disadvantage as small differences in daily lives that amount to significant disadvantage or advantage over time.[7] In sociology, this idea is probably best established in work on gender. Virginia Valian, for example, draws attention to the ramifications of the accumulation of advantage and disadvantage in individuals' occupational careers over time, pointing to how "the long-term consequences of small differences in the evaluation and treatment of men and women also hold up the glass ceiling."[8] What the interviews here point to is something similar—specifically, the trickle-down effect of how seemingly little things can add up to translate into big differences, both material and sociopsychological, for individuals who benefit from family wealth. Over time, accumulative advantages are, as one parent said, "paving the way" for individuals with family wealth, and allowing them "to live worry free," as another said. Previous research on wealth has alluded to this—for instance, referring to the way that wealth "feeds heads," or orients people's future aspirations[9]—but much more work in this area is required to further our understanding.

One way to conceptualize the use of wealth in wealth-holding families is as providing the next generation with *foothold steps of advantage*. Conceptualizing family wealth this way, in the families we interviewed, foothold steps of advantage were created both by small, subtle transfers of wealth (those more day-to-day) and by more massive, obvious transfers (at milestone events); but, over time, these all added up to enable a firmer grip on children's future chances for success, however defined. A good analogy for this legacy of foothold steps of advantage in wealth-holding families is the rock-climbing wall. On the rock-climbing wall, parents use their own family wealth to nail extra foothold steps for their children's climbs. These may be material or nonmaterial, but these footholds are advantageous because they are additional steps that are not provided for other climbers. We all want to secure footholds for our children; we all want to make the path less slippery, less steep, less difficult to climb. Wealth gives some families the ability to provide footholds for their children while other families cannot; this leads to very different climbs, very different experiences, and very different mobility patterns.

Foothold steps of advantage materialized in how wealth-holding families were able to buy in and opt out more easily than the other families, but they also took shape in the tutoring, piano lessons, cultural and social capital, higher-quality housing, better health care, financial guidance, home computers, and all sorts of other things that were more easily acquired—and in operation—within the families with wealth to rely upon. As previously mentioned, in her books, *Home Advantage* and *Unequal Childhoods,* sociologist Annette Lareau discusses how these sorts of things contribute to what she refers to as a "concerted cultivation" of childhood in middle-class families.[10] As she also found, the middle- and upper-middle-class families we interviewed were conscientiously "cultivating" their children's growth by providing family vacations, professional college-admissions preparation, cultural activities, and a myriad of other activities, opportunities, and experiences to their children. Any of these things taken alone would not necessarily impact the life of a child. However, taken together they add up over the course of a childhood, and in the case of the families interviewed here, family wealth was often being relied upon to help facilitate such things.

The families were forthcoming on the subject of wealth privilege; they understood and acknowledged a structure of wealth inequality and the ways that inequality plays out for the next generation in terms of educational trajectories and children's life chances. Taken together and comparing those with and without backgrounds of family wealth, the parents' perspectives, beliefs, and experiences brought to light a sort of "glass floor" connected to wealth privilege. In conjunction with the concept of a "glass ceiling" invisibly keeping disadvantaged individuals from rising, a *glass floor* seemed to keep individuals with family wealth from falling very far. And people were aware of it. Essentially, in families who had access to wealth, parents consciously used it to access advantageous opportunities for their children in their attempts to ensure that the next generation would not only rise from the relatively privileged position in which they already stood, but also not fall very far either. Wealth privilege—the glass floor—was there to stand upon; it served as an invisible safety net, buoying up the families who had it and granting them a sense of security that felt to them like "peace of mind."

Given their acknowledgment of wealth privilege and a structure of wealth inequality, it might be hard to imagine that these same parents truly believed that all Americans have an equal shot at whatever they aspire to, and that people who "make it" do so entirely on their own. The most provocative aspect of the interviews, however, was just that—the families discussed their beliefs in meritocracy with the same forthrightness with which they had discussed wealth privilege.

6

Inequality and Ideology

Interviewer: In your own opinion, how realistic is the American Dream in today's society?

Jacob: I think it's realistic! I think you have to have someone who has the drive to achieve and part of that is people who have a *work ethic*. I think that's what is sort of lacking in a lot of people who don't seem to *want* to work hard for a goal. They want something easy. And so I think it's realistic.

Interviewer: What role does a family's wealth play in someone's ability to attain their dreams in this country today?

Jacob: I think it gives them a couple of legs up. If you have money you can afford to go to a school that helps you in later life. It helps with the contacts. The higher your class and the amount of wealth, you are with people who can be influential in your behalf. No, it *definitely* plays a role. Makes it easier, I think, to achieve.

—Jacob Mitchel, business owner, white, Washington, D.C.

As open as they were in discussing wealth and inequality, the parents' belief in the ideology of the American Dream was the dominant theme of our interviews. This theme emerged throughout the first phase of interviewing, despite it not having even been an original focus of the research. In contrast with the subject of wealth inequality—which *was* intended as the focus—families did not require any questions whatsoever to bring the American Dream of meritocracy to the forefront of their discussions; they often initiated the subject themselves and brought it up repeatedly. It seemed as though they knew at some level that by talking so openly about structured wealth inequality, they were somehow compromising the culturally sacred tenets of the American Dream that they believed in so strongly, and felt compelled to defend their beliefs. In the second set of interviews, families were directly asked about the American Dream, and they talked about their perspectives at length. They were also asked about how they reconcile the contradiction between structured wealth inequality and their belief in meritocracy, and while they spoke about it many of them claimed to have genuinely "never thought about it like this before." Although it was clearly part of their lived experiences, it was apparent in both rounds of interviews that many of the families (if not all of them) had never previously considered the particular subject of this book: the contradiction between the American Dream and the power of wealth.

Inherited family wealth contradicts the American Dream of meritocracy because it creates unearned advantages for some that others do not have. Family wealth ascribes privileges to individuals that they have not earned—wealth privilege flies in the face of the American Dream. How did parents who had received intergenerational transfers of family wealth reconcile their awareness of the wealth gap with their belief in meritocracy? How did parents who were disadvantaged by histories of family wealth poverty make sense of such circumstances in light of their belief in meritocracy? While they openly acknowledged a structure of wealth inequality, these same families simultaneously insisted that Americans wind up where they do based on hard work or lack thereof. They emphasized the importance of family wealth to many people's success; yet, at the same time, they rigorously defended individual merit as *the* determinant of any person's social class positioning. Essentially, the recognition of structured wealth inequality went hand in hand with the dismissal of it—all at the same time.

Conviction in Meritocracy:
Hard Work or Lack Thereof

Carter: The fact of the matter is because you get some assistance from your parents doesn't mean that you haven't primarily achieved anything on your own. The fact of the matter is getting a down payment on a house means you were able to get a house sooner, but you still have to make the payments on the house, you still have to do everything necessary to maintain that house. So yeah, it's a help, but it's not the overriding factor.

Interviewer: You think the overriding factor is your own—

Carter: Your own *psyche*.... At the end of the day, *hard work* is *the* most important ingredient—in *anybody's* success.

Interviewer: Think so?

Carter: Yes. The determination to be successful is like the tide, you know? You can't stop it.

—Carter Martin, attorney, white, Washington, D.C.

Tracei Diamond, a black single mother from St. Louis, spent much of her interview answering "no" to every question regarding any financial assistance she might have received and explaining the lack of any family financial resources available to her. As a full-time banquet waitress at a private country club, Tracei's annual income was $24,000, she had zero net financial assets, and held only a high school degree. Tracei talked about how she sees the members of the country club at functions and events and thinks about how they and their children had advantages that she and her three children simply did not have. She spoke at length, for example, about how the schools "out there" (where the country club was located) were "good schools," how the teachers "really work with them" (the students), and how overall "the education is better." In Tracei's view, for as much as she would like to be able to give her kids those same kinds of opportunities, she simply could not afford the move to such an area. On top of supporting her three children on her own (she was receiving no child support), Tracei also was doing whatever she could to financially support her younger sister and their mother.

Tracei's interview was typical in that she articulated clear recognition of a structured inequality among families that blatantly and categorically translates into unequal educational opportunities for children of different family wealth backgrounds. Yet also typical was Tracei's outright rejection of this inequality and of unequal opportunity. After Tracei had talked about how "wealthy families" get the "better schools," she was asked about how a family's wealth plays a factor in their children's access to quality education. She replied, "It really doesn't have an impact on it. I guess pretty much it depends on *you*, as far as what kind of life you will have for your child." When she was asked if wealth has any impact, she said, "I don't really look at it like that. So, like I say, money definitely doesn't have anything to do with it." When asked to explain further, Tracei answered, "It's basically what the parents want, or whatever, that's the only thing I really can see. It just depends on how they raise them, really." Despite their perspectives that class inequality structures life chances, Tracei and other families interviewed maintained their belief that merit— not money—is what matters; they maintained with conviction their belief in meritocracy.

It was striking to hear disadvantaged parents talk so vehemently about meritocracy, to hear them assert repeatedly that positions in society are earned entirely through hard work and personal achievement, and to hear them deny family wealth inequality as a legitimate concern. But considering that many of these parents had no direct experience with wealth privilege, that they had no awareness of the extent to which wealthy families are using and extending intergenerational transfers of assets, that they did not know for sure how much others are advantaged by unearned resources, then it makes sense how they clung so resolutely to the dominant ideology. What was most remarkable, however, is that those parents with family wealth who had spoken openly of their unearned advantages, who had so plainly seen, felt, and known wealth privilege in motion in their own lives, were at the same time insistent that meritocracy is an accurate and realistic explanation for social stratification in America.

In an interview in St. Louis, Briggette and Joe Barry spoke in detail of the financial help they had received from their parents. They openly declared that these resources had allowed for a lifestyle they would not otherwise have had. After listing extensive financial assistance, the security of family wealth, and the many advantages they have had, the Barrys insisted that the way they had earned their assets was through hard work.

> Interviewer: How did you acquire the different assets that you own?

> Briggette: Worked our butts off to pay for them.... Worked for it. All worked for!

The Barrys were not atypical of the white middle-class families interviewed; on the contrary, they portrayed the sentiments of families like them in the sample. Their socioeconomic positions were due, in large part, to the inheritance and accumulative advantages of family wealth; yet, at the same time, they were adamant that they single-handedly earned and deserved their places in society. These families' insistence that they had "worked their butts off" for what they had was astonishing. They listed in detail the help they had received from their families: financial assistance with major purchases, down payments on houses, school tuition for children, "loans" that were later forgiven, and so on. They cataloged the gifts they had received from family members for birthdays, graduations, weddings, and births of children. They discussed the numerous ways their extended families had been financially generous over the years by providing used cars, old furniture, flight tickets home for holidays, family vacations, meals out in restaurants, kids' back-to-school clothes, and groceries, to name a few. They described the "push" and the "safety net" that come with family wealth: feeling that they have had "a head start" or "an edge" over others, knowing they would have something to fall back on in a financial pinch, and the expectation of future inheritances. While they talked about, listed, and described these things when asked, they repeatedly emphasized how hard they had worked for all that they owned and how much they deserved their stations in life.

Regardless of background, families used the American Dream of meritocracy to explain their assertion that anyone can be anything and do anything and get anywhere with hard work. They stressed that hard work or lack thereof was the determinant in each individual's position in society. But for those with family wealth, what was most notable was how they implied, implicitly and explicitly, that their own advantages as well as the advantages they were passing along to their children were earned and deserved autonomously—through hard work, perseverance, and determination alone.

Chris and Peter Ackerman, a white couple in their early thirties, lived in a white suburb of St. Louis. They had three kids, ages six, three, and two. They had been married for ten years and both worked in management positions on the staff of a local university. Their combined annual income was $83,000, their net worth $210,000, and their net financial assets totaled $91,500. This couple possessed savings accounts, savings bonds, small trust funds for each child, and a boat worth $12,500. They had received significant financial assistance from their families, including help with a down payment on their first home, which they bought when they married. The equity from that house was later used as a down payment for a larger home when they had children. Chris and Peter's parents had financed their college educations; they never had to take out student loans; their children regularly received cash gifts and savings bonds from their grandparents on holidays and birthdays; Chris's parents had often paid for the family to vacation with them; Peter's parents had bought many of their major household appliances for them, as well as their car; and so on. They talked about how appreciative they were of all this help, about how they would not be in the position that they are without it. Despite this acknowledgment, Chris and Peter continually insisted that their wealth had been achieved single-handedly.

> Interviewer: How did you acquire the assets you own?
>
> Chris: By working.
>
> Peter: Saving, working.
>
> Chris: Working and saving, working and saving, working and saving. That's basically how we do it.

The Ackermans and many of their peers simultaneously acknowledged the power of their wealth privilege and avowed that it does not really matter. They were resolute in their explanation that hard work and determination had gotten them where they were. For as much as they were up front about the structure of wealth, they *also* depicted social positioning as independently earned and deserved. As one young mother from just outside of New York City put it, "You know—and I'm not bragging, I'm not saying anything—but it just comes from setting your priorities straight, and taking care of business!" In discussing hard work and individual achievement, people often spoke louder, quicker, and sometimes at a higher pitch. People leaned forward or moved in toward the tape recorder's microphone as if to be sure they were heard clearly on this. They spoke with fervor and conviction when crediting themselves with their own success. For example, throughout much of the interview with Lily and Jonathan Boothe, a white wealthy family from the New York City area, Jonathan had been quite serene. However, when we began talking about the Boothes' perspectives on success and achievement, Jonathan became noticeably more vivacious.

> Interviewer: From what you said about you and your family and where you guys are right now, you're in a great situation relative to other people in the U.S. There are people obviously

that are worse off, have a hard time paying bills, doing things like that. How do you explain your own success?

Jonathan: Well, I did have my own business and I worked pretty hard at it! And we made some pretty good investments in real estate, too. So we're pretty well off.

Interviewer: Okay. How do you think some people make it in this country and other people don't?

Jonathan: I don't know. I guess really sticking to one's ideals of what we want to do with ourselves. And sort of being *focused* on it. Now, the thing is, I think what we need to also come up with is the fact that [in] this country you don't have to be born into richness. You can do it even if you're relatively poor. You can be successful down the road. It's not easily possible in some of the other countries.... I think here the ones that are successful are the ones who really stick with what their goals are and their dreams. And it does take an effort, but they manage.... I mean, I started my own business from scratch. And I've been pretty successful with it.

Interviewer: Okay, so what is the main factor?

Jonathan: Yeah. [*Silent pause.*] Just *working hard*.

Jonathan himself had been "born into richness" and, for example, his business and investments were originally funded by his own father. Although he had been forthright about this and about his awareness of family wealth's value and his gratitude for it (in fact, earlier in the interview in regard to an individual's chances at success he had said that "if you're born into wealth it's probably easier for you"), he also argued that his same position would be "easily possible" for any person born without the privileges that he had been. "Sticking to one's ideals," "being focused" and "motivated," and being "willing to work hard" were themes discussed repeatedly as affluent families explained their perspectives on their own success in comparison to others. Abigail Spence, for instance, discussed in detail the family wealth she'd received from her parents, including substantial help with house down payments, investments, and the funding of her children's educations. Yet, just on the heels of this, she explained that her family's social positioning was the result of her husband Connor's willingness to work hard and his drive to succeed.

Interviewer: So what you said about your house, your family and your kids, and where you live—you guys are in a great situation as far as everything like that. How do you explain your own success?

Abigail: I think Connor has had a big impact on how successful and stable and well off this family is. He works very hard and does whatever it takes to make sure that we've got what we need.

Interviewer: [*Silent pause.*] Why do you think some people make it and others don't?

Abigail: I think it has to do with how hard you're willing to work and how motivated, how driven you are.

Interviewer: So you think it's all in the person and what he or she puts into it?

Abigail: Yeah.

Just as people with wealth credited themselves for their success, conversely, those who lacked family wealth blamed themselves. Conviction in meritocracy worked both ways, and meritocracy could justify both positions. The themes of "sticking to one's ideals," "being focused" and "motivated," and being "willing to work hard" were as consistent in interviews with working-class and impoverished families as they were in affluent families. People blamed themselves for their inability to attain what they wished for and wanted for themselves and their children, even when they were starting from the most disadvantaged backgrounds. One parent from Boston explained that, compared to others, she comes up short because "I did a lot of fooling around." A mother from St. Louis said, "I would say that I am a little bit limited. But it's nobody's fault but my own. So I can't complain." And still another parent lamented, "If I was to make more, better, wiser decisions along the way, I wouldn't have the debt that I have now."

Most people have regrets in life, and maybe if the families who were struggling to make ends meet had made "more, better, wiser decisions along the way" things would have turned out differently for them. Maybe not. But one of the things that stood out the most about this explanation was that many of these families had in fact done extraordinarily well for themselves.[1] More often than not, however, the fruits of unaided self-achievement simply paled in comparison to the results of self-achievement combined with the advantages of family wealth. Still, throughout the interviews, parents from poor and working-class family backgrounds compared themselves to more "well-off" others, blamed themselves, and legitimized their situations by saying they should have worked harder. While to some extent they understood that a structure of wealth inequality existed, and while they recognized the real advantages for those with family wealth, they simultaneously blamed themselves for not having worked harder and done better than they had.

Just as families from across the socioeconomic spectrum blamed and credited themselves for their social class positioning, when they explained their perspectives on how other people end up where they do, they expressed the same conviction in meritocracy by blaming and crediting others. Families from every class bracket used this same basic logic.[2] Here, Grace Conrad, a white mother from the New York City area with very wealthy family backgrounds on both her and her husband's sides, conveys her logic:

Interviewer: On a scale of one to one hundred, with one hundred being the wealthiest Americans and one being the poorest, where do you think your family would rank on that?

Grace: Probably in the seventies.

Interviewer: So on the same scale, one to one hundred, why do you think that the people who are the ones, the fives and the tens—why do you think they're so low on that scale? What are the reasons for that being so?

Grace: I don't know. I would think it's probably has to do with maybe not enough education. Or they possibly could be chronic underachievers, too … it does take quite a bit of effort to educate oneself. You have to be pretty—I don't know what the word for it is—You have to have a *stick-to-it-iveness* to get there.

Notions of meritocracy and ideas bound up with the American Dream were used to explain not just one's own lot in life but also to justify stratification within society at large. And here the conversation inevitably turned to education; parents repeatedly insisted that education makes the American Dream possible for every child—not just that every child has a chance, but that the playing field is level, that education is the Great Equalizer, and that the competition is fair. A great example comes from our New York City area interview with Olivia and Nicholas Holden, a university administrator and a venture capitalist, both from wealthy family backgrounds:

> Interviewer: Okay, what about, say, hypothetically two kids with the same intellectual ability? One coming from an elite private school in the city, one coming from a public school in the city in a poor neighborhood let's say. If they both work hard in school and both get pretty good grades, do you think that they both have the same opportunity to make the same for themselves in the future?
>
> Olivia: Yes.
>
> Interviewer: You do?
>
> Olivia: Yes, I do. Generally, I do.

Although these families had spoken genuinely of their understanding that some kids are unfairly advantaged and disadvantaged by the schools they attend, they also adamantly ignored this fact to argue that they all have equal opportunities. While they claimed that good schools bestow advantages, they also claimed that work ethic is what ultimately matters.

The intensity of these beliefs created confusion and self-doubt for even the most high-achieving parents. An interview with the Johnsons in Los Angeles provides a poignant example: Elaine and Bradford Johnson were in their early forties, had been married eleven years, and had two daughters—Macy was ten and Maya was four. They lived in a predominantly black, middle-class neighborhood. Their condominium development was a secure gated community that they chose because it fulfilled their two biggest priorities: they wanted to feel safe, and they wanted to raise their daughters in a "good neighborhood" where they would not be the only black family. Bradford was a news reporter for a major television network and earned $117,000 a year, while Elaine was home full-time with the girls. Although they had to take out significant student loans, both Elaine and Bradford had surpassed their own parents' levels of education, and both were graduates of private colleges. The Johnsons could easily be held up as perfect examples of the American Dream.

Beneath the poster image, however, they were worried about their situation. The family's net financial assets were negative $14,000.

They had never received financial help from their families and did not suspect that they ever would. Elaine was sending a check to her mother every month to help her pay bills, and they regularly sent money to Bradford's mother, as well. Over the years, the Johnsons had constantly felt pressure to financially assist their extended families, and explained that it was "very difficult" for them to "say no to family." Their biggest concern was that they had not been able to save for a down payment to buy a home, which they had been trying to do for years. The Johnsons felt constantly stressed about these things, and spoke of how they felt no sense of financial security. Bradford said, "I mean, if I lost my job tomorrow, we would be three weeks from living on the street."

Despite their educational and occupational success, the Johnsons had noticed that their white peers seemed much more financially well off. At the end of their interview, Bradford confided that he "just can't figure out what we are doing wrong." They wondered why they had not been able to "keep up"; many of their white friends from college were buying vacation homes while the Johnsons were still struggling to save for a first home; at work functions they had often heard Bradford's white colleagues talk about their investments and Bradford and Elaine wondered how those families had money to invest when they themselves could barely afford to keep up with their monthly bills. They worried about how they would pay for college for their girls and fantasized about taking a nice family vacation someday. They had guessed about the salaries of their friends and colleagues and determined that Bradford made at least as much money. Bradford and Elaine were left feeling baffled by it all. As Bradford explained, "I, you know, in the areas that I drive in or work in, I mean, when I'm driving from Orange County, Laguna, Newport, and I'm looking at these houses and saying, what are these people doing for a living, and how come I'm not doing it? What are all these people doing that I'm not doing? And I thought I was doing pretty well.... I mean, I feel like I should have a lot more, you know? Probably because it is just me—maybe I'm just too ambitious."

Their confusion and self-doubt was so strong that it was almost palpable. Here is the American Dream in motion: Bradford wonders why he is "not doing" whatever it is that others are doing to get to where they are and to have what they have. He compares their uneven achievements with an underlying assumption that they are justifiably comparable. During the interview, it was hard not to stop everything and tell the Johnsons what so many of the interviews with white families had revealed—that they have had a "push," a "safety net," accumulative advantage, a buoy of wealth privilege that the Johnsons just have not had. It was hard not to expose that which was largely invisible to them: that although their college friends and Bradford's colleagues may never speak of it, and some may go out of their way to keep it hidden, the circumstances of many of them were undoubtedly fostered by intergenerational transfers of wealth. It was hard to not read Bradford and Elaine the transcripts from other interviews so that they could see the inside workings of family wealth, the *power of wealth*.

Upholding the Contradiction: The American Dream and the Power of Wealth

Interviewer: So, this is the last question. It's obvious from everything you're saying that you can clearly see how family wealth, family money, family savings enables children through generations to achieve things. You're saying it helps them, it gives them advantages, right?

Suzanne: Yeah.

Drew: Absolutely.

Interviewer: In your own lives and in the lives of people that you know. And you're also saying over and over and over that what matters the most is hard work, and drive and determination and you keep saying 'aspirations.' Do you see how those two things contradict each other?

Suzanne: Yes.

[*Silent pause.*]

Interviewer: Do you, Drew? Because on the one hand you're saying that people make it in America based on how hard they work. But you're also saying that you can see that people make it in America sometimes even if they don't work very hard.

Drew: Yeah.

Interviewer: So you two can clearly see that your kids and you and the people that you know who come from families who have wealth, or some money at the very least, have advantages?

Suzanne: Yes.

Interviewer: You also believe in the American Dream, that people get ahead based entirely on how hard they work. Am I right?

[*Silent pause.*]

Suzanne: Well—[*silent pause*]—it's not an absolute. Not everybody is where they are because of how hard they work. Money.

Drew: But for the most part, yeah.

Suzanne: I don't know. I guess I hope that people are where they are because of hard work. But in reality, I don't know. I don't know.

Interviewer: But in your reality of what you do know—

Suzanne [*interrupting*]: We absolutely have had certain advantages. Our education, and that in itself gives us our opportunities. It's complicated. I think it's a really interesting study because you're right—you say all these things but then you do end up contradicting the two statements. But I think for me it's more like I just hope that people would be that way because that's how I want to instill in my kids.

—Suzanne and Drew Wright, high-tech business owner and high-tech recruiter, white, New York City

A structure of family wealth inequality contradicts the American Dream of meritocracy because while meritocracy explains social position as the result of individual achievement, inherited wealth grants advantages through ascription. In the case of the contemporary United States, historic legacies continue to play out in the present day as white families—especially middle- and upper-middle-class white families—have more wealth to pass along to the next generation than do other families. One particularly interesting arena in which this unfolds is parental decision making regarding children's schools.

The education system is not commonly seen as further rewarding those with wealth privilege and disadvantaging those without. Yet in a system of unequal schooling, wealth can be used (and in the families interviewed who had it, *was* used) as a means to an end: to confer advantageous opportunities to children. All of the parents interviewed believed in the American Dream and saw education as the key to ensuring their dreams for their children, but the decisions they were making about their children's educations were in large part determined by each family's wealth holdings.

Wealth privilege clashes as a material contender to the spirit of the American Dream. And the American Dream clashes as an ideological contender to the power of wealth. Yet the families interviewed upheld both their beliefs in the American Dream and the power of wealth.

> Interviewer: Do you think that the types of schools that you are able to send your kids to puts them at an advantage to others who maybe live in less affluent areas and go to less prosperous schools?

> Cameron: I think that can make a difference, yeah.... I did read recently the results of a survey that indicated that the better school you go to or have a degree from, the more money you're likely to make over the life of your career. So I guess it does make a difference. I think it does. Well, I think it can be overcome but it certainly does give you a bit of an edge to go to a good high school.

> Interviewer: Does where a person goes to school matter for their life chances?

> Cameron: Well, not really. No, I don't think so. If they're willing to work at it.

The interview discussions went to and fro, literally moment by moment, between a deep belief in meritocracy and the defense of its legitimacy on one hand, and an understanding of the reality of structured wealth inequality and its ramifications on the other.

> Interviewer: What makes some people successful in this country and others not?

Sharon: I really think it comes down to how much a person is willing to make sacrifices, work and get trained, get educated, do whatever it takes to make something of themselves.

Interviewer: And what about family wealth? What do you think is the place of that in someone's attainment of success?

Sharon: It can give people an advantage to having access to better schools, better neighborhoods, better class of people.

Interviewer: Can the financial help, in terms of wealth, that some people receive from their families give them certain advantages in achieving the American Dream?

Sharon: I tend to think it isn't all much of an advantage in many ways.

Interviewer: Has everyone with economic privilege worked hard to achieve that position?

Sharon: I think so [pause]. There's those that are wealthy that have inherited it, but I would still say that they have achieved it.

Interviewer: Do you think those people that inherit family wealth—do you think that's an achievement? Do you think they can say, "We achieved it"?

Sharon: I would think not.

Sharon and the families interviewed as a whole expressed their perspectives as a simultaneous back-and-forth between the American Dream and the power of wealth. In addition to discussing each separate topic at length, the subjects of structured wealth inequality and meritocracy were tangled together as families attempted to make sense of it all. Rather than "choosing" an allegiance to one side or another of this complicated paradox, parents generally insisted on both—they tried to hold it all in one hand—despite the contradiction.

In their interview, Pamela and James Gordon, one of the families interviewed from the Washington, D.C. area, articulated what was the prevailing stance of the two hundred families interviewed; in looking at long portions of their discussion we can see them *upholding the contradiction* between the American Dream and the power of wealth.

James: Wealth somehow opens the road for you and smooths it very, very easy. And I think you can achieve and this country gives you a chance to do everything you want if you are capable and wealthy and able to pay for it. I mean, I started with nothing. Although my father was wealthy, yes. I started with nothing. And I believe this is what the American Dream is! They give you a chance to be what you want to be, to become what you want to be. So I feel, no, I think this land gives you the opportunity, not what is passed on from your parents.

Interviewer: Just to go back to this wealth question one more time: Do you see the ways in which a family that does have wealth can pass down certain advantages to their children that others who are not as wealthy can't?

Pamela: Definitely. No question about it.

James: Definitely. Because you are giving him a tool to smooth his way. And to open up things much easier than the underprivileged.

Pamela: Exactly, yeah. Definitely.

Interviewer: Do you two believe that those without stable economic situations have a harder time achieving success?

Pamela: Not if they are persistent and they have dreams. No. Because you hear stories and you see people that come from really very harsh backgrounds, but like I said if they have goals and they have dreams, nothing can't be achieved. You have to have these dreams in your head. And then you hear of these public schools in D.C. that are really bad and they are in very poor neighborhoods and there's that kid that just graduated from high school this year and he got three different offers from Ivy League schools because he was so intelligent! And he tried to do the best he can. And he got a full scholarship from Georgetown, from UNC, and from other different schools.

James: That proves the viability of the American Dream right there!

Pamela: Hard work! You have to have motivation and give it your all. Some people are willing to take the extra mile, others are not.

James: Hard work somehow secures for you success. And provides you an edge on others who do not. And this is why you will excel.

Interviewer: Does the financial help in terms of wealth that some people receive from their families give them a great deal of advantage in achieving the American dream?

James: Obviously.

Pamela: Yeah, definitely.

Interviewer: Do you think that everyone with economic privilege worked hard for it?

James: Not necessarily.

The Gordons wanted to be clear that they were big believers in the American Dream, in the belief in "hard work" and "motivation" as the "true ingredients" for "why you will excel." And, like so many families interviewed, James pointed to himself as proof—in this case, proof of his success (although in interviews with disadvantaged families it was not uncommon to find them pointing to themselves as proof of failure). James claimed he had "started with nothing." Of course, he continued, "Although my father was wealthy, yes." But again, in upholding the contradiction, he repeated, "I started with nothing." James clearly denied the power of wealth in his adamancy about meritocracy. At the same time, James and Pamela were clear in their view that there is "no question about it"—that family wealth can "open up things much easier" in order to "smooth [the] way."

And Pamela and James, like many families, relied upon token examples—stories they had heard of individual people "that come from really very harsh backgrounds," who, unaided, had managed to achieve great things through hard work. These token stories are called upon to deflect from the many more that contradict them, and thus, as James said, serve to prove "the viability of the American Dream."

These stories are iconic in our culture so that, although they are few relative to the massive patterns that defy them, they are easy to come up with. And they easily gave Pamela, and James, and all who used them in this way, the "proof" they were looking for to substantiate their arguments. But rarely do we deconstruct such stories to consider what they actually bear out, nor compare them objectively with the patterns to which they dull in comparison. While Pamela and James fluctuate back and forth between their belief in the American Dream and their acknowledgment of structured wealth inequality, they use these stories and their own life experiences (despite that the two often directly contradict each other) to seemingly thread it all together. Ultimately, no reconciliation is usually made, and Pamela and James—and the other families interviewed—completed their discussions without any resolution.

In upholding the contradiction, the families interviewed explained their positions and opportunities as being the result of hard work or lack thereof, and yet, at the same time, they acknowledged their understanding of the power of family wealth—and often some interconnection between race and class as well—in shaping life chances.

> Daniel: Whether we like it or not, I mean there is this race problem, it is there, it's just not in the open anymore. And most definitely what I'm talking about is not just being black or white. I mean just not being that so-called white American has a role to play in your success. Although the thing about it in this country is that with all these problems, there is just so much available that I guess everyone has a chance. But not necessarily everybody will get a chance.... For sure, the one which has got the better-to-do parents will have better chance.

> Interviewer: Do you think there are some ethnicities, races, groups in this country that are more disadvantaged than others?

> Daniel: Yeah.

> Interviewer: So you think there are certain groups as a whole, not just individuals, but groups as a whole that have a harder time making it today in this country and in achieving success to whatever level they want?

> Daniel: Sure. Definitely.

Interviewer: Okay, now, what about the American Dream? The idea that with hard work and desire, individual potential is unconstrained, that everyone regardless of background gets equal chance to get ahead based on their own individual achievement. What do you think of that?

Daniel: That's a very good definition.

Interviewer: [*Silent pause.*] Do you believe that the American Dream is true for all people and that everybody does have an equal chance?

Daniel: Yes. Everybody has an equal chance, no matter who he or she is.

Parents upheld their belief in meritocracy, despite that their own experiences often directly contradicted it. For them, it was more than just rhetoric; they genuinely believed in its legitimacy. At the same time, they upheld their belief in the power of wealth, despite their ideological understanding of a contradicting social reality. Unless it was pointed out to them, the families interviewed never seemed to notice either this paradox or the disjointed logic of their perspectives. The "taboo" of wealth and the invisibility of intergenerational family wealth help to explain how it is that families with backgrounds of poverty did not "see" the contradiction. However, the insistence upon upholding the contradiction seems especially perplexing in regard to the wealth-holding families, since they were so transparently and directly benefiting from wealth privilege in their own lives. What happens when these families are confronted with the contradiction?

In the second phase of interviewing, twenty relatively wealthy families were asked to reflect on their own contradictory reasoning. They were directly faced with the contradiction between structured wealth inequality and the notion of meritocracy and were asked explicitly about how they made sense of this paradox. This challenge caused some people to become slightly frazzled, but they always recovered—most, quite gracefully—and continued to insist on their belief in both. Even when directly confronted with the intrinsic incongruity of this contradictory belief system, the families interviewed uphold both simultaneously; the American Dream and the power of wealth were not presented as dichotomous, but rather were woven together complexly in parents' worldviews and perspectives, in the way they explained and described their experiences, and—I do believe—in their actual belief systems. And these belief systems were the basis for their decision making—at least where schools for their children were concerned. These families upheld the contradiction between the American Dream and the power of wealth, even when they were confronted with the suggestion that their beliefs were inherently contradictory.

> Interviewer: In other interviews we found that in terms of private family wealth, some people received a lot of help from families in getting what they have. Yet these same people believe that they've earned their position through hard work. Do you see how the two are contradictory?

> Emily: I see that they are contradictory. I can also see how you can rationalize them. Because, clearly, if your parents give you the opportunity to get an education and but for that opportunity you wouldn't have achieved what you achieved. But then you got the education and then you got this great job and you really did what you did and were successful in terms of reaching whatever your goals were in life. So then I don't think they're so exclusive or inconsistent. Because they gave you the underpinnings, but you didn't rest there, you went on with it. So I think we still think that we achieve.... In my case, my parents gave me the money for the down payment on a home in Washington. I paid them back. And when I sold that house, I turned it over to buy this house. So I had that help. I couldn't have bought that first house without it. And yet they were paid back and I had a really lovely old house. But I didn't stop with just that. So I can see where you can compare the two and still feel like you did this yourself, even though you got that boost.

Emily Mitchel explained how both ideas, although contradictory, fit together in her mind so that they worked in concert. Emily's perspective was unusually articulate, but her's was just one of many similar perspectives. When directly challenged, rather than try to reconcile the two in their minds, people upheld the contradiction by saying that they understood it and still believed in both the American Dream and the power of wealth.

A Persistent Paradox

Interviewer: In prior interviews we see that in terms of private family wealth, some people received a lot of help from families in getting what they have and getting to where they are. Yet these same people believe that they've earned their positions entirely through hard work. Do you see how the two ideas are contradictory?

Molly: Well, class is a concept I just can't get my mind around. I just saw examples of it in Britain [on vacation]. But, hmm. But I've never felt like I had to parade my wealth and wear designer clothes or anything. No. I don't think that's a big deal. It hasn't been for me.... But, I do feel that when we die, our wealth will be passed down to our children and hopefully grandchildren. And I think that they will use it wisely and pass it on, too.

Interviewer: Do you believe that your position in society has or will provide some underlying advantages for your children or grandchildren?

Molly: Hope so!

Interviewer: On a scale of one to one hundred, with one hundred being the wealthiest Americans, where would you say your family ranks?

Molly: Gosh! Ninety-two! [*Laughs.*] Plucked out of the air!

Interviewer: So looking at the same one to one hundred, for the people that are at the five, ten, twenty, why do you think they're there?

Molly: Bad luck. Bad genes. Poor habits. Poor choices. Lack of initiative.

—Molly Stone, homemaker, white, New York City

More than anything else, the interviews revealed a complex relationship between the ideology of meritocracy and structured wealth inequality in the contemporary United States. They disclosed complexities not only in terms of the logic of our system, but in how fluid and contradictory the act of sense making can be. The parents understood that within interlocking structures of wealth inequality and school inequality, educational opportunity is not evenly distributed. Yet, at the same time, they genuinely saw the system as a meritocracy, in which hard work is rewarded and equal chances are ensured through the Great Equalizer of education.

Previous research has yielded very different results from those here. Most of the scholarship that exists on Americans' perspectives on inequality generally asserts that people either believe one thing or another.[3] It is normally assumed that individual attitudes are more or less clear-cut, with their views conceived of as dichotomous oppositions. A prevalent example of this comes from the literature on stratification beliefs, which suggests that people either hold individuals or society responsible for one's position in the hierarchical social world. This research has focused almost entirely on people's beliefs about, and attitudes toward, poverty. Sociologist Joe Feagin, for example, argues that there are three basic types of beliefs about poverty: individualistic beliefs, which assert that poverty is the result of deficiencies and characteristics of poor individuals themselves; structuralist beliefs, which assert that poverty is the result of politico-socioeconomic systems that subordinate the poor; and fatalistic beliefs, which assert that the poor suffer from disabilities or from bad luck or happenstance.[4] Feagin's studies, as well as those of other sociologists and social psychologists, show that Americans predominantly use the individualistic framework to explain why some people are poor.[5] These individualistic explanations center on the belief that poverty results from lack of proper work ethics, laziness, socially deviant behaviors, or other such personal problems.

Americans' individualistic explanations are thought to stem from the nation's "dominant ideology" of the American Dream.[6] The dominant ideology of American society, or the "achievement ideology," emphasizes notions of individualism, equal opportunity, and personal achievement. Joan Huber and William Form define the dominant ideology: "American culture contains a stable, widely held set of beliefs involving the availability of opportunity, individualistic explanations for achievement, and acceptance of unequal distributions of rewards."[7] It is, in effect the American Dream of meritocracy. James Kluegel and Eliot Smith outline the basic tenets of this dominant ideology: "First, that opportunity for economic advancement is widespread in America today; second, that individuals are personally responsible for their positions; and third, that the overall system of inequality is, therefore, equitable and fair."[8] As with other ideologies, the American dominant ideology is understood as serving to justify and legitimize inequality as an important social process in the reproduction of stratification. Kluegel and Smith, as well as most others, argue that the dominant ideology is prevalent and stable within the population, but that a person's individual position within the stratification system shapes his or her attitude toward inequality. Most of this work reflects that people of higher status subscribe more strongly and with more fervor to individualistic explanations, the argument being that these groups have a vested self-interest in maintaining their advantageous social standing.

Recent studies have started to show more nuanced results, and these go far to validate the findings presented in this book. Two important things are happening in the recent work on stratification beliefs: research has begun to document that Americans in fact buy into *both* individualistic and structuralist explanations for poverty; and new research is beginning to incorporate perspectives on *wealth* into the analysis, examining not just how people make sense of poverty but how they make sense of wealth as well.

Regarding research findings that Americans believe in both individualistic and structuralist explanations for inequality, a few recent studies are important to highlight here. Based on a study of workers in Indiana, Brian Starks argues that Americans' individualistic explanations for inequality are declining. In contrast to much of the previous literature on the subject, he found that those most disadvantaged are the least likely to subscribe to the dominant ideology. He also notes, significantly, that people's views are shaped not only by their own experiences, but by their observations of the experiences of friends and family as well. He concludes that "many workers are currently disillusioned with the American Dream."[9] Starks's study is important in showing that Americans aren't wholly "under the spell,"[10] nor 100 percent transfixed with the American Dream, but that they waver in their beliefs. Lawrence Bobo and others have shown that disadvantaged groups, specifically racial minorities, do not subscribe entirely to the dominant ideology, but instead to a combination of both individualistic and structural explanations for poverty; these findings suggest that beliefs and attitudes are much more inconsistent than scholars previously had thought.[11] Other researchers have documented that all Americans (not just disadvantaged groups) hold ambivalent and contradictory beliefs simultaneously. In a study of North Carolinians, Katherine Ann Hyde argues that "[a]ll the participants have a complex relationship to the dream ideology, given that their lives both support and challenge the ideology." She goes on to say, "It's possible that the participants clearly understand the nature of the concrete struggles in their lives, which conflict with the dream's premises, while also buying into the dream."[12] Matthew Hunt's 1996 study of Southern Californians reported a "complex set of results," documenting that blacks and Latinos are more likely than whites to believe in both individualistic and structuralist explanations for poverty, and that most all people endorse these beliefs simultaneously.[13]

These studies are important new developments as they suggest that Americans are aware of the inconsistencies between ideology and reality, not wholly buying into the American Dream nor fully critiquing structural inequality. They show that there is not nearly the consensus on individualistic explanations as was previously believed. These studies suggest that, while people may still believe more strongly in individualistic explanations, they can—and do—subscribe simultaneously to both individualistic/ideological and sociostructural explanations for inequality. Based on this evidence, a handful of scholars are now arguing that "inconsistency of the belief systems" or a "dual consciousness" exists in regard to Americans' stratification beliefs.[14] This research confirms what the family interviews show here: that neither consensus nor consistency exists between individualistic/ideological and structural beliefs, and that—more often than not—these perspectives are combined. Beliefs about inequality are not either/or; on the contrary, people often hold multiple perspectives simultaneously.

Last, and most important, some research on stratification beliefs has begun to explore Americans' perspectives on wealth (whereas traditionally studies have focused on perspectives on poverty). Although I am only aware of three such studies, these are most important in validating the findings of the family interviews presented here. First, Kleugel and Smith's 1986 study, while emphasizing beliefs about poverty, did include beliefs about wealth. Their findings regarding wealth were similar to their findings regarding poverty: based on data from over two thousand phone interviews, they argued that people subscribe to both individualist (hard work, drive for achievement) and structuralist (inherited money) explanations for wealth, but that individualistic beliefs are much more popular. Kevin Smith's studies from the late 1980s document findings consistent with Kluegel and Smith's.[15] In phone and mail surveys with two hundred adults in Texas, he and Lorene Stone found that individualistic beliefs about both wealth and poverty were predominant. Smith and Stone argued, however (as others noted above have), that there is much more overlap between the two perspectives than most of the literature accounts for. "Today," they write, "few people believe that wealth and poverty are caused by a single factor or even a couple of factors ... overlap exists."[16] They contend that "personality traits as well as the social structures and situations that mark the wealthy and poor" are part of a "cultural metatheory" that blends individualistic explanations with structuralist ones.[17]

The most recent study of beliefs about wealth comes from sociologist Matthew Hunt, who noted the "curious" lack of research on beliefs about wealth and asserted the importance of such studies. Using survey data from over a thousand residents of Los Angeles County, Hunt attempted to uncover "lay explanations" for wealth as well as poverty. His findings were similar to those of Kluegel and Smith in that respondents favored individualistic beliefs to explain wealth but also viewed structural beliefs as important. It is interesting to note that Hunt's respondents blamed the structure less for wealth than for poverty, and minorities were more likely than whites to blame the poor for their own plight. Hunt argued that a "dual consciousness" exists that allows Americans to hold conflicting beliefs simultaneously.[18]

This recent research yielded results similar to those described here: they reveal that Americans do indeed believe in *both* individualistic/ideological explanations (i.e. the American Dream) and structural explanations (i.e. the power of wealth) about inequality, and they hold these views about *wealth* as well as poverty. These studies, however, have been based almost exclusively on quantitative research methodologies. Until now, no one had spoken with people in person and at length about their perspectives on wealth and the American Dream. The results of this study, while to some degree validated by other research, are the first to show in any depth the extent to which individuals both acknowledge the power of wealth and believe in the legitimacy of meritocracy. The interviews suggest that in their sense making, American families are upholding the contradiction.

The interviews herein bring to light two important points in regard to how families hold such contradictory perspectives at once. First, they reflect the *power of ideology*. Ideology is "the public's best effort—at any given time—to make sense of, comprehend, and explain the problematic world of everyday life."[19] But ideology is more than just a set of ideas about how our social world works; it is a set of ideas that is used to legitimate and justify social inequalities. Belief systems become ideological when we use them to justify and mask structural inequality.[20] To be successful, though, ideologies must be more than simply illusions; they must put forth a vision of social reality that is recognizable and believable—and, as we know, each of us could tell a story of someone who pulled themselves up from their bootstraps and became the quintessential American self-made man (or woman, as in the case most often cited to me—that of Oprah Winfrey). These token stories and the ideological notions themselves bombard us daily and seem to be present everywhere we look. On the surface an ideology may appear to be nothing more than a set of beliefs. But ideologies are deceptive in their force.[21] And in the United States, ideologies about the meritocracy of the social system are particularly strong, and particularly deceptive.

These interviews reveal the power of the ideology of the American Dream, for even when it flew in the face of lived reality, even when it contradicted actual experiences, the parents interviewed still believed in it, guided their actions by it, and used it to explain the situations of themselves, their children, and others. It is not that we are all duped, in denial, or so anti-intellectual that we do not, or cannot, see the flaws of the ideology, but rather that the ideology is so strong and so ingrained that we unself-consciously succumb to it. Especially now, in the Post–Civil Rights Era, the ideology of meritocracy is predominant in our mainstream culture; it has been presented to us from every angle as a legitimate belief system since some of the earliest points in our lives that we can remember. The families interviewed were not unaware of structural inequality, and they did not think that this structure was fair. But this awareness and acknowledgment did not dilute their insistence in the authenticity of meritocracy, despite the contradiction to it that wealth privilege presented. And it did not temper their use of meritocracy to explain, justify, and legitimize social standing—no matter how "high" or "low" they found themselves in relative social class rank. In making sense of lives and the world around us, the power of ideology is strong: when the ideology seeps in from every facet, when it becomes the easy explanation to fall back on, when it appears to be perhaps the only explanation, it becomes difficult to not surrender to it. The families interviewed did not seem to fully surrender; however, they did not attempt in any real way to reconcile the American Dream and the power of wealth.

Second, the interviews herein show the *power of hope*. For these families the American Dream *was* hope. It held out hope that what is wanted will happen, and that what is wanted can be expected.[22] It held out hope that children's life chances were all equally unconstrained. It held out hope that the world is just. To think otherwise (to think that the world is not just) would be heartbreaking to any parent. And, I believe, many parents fear that to think otherwise could potentially—if conveyed to children—break the spirit of any child. So they hold on to the American Dream, they hold on to their hope. This hope was reflected in the parents' perspectives regarding themselves, the social system they are acting on and within, and—most importantly—their children.

An illustration of this deep-seated hopefulness comes from one of the most memorable interviews I conducted, with Thomas Saucier, a white father who had lived in Boston his whole life. He lived in a rented apartment with his fiancée Tammy and their young son in a working-class, blue-collar neighborhood. Sitting on the small porch overlooking an alleyway, Thomas told me about his work as a line cook in a diner and Tammy's two jobs—waiting tables at night and cleaning houses during the day. Over the years, they had received little financial help from their families, and they were barely getting by on minimum wage. Yet Thomas had lots of ideas and hopefulness about his family's future—particularly when it came to his son:

> I guess the more money you have, the more things you can do, right?... There are some things I'd *like* to do. I'd like to set up a U-plan for my son. You know, one of them college savings things? Where it's, you know, *lock in today's rate for tomorrow* type of thing? You know, I see the ad and I'm like, that's something I'd like to do! But it's not in the cards right now. But something like that, like, that's something I'd like to do.... I'd like a nicer car, and a nicer apartment, maybe buy a house.... Yeah, I would just hope that, you know, that I make more money in the future, so that he can go to a school that's, that I *want* him to go to. That he would go to a private school as opposed to a public school. And I'd try to buy a house at the same time. You know, that's a big increase in money, but it *could* be done. It happens all the time. So, that's all. That's all I'd like to have happen.

While they were aware of a structure of wealth inequality, and of the resulting advantages or disadvantages that their kids were faced with, parents—Thomas being just one example—wanted nothing more than to ensure the best possible futures for their children. Despite their differences in possibilities and social positioning, privileged and underprivileged families alike were holding out hope. As a young black mother from Los Angeles said, "You do the best you can, and you try to be optimistic, and you just keep going."

The power of ideology keeps us from challenging privilege, even when we acknowledge inequality; the power of hope keeps all parents "wanting and wishing," "wanting and expecting" the best for their children's futures. Ultimately, this has created a context in which disadvantaged families are wholly blamed for their own plight, and—perhaps even more important—families of privilege continue their legacies without being questioned.

As Jonathan Boothe, the wealthy white businessman whose father funded the lucrative enterprise that Jonathan started from scratch, summed up at the conclusion of his interview: "The American Dream is possible for everybody. It's unfortunate some people do have to start right at the bottom, but they can do it!"

7

An Unresolved Conflict

After more than two hours of discussion, the interview with Steve and Jan Hadley in St. Louis was ending. Beyond the windows of their family room it was dusk outside. Their white suburban neighborhood was quieting down as families regrouped for dinner in their houses. The Hadley children were anxious for dinner themselves and anxious for their parents' attention, and Steve and Jan had told seemingly everything there was to tell about their family's wealth and their school decisions. The tape recorder was about to be turned off. Suddenly, Steve asked if he could add something. Sitting forward in his chair with a focused look on his face, his entire demeanor had shifted. Throughout the interview he had taken a laid back, jovial tone, but Steve abruptly had become intensely serious.

> Steve: Um, uh, I don't know—all of a sudden, going through, walking through this, I've gotten, uh, to feel like I'm one of the little, not an individual, but kind of a mainstream middle class. You know?... You have a house in the suburbs, you, you, in our case, live in a white neighborhood and go to a white school system. Um, uh, I didn't really look at it like that before. But I, I guess it just kind of fits, I want to say—mainstream—of what's um, we, we fit right into a very large class of people.
>
> Interviewer: That's probably very true.

Steve: But it didn't start out to be that way. I mean, we didn't *consciously* think of it that way. But we certainly did fit the mold.

Jan: Well, it's the background that we grew up in too. I mean, it's very similar to that.

Steve: Yeah [*silent pause*]. So, um, I don't know.

Jan [*turning to Steve*]: It shouldn't be a shock to you, dear.

Steve: Well, no, it's not a shock. It's just, uh, I hadn't really thought of that, that before.

The way wealth is passed along and utilized in families is a patterned, dynamic process that is structured along race and class lines, and because of its intergenerational dimension, the black-white wealth gap is persistent and enduring over time. In the previous pages, we have looked at how this plays out in one institutional arena—education, specifically school choice making—and we have seen how an historic legacy of family wealth inequality enabled most white parents to provide educational advantages to their children that most black parents simply could not. In particular, parents whose own families of origin were wealth-holding families were able to draw on their own privilege to perpetuate the advantages and opportunities that wealth fosters and purchases. These families were disproportionately white, and wealth for them was a means to an end—a way to pass privilege along to the next generation, a way to do as much as they possibly could to help their children get ahead.

While parents' school decisions were indeed individualized, they were also highly patterned within a context of structured inequality. Different families had different sets of choices. Families who had "bought in" or "opted out" had the wealth resources to act on those decisions, they tended to be white, and they generally chose whiter, wealthier schools. The families who were "making do" and "feeling stuck" were constrained from making the decisions they wanted to make because they had comparatively fewer assets to rely upon and comparatively less wealth privilege to maximize. These families were disproportionately black and most often found their school options limited to relatively underfunded educational systems serving relatively underprivileged populations. These findings do not suggest that merit and achievement do not matter—they do, of course, matter greatly. Rather, the interview data reveals how *nonmerit* factors also matter—greatly.

Within a structure of unequal education, family histories of wealth and poverty had very real consequences for the educations and life trajectories of children. This poses a challenge to the American Dream of meritocracy. Even if every individual is indeed given *a* chance at success, the pattern is that some groups have *better chances*, and this—this pattern—is the problem; the playing field is not level. While they did not necessarily notice how their "choices" fit together into a bigger picture, the parents we spoke with, in their attempts to achieve the best schooling for their children, ended up reproducing the same inequality that they lamented. In this study, we saw these patterns surface from interviews with just two hundred families. But in a country of millions, the ramifications of these patterns are massive: while we do not necessarily intend it, our collective action (or collective inaction, as the case may be) further perpetuates the race and class inequalities that we have inherited.

Social Reproduction: Intentioned or Not

Wealth creates options, opportunities, and advantages, and lack of wealth constrains these. Wealth might trickle down in small amounts over time, but ultimately it is a powerful enabling force for families and children: it enables them to *choose* what they believe is in the best interest of their children's futures, it enables them to *act* on their decisions, and, notably, in a competitive environment it enables them to do these things more easily than other families who do not have wealth on which to rely. Using wealth to propel advantages for one's own children over other people's children, no matter how well intended, further perpetuates cycles of inequality. When families pass along wealth to the next generation—whether in small or large amounts, whether from day to day or at milestone events—they pass along privilege. Social reproduction takes place as the power of wealth is passed down from parents to children to grandchildren. Concurrently, families without wealth to transfer are comparatively limited in the opportunities and advantages they can provide. Regardless of how much they may want to choose the best for their children, regardless of how badly they wish they could give them advantageous opportunities, they are not as easily able to act on those choices. In the particular context of school decision making, although perhaps entirely unintentional, families' "choices" (or lack thereof) contribute to the maintenance of social stratification.

The 260 parents we spoke with were not blinded to the structural inequality of family wealth. While they did not necessarily know the depth or breadth of how it was playing out in families beyond their own, they recognized that it existed, acknowledged it, and many even expressed that they "felt bad" about it because it was "so unfair." However, they simultaneously denied that it mattered by vehemently arguing that individuals' social positions are the just results of a meritocratic system. Notably, they did not claim that the logic of the system was logic of luck,[1] and none of them made an argument that the wealth they had inherited was somehow deserved since their ancestors had earned it.[2] Instead, they genuinely claimed that each person's success is determined by individual hard work and achievement. Parents from across the race and class spectrum saw the American Dream as more than just rhetoric, an ideal, or even a creed; they understood meritocracy as a legitimate explanation for how our current system works. They had conviction in their belief that people's social positions are justified by meritocracy, despite that their own experiences and the experiences of others most often contradicted this. Rather than trying to reconcile their ideological beliefs with their lived experiences, they upheld the contradiction. They recognized that family wealth privileges some individuals over others *and* they considered individuals' relative social positions to be earned and deserved. While the American Dream and the power of wealth lie in contradiction, they were woven together in families' perspectives, beliefs, decisions, and experiences.

As contradictory as the American Dream and the power of wealth are, their confluence is immeasurably potent. They were fused together in parents' thoughts, words, and deeds as they individually made sense of inequality and contributed to the large-scale social reproduction of it, intended or not. Here we have examined just one site where this plays out; yet, in even that one arena, we can see how the families were (knowingly or not) participating in a process of perpetuating inequality: through their collective action regarding school decisions made for their children, their individual actions both were shaped by structural inequality and contributed to it. Ironically, their school decisions—while guided by love and intended to better their own children's chances—ultimately resulted in further cementing unequal opportunities for different groups of children. School decisions in individual families contributed to the intergenerational transmission of structural inequality by disproportionately ensuring better education (and thus, presumably, better chances at success) for white and wealthy children.

Family wealth and lack of it heavily shaped parents' decision making, but school decisions were also influenced in ways that extended well beyond family economics. Motivations for educational choices were often racially charged or heavily encumbered by class prejudice. White families purposefully used their wealth to place their children in not just what they perceived to be better schools, but what were conscientiously whiter schools, located in more affluent neighborhoods. Black families, too, were cognizant of the racialized dynamics in schools and in neighborhoods and were often unwilling to place their kids in all-white environments for fear of isolation, prejudice, or racism. Race here was not only about traditional racism per se (although it surely played a part for many families). As Eduardo Bonilla-Silva reminds us, "Although 'racism' has a definite ideological component, reducing racial phenomena to ideas limits the possibility of understanding how it shapes a race's life chances."[3] Families were making decisions within highly racialized and classed *structures*—structures that *reward* families for acting to perpetuate race and class inequality.

This marks a paradigm shift from past literature that has focused on people's ideas. While I do not intend to downplay the power of ideas (in fact, not at all; the power of ideology is central to this work), I do however want to move the focus away from "old fashioned" racism or classism as the assumed motivators of behavior. Although racism and classism were disturbingly prevalent in the interviews,[4] in my view the racialized and classed structural dynamics at play were more powerful in perpetuating macro-level patterns of inequality.

To refer to a "racialized" or "classed" structure implies a *system*. This shifts the focus from individual or attitudinal phenomena and toward social structures, systems of power, and patterns of ascribed inequality. Rather than pointing to individuals' racist or classist attitudes or beliefs as the roots of the problem, the interview data here suggests that a *structure* of race and class inequality that *advantages* some for their race and class positions and *disadvantages* others is at the core. A structure of patterns, systems, and institutions privileges some families and disadvantages others categorically and systematically. For example, a structure of unequal schooling rewards historically privileged families for the school decisions they tend to make within it by conferring to their children better educational opportunities and chances for success. Individuals make decisions in a highly structured context that provides incentives for people to—as the father quoted at the opening of this chapter said—"fit the mold" of "the mainstream," even when they do not "consciously think of it that way"; the structure rewards microlevel actions that perpetuate the macrolevel inequalities.

Meanwhile, the American Dream of meritocracy presents the social structure as an open and egalitarian system—an inclusivist, egalitarian, open society; it veils the social forces that impact our individual circumstances. We incorporate the ideology into our thinking, use it to make sense of our lives and pat ourselves on the back or blame ourselves; we rely on it to explain the situations of others, depend on it to justify and legitimize the structure of society, and utilize it in our decision making. This has been historically successful in helping to imply that the United States is a "color-blind," "classless" society, and in offering up hope for people to cling to. But it has been relatively less successful in diminishing race and class stratification.

If some groups' socioeconomic positions continue to be even *partially* based on ascribed factors, then stratification is perpetuated and meritocracy does not exist. If the American Dream allows us to deny this reality, then both the inequality and the ideology are left to go unchallenged. Paradoxically, something that we all believe in so strongly, something that unites us as a common thread, something that inspires great achievement and gives us tremendous hope also contributes to maintaining exactly that which it claims does not exist: the inherited, intergenerational transmission of inequality.

The American Dream and the power of wealth collide in decisions regarding children's education. These decisions serve as one mechanism through which stratification is reproduced, whether intentionally or not. Within a competitive system rife with race and class inequality, intention is not always necessary to perpetuate social patterns. Many white and wealthy parents did not intend to be racist, classist, discriminating, or exclusive, and would feel awful if they understood their actions as contributing to social inequality. In fact, most of these parents did not even consider the larger-scale implications of their decisions, as they were instead consumed with trying to be good parents, focused on their own children, and concerned with their individual family situations. Similarly, families limited by a lack of wealth did not devalue education, nor did they intend to disadvantage their own children. They expressed no desire to take away opportunities from well-off families, and they never blamed wealthy parents for providing their children with advantageous schooling—they simply wanted the same kinds of opportunities for their own children. Clearly, the problem is not about people's efforts at being good parents. Rather, the problem is about how wealth situates different groups differently, what kinds of schools are available to families of different groups, and how we justify and legitimize a system of intergenerational inequality. While there is nothing wrong with trying to provide the best for one's family, this heartfelt desire ultimately ends up contributing to a structure of inequality that is much larger than any one particular parent or child.

If we want to confront these social problems head on and make progress toward ameliorating them, we must understand that millions of personal decisions, when taken together and looked at analytically, become a very public issue.

Unequal education, the wealth gap, and the ideology of the American Dream are complex social problems, complex public issues. While they certainly do not tell the whole story, together they compose an important piece of the story of intergenerational inequality in the contemporary American society.[5] What, if anything, can we as individuals, families, communities, and as a society do about them? My own goal here has been not to solve these problems, but to identify and clarify them so that we can better wrap our minds around them, better understand them. The family interviews indicated (and it seems to me to be true) that most of us in our day-to-day lives do not normally stop to think about how what we say, what we believe, and what we do fit into the larger social world of which we are a part. But not only are our perspectives and experiences influenced by the social world, they contribute to the maintenance of it as well. While my hope is that any reader will come away from this book with more questions than answers, it is important to elucidate some of the key avenues for social change to which this study points. The first, and disconcertingly the most simple, is the challenge to our social system that unequal education presents.

The Predicament of Unequal Education

We believe education is the key to the American Dream and the hope for our children's future, but a structure of unequal schooling creates a predicament for us all. Our predicament is this: the core values of egalitarianism, inclusiveness, equal opportunity and individualism central to the American Dream rely on equal education to mediate the effects of uneven family backgrounds; yet we have a system of unequal education. We look to education as the Great Equalizer in our society, as the institution that levels the playing field for all children regardless of their family of origin, but we also recognize that schools are not equal. While we are proud of the American Dream and hold our beliefs in it with conviction, within a system of unequal education, meritocracy is merely an out-of-reach ideal. As long as schools are unequal in quality, resources, curriculum, facilities, staffing, and so on, and as long as children have categorically unequal access to them, we will inevitably have categorically unequal outcomes.

While surely, as many scholars argue, parenting, family structure, culture, community effects, and a host of other dynamics play roles in children's varying educational, occupational, and life outcomes, the basic concept of disparate schooling undoubtedly contributes. The fact that certain families are faced with inexcusably poor schooling while others can access highly enriching educational environments creates systemic inequalities for children that continue to affect them throughout their adult lives. Some might argue that a plausible solution would be school choice policies, or voucher programs, that would supplement parents' financial resources so that more families would have more choices in regard to school decisions for their children. While at first glance this may appear to be a simple solution, as we have seen, many families with wealth resources in place are already choosing schools, and when they do they tend to choose schools that intensify rather than abate core problems of segregation, exclusion, and inequality. As Thomas Shapiro and I have argued elsewhere, our data show that in voucher programs white and affluent families will only continue to use their resources to "further exacerbate class and race inequalities in a more systematic and government-subsidized fashion." In regard to asset-poor parents, the addition of the small vouchers they would receive would "do virtually nothing to help these families move to the schools they most desire for their children."[6] Vouchers in existing and proposed programs are generally so small that they would not even cover one-third of the cost of per-pupil funding at the best public or private schools, and they would definitely neither cover the down payment on a home to "buy in" nor the finances required to "opt out."

As it stands, disadvantaged families have seriously limited options, and privileged families—as their choices directly benefit themselves and their children—have no real incentive to alter their patterns. In fact, they are offered irresistible incentives *not* to alter them. Excellent schools in affluent neighborhoods act like magnets pulling in wealthy families and perpetuating cycles of segregation, exclusion, and inequality. As one white middle-class parent said, "I would like to be part of the solution ... but I'm not going to put my family at risk to be part of the solution." Another said, "I think that all kids should have a good elementary school and high school to go to, but I'm not sure that I'm able to fight the system that much." Given the incentives and rewards in place for them, privileged families would be, as a third parent said, "swimming upstream" to not be choosing whiter, wealthier schools. Few would blame these parents for doing the best they can for their children, but the scenario here is truly a predicament for us all. It is not that wealthy families should be kept from accessing excellent educational opportunities, but rather that everyone should have equal access to these opportunities.

Equal education would not take family wealth and its privileges entirely out of the equation—wealthier families still would be able to supplement schooling with additional opportunities and advantage their children in other ways. But it would at least help to mitigate the power of wealth a bit. Making schools less profoundly different would not ultimately fix the problem of perpetuating social inequalities, but at least we would know that we were providing all children with what we as a country claim to value: high quality education for every child regardless of family background. A system of equal educational opportunity would mean that no matter how wealthy or asset-poor a child's family is, his or her school's quality would not hinge on that. If excellent schools were equally accessible to everyone, then much of the frenzy surrounding school decisions would be eliminated, and the ramifications of race and class inequality might at least be diminished.

To make steps toward more equitable education, the power of family wealth in school decisions must be recognized and tempered. Equitable education for all children would ultimately have to include equality of opportunity, some degree of integration, and fair distribution of resources among states, districts, and schools, not to mention a whole host of other changes. It would have to dismantle what Jennifer Hochschild refers to as the "nested" character of inequality and separation.[7] It is truly overwhelming. But while integration and the redistribution of educational finances, facilities, and resources would not single-handedly transform structured inequality, they would certainly help and they would certainly be steps on the road toward actualizing what we claim.

However, rather than embracing the goal of equitable education, our country continues to lean farther and farther away from efforts toward that goal.[8] It takes only a glance at a current newspaper or a sound bite from the evening news to see how instead of committing our education agenda to equal educational opportunity, individual parents are being blamed for not being involved enough in their children's schooling and for not making good enough choices on behalf of their kids. Even the families we spoke with purported this in their comments, such as one mother from the New York City area who commented that "anyone who really values education wouldn't allow their kids to go to weak schools, and would make sure their children are well educated ... so the parents are to blame." The data presented here, though, shows that parents—asset-rich and asset-poor alike—do value education, have equally high hopes for their children, and want the best for them.[9] Parents' educational values, and their love for and commitment to their children cannot be measured by the material objects and schooling opportunities that they can or cannot provide.

To create legitimate structures of equal opportunity, we must either operationalize equitable education or find some other institutional arena to act as a leveler. Until we do, it is not realistic, fair, or just to claim that every child has equal opportunity for success, equal life chances, and that each individual autonomously earns and deserves their relative social position. We can choose to face the predicament of unequal education head on, acknowledge it, question it, and grapple with it. Or we can choose not to.

In discussing with people the subject of this book, I have often been asked about the policy implications of my research. When I suggest that a solution to the problem of contemporary race and class inequality must include a transformation of our educational structure so that all children have equal access to high-quality education, many people tend to respond that I am being impractical, naive, or idealistic. I find this ironic, since a system of equal education is something the majority of Americans claim to believe in so fervently. Equal educational opportunity is indeed one of the foundational principles of our social system, so it is curious to me how few people take equal education—as a policy goal—seriously. Structural problems require structural solutions, and anything less will not drive positive social change in the long run. I do not underestimate how complicated this goal would be to achieve, nor how much would be involved; however, I advocate, as political scientist John Roemer does, "the view that one must know what the ethically desirable policy is before compromising for the sake of political reality."[10] We should, at a minimum, consider equal education as a solution for the predicament of unequal education. If we believe so fully in the tenets of the American Dream (or, at the very least, the ideals of it) then constructing a system of equal education should not be such an unrealistic notion.

The Dilemma of Family Wealth

As complicated as the predicament of unequal education is, the dilemma of wealth—the way it is acquired and passed along in families, and the way it is used by them to create advantageous opportunities—is arguably even more complex. And, unlike education, which we at least have some national discourse about, the dilemma of wealth is further exacerbated by the fact that we do not talk about it, the fact that we live "in a class society committed to the denial of class."[11]

For as much as we may wish it were not true, the fact is that family wealth allows some families to, as one parent said, "smooth the way" and "open up doors" for their children much more easily

than others. This sets up an unfair competition that is p⟨
evident in the arena of education. Given the importance of
in today's society and the condition of segregated, unequal sch⟨
the consequences of the widening wealth gap are severe. Since this is
not only a wealth gap but a stark racial gap as well, the advantages
and disadvantages for children are largely divided along class and
race lines, categorically placing different groups of kids behind different starting lines. And today, rather than decreasing, the wealth
gap—a powerful distributor of race and class inequality—is growing. This book is written in the context of the most massive transfer
of wealth the world has ever seen: certain segments of the baby boom
generation are currently in the process of receiving the greatest collective wealth inheritance in our nation's history.[12]

The intergenerational transfer of wealth is a major key (some
would argue *the* major key) to the intergenerational reproduction of
race and class inequality in the contemporary United States. Ironically, through wealth transfers in families—which are often given
out of love, loyalty, commitment to family, and hopefulness for the
future—we also transfer the troubles, ills, and hopelessness of race
and class inequality to the next generation. As long as a family's level
of wealth has a determining impact (even a partially determining
impact) on the life trajectory of a child, then we will continue to witness discrepancies between social groups that are based on ascription
rather than achievement or merit.

Our dilemma is this: while we believe in the idea of an egalitarian
system where individuals self-reliantly earn and deserve their relative
places in the social order, we also like the idea of being able to pass
our wealth along to our own children. As opposed to the predicament of unequal education, where the vast majority of Americans
seem committed to at least the ideal of equitable education, we do not
at all seem to agree on ideals regarding the intergenerational transmission of wealth. While we value the notion that race, class, or family background should not help or hinder one's life chances, we also
value doing the best we can for our own children. We are left facing
competing and unpleasant alternatives: Do we take intergenerational
transfers of wealth out of the equation, thereby restraining ourselves
from giving all we can to our own children, but moving closer to
ensuring a truly democratic system for all? Or, do we take the notion
of meritocracy out of the equation, thereby allowing families to give
all they can to their own children, but abandoning the possibilities
for egalitarianism and true equality of opportunity? Neither choice
seems one that many of us would make easily. But to sincerely confront
the dilemma of wealth, we will need to confront the contradiction

that the power of wealth presents to the American Dream. Any true equity or justice in this realm would require an extreme redistribution of wealth. While this is indeed a radical suggestion, it must be considered if we are to take the goal of fundamental social change seriously.

Wealth inequalities, the mechanisms contributing to them, and potential policies to ameliorate them have been the focus of significant research, debate, and policy projects over the past decade, but rarely are radical possibilities taken seriously in the mainstream. The reparations movement, for example, is a case in point. While proponents present a judicious case for a reparations effort to ameliorate systemic, structured wealth disadvantage for African Americans, implementation of such policy is seldom considered in earnest.[13] Asset-based policy, generally much less extreme in its goals for wealth redistribution, is currently the solution most advocated by scholars and policy analysts.[14] This policy direction aims to attack social problems related to unequal distributions of resources from a wealth perspective rather than from an income orientation. Much of this work has concentrated on understanding how to alleviate poverty and has centered on helping poor families develop assets, attempting to foster wealth accumulation among disadvantaged populations, and documenting that when given a chance poor families can—and do—save to build assets.[15] But for as much as the persistence of the wealth gap is surely to some extent the result of poor families' relative inability to save, it is equally (and, if the interviews conducted for this book are any indication, perhaps more so) the result of wealthy families' relative ability to bestow financial advantages to the next generation. While surely the asset policy approach is a vital shift from prior paradigms, we have much to learn about how best to design and implement programs that aim to decrease the effects of the wealth gap overall.

Wealth-based policy needs to look carefully not just at how to help poor families develop assets, but at how to deal with the privileges that asset ownership confers to wealthy families. Encouraging asset-poor families to save does nothing to diminish the accumulative advantage of wealth privilege. Furthermore, wealth-based policy has not yet squarely confronted one of the biggest dilemmas of all: the intergenerational transfers in reverse that are prevalent in many poor communities, and as we saw, in many of the black families with whom we spoke. Asset-based policy will need to seriously consider the dynamic here; if poor families are pressured to save for themselves alone, then the community and kin networks that have historically been so resourceful would be pragmatically discouraged rather than celebrated.[16] Put bluntly, in my view, our wealth policy goals should not be so much about trying to get poor families to be pragmatically more like wealthy families (more determined about saving money in order to place the next generation in advantageous positions), but should be about trying to get wealthy families to be philosophically more like poor families (more committed to sharing resources for the betterment of others beyond themselves and their own children).

In addition to asset building policy, inheritance tax policy is an important consideration in regard to approaching the dilemma of wealth. Tax law has been suggested as a means for regulating bequests and asset transfers. Proponents suggest creating wealth-transfer taxes that would lessen the effects of inheritance.[17] One such proposal, for example, calls for tax reform to treat bequests, inheritances, and other major transfers of wealth as taxable income. This would involve taxation through recipients' annual income tax returns.[18] Thomas Shapiro, for instance, suggests an "Opportunity Act" that would distinguish between earned and inherited wealth and create a flat tax for all that is inherited.[19] Such efforts would be crucial steps if we were to genuinely attempt to begin shrinking the wealth gap.

If we are truly going to succeed or fail based on our own individual hard work, achievement, or lack thereof, we need to eliminate wealth privilege from the equation. This is explosively controversial. The dilemma of wealth has serious implications, in part because no one wants to be told they cannot pass their wealth along to their children—no one wants to be told they cannot better their children's life chances. And few people support the idea of a radical redistribution of wealth. However, if we continue to hold on to our inherited wealth and pass it along to our children we continue to structure an unfair set of opportunities and life trajectories for kids of different backgrounds. As sociologist Jenny Wahl notes, "If people spent all their wealth on themselves and neither nature nor nurture mattered, then only your own characteristics and luck would determine how you fared. But if parents pass something on, the story changes."[20] How will we reconcile the power of wealth with the American Dream?

The Quandary of the American Dream

The American Dream can inspire us in our own lives, but perhaps an even stronger inspiration comes from the hope it cultivates for the next generation. We all want to see kids succeed; we all want to see young people achieve great things. But when that generation includes our own children, we are even more enchanted with the dream. Perhaps the most profound quandary this book presents is the basic question of what to teach our children. Do we continue to encourage belief in the American Dream, or do we acknowledge those structural inequalities that contradict it? Does the American Dream represent a realistic hope, or a false hope for the next generation? Is it fair to teach our children that each individual makes it on his or her own in America, and then systematically give some of them privileges that others do not have?

On the one hand, we know that whole social groups are categorically and systematically privileged over others. On the other hand, the American Dream inspires us to believe in the boundless possibilities of the future. There is a sense, I think, that we almost *have* to carry on the American Dream. Not only is it what makes the United States so special in the minds of people here and throughout the world, but it inspires so many of our individual aspirations. Laura Cannon states it well: "The story of the American Dream lurks as a backdrop to many lives. Whether the Dream is bitterly rejected or wholeheartedly accepted, it is ever present."[21] But peeling away the various layers of inheritance and intergenerational dynamics tells us something about how inequality operates and what we think of as legitimate or illegitimate.

In the contemporary United States, the American Dream is a belief that unifies us all at some level. The quandary is that it also helps to divide us by acting as a mechanism for our collective denial that structured inequality exists. The American Dream allows privileged families to maintain a sense of entitlement regarding that which they neither wholly personally achieve nor wholly merit: the wealth they receive from the generation before them. The ideology legitimizes structural inequality so that it goes unchallenged, allowing for invisible, often even unintended, social reproduction. It is in this context that we see the central role of ideology in the perpetuation of inequality; for even a system constructed on social inequalities must appear justified, at least to some extent, in order to be maintained. People of privileged positions, people in positions of power, are able to use the American Dream to justify and legitimize their positions and pass along a sense of entitlement to these positions to their own children. In so doing, they neglect the power of wealth in shaping the life trajectories of themselves, their own children, other people, and other peoples' children. This, in effect, allows them to assuage any sense of guilt, compassion, or empathy they might otherwise feel about their own experiences and the experiences of others. And it allows them to assuage any sense of social responsibility or moral obligation they might otherwise feel toward using their power in altruistic, generous ways in the interest of progressive social change for the greater good.

Some will say that what makes this society so noble and so unique is not that everyone makes it, but that despite inequality in family backgrounds all citizens at least have a chance. Perhaps simply having a chance, however it is defined, is enough for us to be satisfied with our social system. Nevertheless, the idea that everyone has a chance simply does not compare to the idea that everyone has an *equal* chance, that no group is unfairly privileged or disadvantaged over another. An equal chance would mean that people truly would advance based on their own doing; that we would not be encumbered by our parents' positioning nor enhanced by it; and that some families would not be able to propel their privilege on to their children while others are left on their own. If we find ourselves committed to the ideal of meritocracy, then *a* chance is not good enough.

Ultimately we need to ask if we believe in the American Dream enough to make it real, or if instead we are ready to let go of it. Is meritocracy ultimately a straw man, or is it actually possible? If it is possible, would it even be desirable for such a system to exist?

I personally believe that to challenge the social reproduction of race and class inequalities, we must directly confront the structures themselves—we must recognize them and acknowledge them. To do so *would* be to discredit the American Dream. I myself am comfortable with that and am comfortable in teaching my children that. I believe that meritocracy is an ideological myth that could never be attained, and that it would not be desirable even if it could be achieved.[22] But my beliefs alone are negligible in the face of a dominant cultural ideology. We are sorely missing a major piece of the puzzle if we underestimate the power of this ideology. Race and class inequality is perpetuated in contemporary American society in part because the ideology of meritocracy is woven so heavily into our mind-sets so that we do not have to confront it nor the structures it masks. The American Dream is firmly rooted, central, and pervasive, and it acts as a mechanism through which stratification is perpetuated. Most likely Americans are probably not willing to give up on one of the things that unite them the most.[23] The American Dream is much more strongly ingrained than might generally be recognized.[24] So I agree with what Jennifer Hochschild and Peter Scovronick have recently argued—that we must work *with* the American Dream rather than against it if we have any hope for positive social change where equalizing children's life chances are concerned.[25] When juxtaposed to the power of wealth, the American Dream presents a real quandary for us: are we inspired enough by the ideals of the ideology to realize them for our communities, our families, our children?

At an Impasse

While most of us are morally committed to a society wherein all people have equal life chances and success is determined by individual achievement, our conviction in the ideology of meritocracy ironically allows us to disregard the hurdles we need to overcome in order to truly achieve those principles. Those hurdles are hard to grapple with because they are unavoidably structural in nature. They demand structural transformations in order to see real, lasting, positive social change. Further, since many of us who are in positions of power to implement social change are directly benefiting from the existence of the very structures that require alteration, it is hard to imagine the dissolution of them.

The American Dream and the power of wealth are so much part of the fabric of our society that we do not often consider them, let alone the ways they interrelate with our social institutions or our own roles in perpetuating them. Our beliefs and experiences are patterned in ways that are not always obvious, especially to us ourselves. Yet, by not wrestling with this paradox, by not gravely struggling to overcome it, we are—whether it is purposely or inadvertently—helping to maintain it. In our collective action and inaction; in our choices and in our standing back and letting it all happen; in our frenzy to do the best we can for our own families and in our presumption that we have no way to alter the status quo; in our indifference to the paradox—as if it were our shared fate, we are helping to maintain it. But the words of the classic American sociologist C. Wright Mills continue to haunt us: "The sociological meaning of 'fate' is simply this: that, when the decisions are innumerable and each one is of small consequence, all of them add up in a way no man [sic] intended—to history as fate."[26] What will our own history be? Can we change the course of it?

School decisions are just one arena in which the American Dream and the power of wealth play themselves out, but it is an important one because schools are where routes of access—to success, to mobility, to fulfillment of individual promise—are supposed to be equalized and actualized for all children. Instead, sets of opportunities for children of different race and class backgrounds, structurally unequal from the start, further perpetuate structured inequality. The ideology of the American Dream, perhaps strongest around the arena of education, legitimizes race and class inequality by presenting these not as structures but as the inconsequential ramifications of meritocracy. In a context in which education is seen as the key to success and schools are persistently segregated and unequal, school decisions become pivotal for the life chances of a child. The ideology of meritocracy and the reality of the wealth gap operate together, and in the simple act of sending children to school, we contribute to perpetuating inequality.

The interviews at the heart of this book give us a glimpse into how people make sense of their social world and come to make decisions in the context of it. Interviews, especially long interviews that encourage multifaceted discussion, allow people to express perspectives that are complex, multidimensional, and even contradictory. The biggest contribution of the families who gave us their perspectives and shared their experiences is that for the first time we have seen in depth how parents make sense of the contradiction between the wealth gap and meritocracy. For these parents, this was a potent contradiction: inherited family wealth ensured that white and wealthy children would disproportionately receive educational advantages, and yet the dominant ideology assured that all children would grow up in a meritocratic society. Here we have a firsthand account of how two hundred families made sense of this contradiction, the contradiction between the American Dream and the power of wealth.[27]

The families here do not, of course, represent all families living in the United States, but they do offer a new level of insight to the intergenerational transmission of race and class inequality. And, while the interviews cannot be generalized to capture the stories of us all, they are a lens through which to examine ourselves, our perspectives, and our own experiences. Although not intended as a representative sample, I think that the interviews presented here resonate for a lot of us. I have spoken about this work to many diverse audiences, and I always receive similar reactions: this material seems familiar to people, it resonates with them personally, and they relate to it in some profound way—often people tell me so. The interviews seem to unearth and articulate what we somehow already knew or suspected: that the American Dream and the power of wealth interrelate, contradict, and complement each other, that they collide as we pass along all that we can to the next generation.

It is easy to get entrenched in that which divides us, so we tend not to focus on those things that unify us. This is true for even the most analytical person or scholar; as Dalton Conley has noted, "rarely do social scientists ask how the rich and poor are similar,"[28] and sociologists seem especially prone to this tendency. But, despite how much separated them, the families in this study had much in common. Parents shared their bedrock beliefs in the values of the American Dream, and they shared their yearning to give their children the best chances they possibly could. Yet, by defending so staunchly the legitimacy of meritocracy and by focusing so intently on their own children, these parents were continually disregarding the patterns they were perpetuating for a whole new generation.

Prospects for altering legacies of ideology and inequality are tremendously challenging. But if we claim a meritocracy exists while we know it does not, if we acknowledge the structure is unjust and unfair, if we know all this and still do nothing, we are then taking a profoundly immoral stance. When we can claim to be uninformed, then perhaps our apathy toward injustice is justified. But once we are informed of the consequences of our actions, and still we make the same decisions, then we have no honorable defense to evade responsibility. Our collective inaction is then a force. What will we do? We have inherited powerful legacies and, intended or not, we will leave legacies ourselves. What do we want to pass along?

We are holding out hope, but we *are* at an impasse. As we look in the eyes of the next generation, we must ask what legacies we ourselves will leave. And we must answer this honestly—with strength and conviction—for not just our own, but for all of our children.

Appendix: Methodology

From 1998 to 2001, while a doctoral student in sociology at Northeastern University, I worked as a research assistant managing the qualitative data portion of the Assets and Inequality Project, a research project generously funded by two grants from the Ford Foundation (Thomas Shapiro, principal investigator). The project was constructed as a follow-up study to Melvin Oliver and Thomas Shapiro's 1995 book *Black Wealth/White Wealth* and was designed to further empirical understanding of how American families acquire and use assets. Thomas Shapiro's 2004 book *The Hidden Cost of Being African American* and several research papers that he and I coauthored resulted from this project. In addition, my 2001 doctoral dissertation relied entirely on the qualitative data that we collected. While I have tried to minimize overlap between interview quotations incorporated into *The Hidden Cost of Being African American* and this book, some of the data so typify or represent specific concepts that they are ultimately used in both texts.

As a sociologist, my major interest lies in what is happening in real life with real people when it comes to the reproduction of race and class inequalities in contemporary American society. I have always believed that dominant cultural ideologies play a major role in the perpetuation of inequality in that they foster people's legitimation of social structures that advantage and disadvantage them, thus allowing those structures to go more unquestioned and unchallenged than they might otherwise if the ideologies were not acting to support them. From the beginning of my work on the Assets and Inequality Project, it was striking to me the extent to which the black and white families we interviewed of different class backgrounds seemed to cling to the American Dream not just as rhetoric, but as a legitimate explanation for social inequality. What I was always most interested in was how privileged families justify advantage and teach their children about inequality. Even after completing the research, I continue to be surprised with how the families we spoke with during both phases of interviews actually believed that in post–civil rights America the playing field is truly level. In writing this book, my intent was never to convey the percentages of black and white families who do or do not have financial assets capable of propelling significant educational opportunities for their children (those statistics can be found elsewhere), nor to document the number of people who hold deep conviction in meritocracy (those numbers too can be found elsewhere). Rather, it was to better understand parents' assessments of their own opportunities and constraints, how families make decisions regarding schools for their children, how they act (or feel constrained from acting) on those decisions, and how they make sense of their experiences and the experiences of others.

Previous literature documents the gaps and quantifiable patterns of race and class/wealth stratification. But we do not know much about how these patterns are reproduced. *How* is inequality sustained and perpetuated? *How* do these patterns work themselves out in living, breathing, complicatedly real life? Qualitative research can get to the *how* in these questions. And qualitative research can help us understand questions of *why*. We know, for example, that white families often flee urban areas for suburbs when their children reach school age, but *how* and *why* do they do it, and on what terms? We know that schools are racially segregated based on de facto segregation, but *how* does this happen, and *why*? Quantitative research tells us about the extent of assets that different groups of American families own but it does not tell us the story of *how* these families acquired them, or *how* they decide to use them, or *why* they use them as they do. And, while public opinion polls are important to understanding the basic contours of people's conviction in ideological beliefs, they do not help to explain these belief systems from the perspective of people who actually hold them, are inspired by them, and act on them. Thus, while survey analysis is crucial for documenting and understanding much about wealth inequality and ideology, it fails to capture the grounded social processes at the interactional level that I am interested in understanding.

During two phases of interviewing, 260 individuals were interviewed from five major U.S. metropolitan areas. Chapter 1 discusses the research process. Below, the demographic characteristics of the families interviewed—the parents whose quotations appear throughout this book—are noted.

Qualitative Solutions and Research's Non-Numerical Unstructured Data-Indexing, Searching, and Theorizing program, version 4 ("NUD*IST"), distributed by Scolari Sage Publications Software, was used to manage the interview transcriptions, code the data, and to create interview and coding memos. NUD*IST and other software programs like it are valuable resources to help analyze large volumes of qualitative data, reveal patterns, and manage multiple streams of information and ideas that result from interviews on complex subjects. NUD*IST was used to ask questions and build and test hypotheses and theories about the data flexibly, and to check and cross-check data themes for theory validity as ideas evolved. Of the interviews yielded from the first phase of interviewing, 175 of them were coded using NUD*IST (seven interviews were not included due to technical problems with the recordings that made transcribing them impossible). All of the second-phase interviews were entered into the NUD*IST database. While NUD*IST served as an invaluable tool, as Renata Tesch notes, "The thinking, judging, deciding, interpreting, etc., are still done by the researcher. The computer does not make conceptual decisions, such as which words or themes are important to focus on, or which analytical step to take next. These analytical tasks are still left entirely to the researcher."[1] Ultimately, the strengths and weaknesses of the analysis are mine and mine alone.

Wealth, including savings, investments, and assets of all kinds, was self-reported, as was family income. *Income* here refers to the combined annual income of a household unit. Wealth is reported throughout the book as net financial assets. While there is no consistent measure of wealth used in the literature, Oliver and Shapiro have argued that net financial assets is a more reliable measure of a family's well-being:

The first, *net worth* (NW) conveys the straightforward value of all assets less any debts. The second, *net financial assets* (NFA), excludes equity accrued in a home or vehicle from the calculation of a household's available resources. Net worth gives a comprehensive picture of all assets and debts, yet it may not be a reliable measure of *command over future resources* for one's self and family.... Net financial assets, by contrast, are those financial assets normally available for present or future conversion into ready cash.... In contrast to net worth, net financial assets consists of more readily liquid sources of income and wealth that can be used for a family's immediate well-being.... Net financial assets seem to be the best indicator of the current generation's command over future resources, while net worth provides a more accurate estimate of the wealth likely to be inherited by the next generation.[2]

Interviews included in-depth discussions about family wealth and intergenerational transfers. Despite the extensive financial information interview participants provided, a challenge remains in regard to analyzing family wealth: a sound formula has yet to be created that would accurately depict how much of a family's wealth was originally unearned. In wealth-holding families, major milestones in life such as an eighteenth birthday, a college graduation, a wedding, or the birth of a grandchild are often marked by substantial gifts or transfers of assets. These intergenerational transfers are sometimes remembered years later as significant in the growth of a family's wealth port-folio, and sometimes not remembered (or considered significant) at all. Also quite common for members of wealth-holding families is to receive financial assistance, gifts, loans, and the like that happen so frequently, or are such a normalized part of their lives, that they are not necessarily conceptualized by them as "help" nor believed to be of significance. In such instances, families probably did not think to mention all of the intergenerational transfers they have received—despite how much we probed them to do so—when explaining how they acquired the wealth that they have.

Even more complicated for research on wealth is that when wealth gets passed along in families—in either small or large amounts—it accumulates over time and is often invested and built upon. As I argue in the book, down payments; paying for college, gifts, furniture, meals out, new clothes; help here and there; and so forth take on an accumulative effect over time. Wealth received at major milestones and the accumulated advantage of family wealth are two different yet potentially equally important dimensions of wealth privilege. How do we measure what percentage of a family's wealth originated from their extended families? How could we cal-culate how much of a family's wealth portfolio is rooted in unearned assets over time? How can we determine the extent to which families have relied upon family wealth in material and nonmaterial ways throughout the course of their experiences? We have yet to determine such formulas. For these reasons, while I do not believe the wealth data presented in this study are misleading, they are probably very conservative estimates of intergenerational transfers of money, family wealth, and unearned assets. Essentially, realities of family wealth in America, and the extent to which the wealth gap is playing itself out, are probably much more extreme than this study portrays.

General Demographic Characteristics
of Families Interviewed

Phase One: January 1998 through June 1999

Interviews
   182: Total number of interviews (232 individuals)
   175: Total number of interviews in NUD*IST qualitative database

> *Note:* All numbers below refer to totals of the interviews within the database.

City/Metropolitan Area
   49: Boston area
   62: Los Angeles area
   64: St. Louis area

Family's Race
   85: Black
   75: White
    5: Biracial (at least one respondent self-identified as "African American and white")
   10: Hispanic

Family's Social Class
   72: Working class and poor
  103: Middle class and upper middle class

Household Structure
   79: Total single-parent families
      46: Single parent, never married
      33: Divorced or separated
   92: Total two-parent families
      83: Two parents, married
       9: Two parents, living together unmarried, coparenting
   22: Total shared or extended families, kin living in home

Occupation of Respondent 1 (Single Parent, or Woman/Mother in Household, If a Couple)
   35: Upper-income white collar or professional
   60: Lower-income white collar
   23: Upper-income blue collar
   12: Lower-income blue collar
   16: In home/homemaker/no work outside home
   27: Unemployed

Occupation of Respondent 2 (Spouse of Respondent 1)
53: Upper-income white collar or professional
18: Lower-income white collar
5: Upper-income blue collar
10: Lower-income blue collar
0: In home/homemaker/no work outside home
4: Unemployed

Level of Education (Highest Degree Earned by Respondents in Household)
14: Less than high school
17: High school
57: Some college
44: College
26: Public college
18: Private college
40: Graduate or professional school

Precollege Education of Respondent 1
101: Public: attended public elementary and high school
18: Public and private: attended some public and some private elementary and high school
10: Private: attended private elementary and high school

Precollege Education of Respondent 2
59: Public: attended public elementary and high school
8: Public and private: attended some public and some private elementary and high school
6: Private: attended private elementary and high school

Basic Family Background—Class Background of Respondent 1
14: Poor
73: Working class
86: Middle class or upper middle class

Basic Family Background—Class Background of Respondent 2
3: Poor
26: Working class
49: Middle class or upper middle class

Home Ownership
88: Rent
84: Own

Children's Schooling
105: Public school
32: Private school
2: Public and private: combination of schooling
38: Not yet attending school

Phase II: June through August 2003
Interviews
20: Total number of interviews (28 individuals)
20: Total number of interviews in NUD*IST qualitative database

City/Metropolitan Area
9: Washington, D.C.
11: New York City

Family's Race
17: White
1: Biracial (at least one respondent self-identified as "African American and white")
2: Other (at least one respondent self-identified as "Middle Eastern")

Family's Social Class
20: Middle and upper middle class

Household Structure
20: Total two-parent families, married

Occupation of Respondent 1 (Single Parent, or Woman/Mother in Household If a Couple)
7: Upper-income white collar or professional
13: In home/homemaker/no work outside home

Occupation of Respondent 2 (Spouse of Respondent 1)
20: Upper-level white collar or professional

Level of Education (Highest Degree Earned by Respondents in Household)
12: College
2: Public college
10: Private college
8: Graduate or professional school

Precollege Education of Respondent 1
    16: Public: attended public elementary and high school
    4: Private: attended private elementary and high school

Pre-College Education of Respondent 2
    18: Public: attended public elementary and high school
    1: Public and private: attended some public and some private elementary and high school
    1: Private, attended private elementary and high school

Basic Family Background—Class Background of Respondent 1
    2: Working class
    18: Middle class or upper middle class

Basic Family Background—Class Background of Respondent 2
    3: Working class
    17: Middle class or upper middle class

Home Ownership
    20: Own

Children's Schooling
    8: Public school
    12: Private school

Notes

Chapter 1

1. Proctor and Dalaker 2003.
2. See Berrick 1995; Edin and Lein 1997; Ellwood 1988; Kozol 1988.
3. Proctor and Dalaker 2003.
4. See Ehrenreich 2001; Johnson 2002; Levitan and Shapiro 1987; New-man 1999; Rank 2004; Shipler 2004.
5. Marx 1867.
6. I use the term *family wealth* throughout the book to refer to the wealth within a family, including immediate family and extended family that has been used, is being used, and/or has the potential to be used to pass along intergenerational transfers over time. This conceptualization helps give a sense of family background where wealth is concerned. This is a different concept than the terms "family money" or "old money" often used to describe those families who have *lots* of money, or money that (as one participant said) "goes way back." Only a hand-ful of such "old money" families were interviewed for this book, but many of the parents interviewed had backgrounds of family wealth. As we will see, even small amounts of family wealth make big differences for the life chances of a family's next generation.
7. Class is more than simply a materialist phenomenon, it is a struc-tural, hierarchical phenomenon involving distinctions between strati-fied groups or individuals. While social class status and identification involves ownership of property and valued resources, and while it involves control over property and valued resources, it must also be understood in a fuller context to include such dimensions as economic status (income, wealth portfolios); socioeconomic status (education, occupations, prestige); power and control (social and political power); social and cultural capital (values, tastes and preferences, social networks); life chances (expectations, life trajectories of families and children); etc.
8. Devine 1998, 2004.

9. Sherraden 1991. Also see Sen 1999 for a discussion of his conceptualization of similar ideas.
10. Sociologists generally define something as "structural" if it is an enduring pattern of social life rooted in more-or-less recurrent sets of social arrangements within society.
11. Bradshaw and Wallace 1996; Wolff 1995.
12. Keister 2000, p. 3.
13. Scharf 2004; Wolff 2001.
14. McNamee and Miller 1998.
15. Keister 2000.
16. Shapiro 2004.
17. Shapiro 2004; Wolff 2001.
18. Keister 2000, p. 220.
19. In the pages that follow, race is discussed by addressing the dynamics between only black and white Americans. The terms *black* and *white* are used conscientiously on my part as descriptors for the two racial groups. I choose to use this language in part because it seems most reasonable to me, but mostly because these are the terms that the interview participants in this study used to describe themselves. For consistency purposes, *black* and *white* are used both in the interview data and throughout the text to describe individuals and groups of the two different racial and ethnic backgrounds. Of course, the United States is a multiracial and multiethnic society. So why examine the topic here with attention paid only to blacks and whites? First, there are practical reasons to justify it: by focusing the analysis to black and white the project is simplified so that a study such as the one presented here—an in-depth examination of race and class in the contemporary United States—is pragmatically possible. But this alone is not good enough reason to warrant the oversimplified analysis. More important, in the contemporary United States, blacks and whites demonstrate the greatest disparities between racial groups. Most social scientists agree that the black-white racial divide is a special case, in that it is more extreme than most disparities among other racial and ethnic groups; as one example, blacks have been shown to be "hypersegregated"—more residentially segregated and isolated than any other racial group (Massey and Denton 1993). As Sam Roberts concludes, "For all the pretense of egalitarianism in the United States, gaps have always developed and, to one degree or another, persisted: between rich and poor, between North and South, between older groups of immigrants and greenhorns, between Americans of European stock and everyone else. None have been more enduring and insidious than the gap between blacks and whites" (2004, p. 165). The history of black slave owning by white slave owners has made the black-white racial divide unique in our society and particularly intense socially, economically, and politically. The legacy of slavery has carried through to the present day, especially in regards to the racial wealth gap

(Oliver and Shapiro 1995). Despite efforts to curtail it, a huge chasm remains between blacks and whites in this country. The wealth gap is perhaps one of the most significant aspects of this chasm.

20. Oliver and Shapiro 1995.

21. Others, too, have made important contributions to our understanding of the relationship between race and class by documenting the patterned gaps in wealth ownership between white and black families. See, especially, Conley 1999.

22. U.S. Census Bureau, Statistical Abstract 2003.

23. Conley 1999; Oliver and Shapiro 1995.

24. Shapiro finds similar results when analyzing net financial assets as opposed to net worth: the typical black family owns $3,000 net financial assets, compared to the $33,500 owned by the typical white family. See Shapiro 2004 for more results. Also, note that throughout this book wealth is reported as net financial assets (see Appendix).

25. Shapiro 2004.

26. Conley 1999; Keister 2000; Neckerman 2004; Oliver and Shapiro 1995; Shapiro 2004; Wolff 1995; Wolff 2001.

27. See Conley 1999; Keister 2000; Oliver and Shapiro 1995; Shapiro 2004.

28. Blinder 1988; Cox and Rank 1992; Gale and Scholz 1994; Keister 2000; Kotlikoff and Summers 1981; Kotlikoff and Summers 1988; Wilhelm 2001. Note: An exception is Modigliani (1988a; 1988b), who estimates such transfers as accounting for less than 20 percent.

29. Schoeni 1997.

30. Conley 1999, p. 47.

31. See Smith 1995.

32. Shapiro 2004.

33. Cox and Raines 1985; Gale and Scholz 1994.

34. Poor families (as measured by income or by asset poverty)—including white families—have been the focus of much analysis and literature both in and outside of academe. Much less often are wealthy black families at the center of examination, although of course there are and always have been wealthy black families in the United States. For an illustrative exception to this, see Graham 2000.

35. For discussions on what wealth can provide for children, see Conley 1999; Haveman and Wolfe 1994; Lareau 2003; Miller-Adams 2002; Oliver and Shapiro 1995; Shapiro 2004; Shapiro and Wolff 2001; Sherraden 1991.

36. Many scholars have noted this point (see, for example, Conley 1999; Cooksen and Persell 1985; Lareau 2003; Miller-Adams 2002; Oliver and Shapiro 1995; Shapiro 2004; Shapiro and Wolff 2001; Sherraden 1991), although no conclusive empirical evidence on this subject has been documented thus far in the research literature.

37. See Bowman and Ladd 1998; Hochschild 1995; Kluegel and Smith 1986; Ladd 1994.
38. Davis and Smith 1999, as cited in McNamee and Miller 2004.
39. Throughout the book, I use the word *ideology* to refer to the dominant scheme for the general public's understanding of, and explanations for, the operation of the social order. The concept is used analytically rather than judgmentally. My goal here is not to imply that the belief systems I am scrutinizing are false, nor to imply that any particular group is responsible for the existence of them. For more on this sort of conceptuatlization of ideology, see Prager 1982. For more on ideology generally, see McLellan 1995; Therborn 1980.
40. Wealth practically ensures, for example, better schools, safer neighborhoods, more experiential opportunities, access to higher-quality healthcare, exposure to more well-connected professional networks, etc.
41. See Feagin 1975; Huber and Form 1973; Kluegel and Smith 1986.
42. See Della Fave 1980; 1986.
43. Grusky 1994, p. 3.
44. See Centers 1949; Jackman and Jackman 1983; Vanneman and Cannon 1987.
45. Cullen 2003; Delbanco 1999; Hochschild 1995; Hochschild and Scovronick 2003; Schwarz 1997.
46. American public schools today are not only heavily segregated by race and class, but are increasingly so. See Orfield, Eaton, and the Harvard Project on School Desegregation 1996; Orfield and Yun 1999.
47. With relatively few exceptions, sociology has historically and contemporarily been negligent in studying the privileged. One of the most major exceptions in classical sociology is Mills 1956. Examples of recent work on privileged populations include Brantlinger 2003; Cookson and Persell 1985; Kendall 2002; Lamont 1992; Sherwood 2004.
48. Conley 2003, p.2.
49. Quote cited is from MacLeod 1987, p. 6. Others who have recently noted the paucity of studies of class advantaged populations and have focused studies on privilege include Brantlinger 2003; Kendall 2002; Ostrander 1984; Sherwood 2004. Studies of race advantage have recently become more common, as a sizable body of research on white privilege has taken shape. See, for example, Doane and Bonilla-Silva 2003; Fine, Weis, Powell, and Wong 1997; Kincheloe, Steinberg, Rodriguez, and Chennault 1991; Lipsitz 1998; Rothenberg 2002.
50. MacLeod 1987, p. 248.
51. For some of the most noteworthy examples, see Wilson 1978; 1987; 1996; and Willie 1977; 1979; 1985; 1989.

52. For further discussion, see Collins 1993. Collins argues that ranking and quantifying inequality only obscures the multidimensional connectedness of it.

53. This is paraphrased from Thomas and Thomas 1928. Race and class are socially constructed realities that have great significance in social life both in terms of perceptions (how we perceive ourselves and others and how others perceive us), and actions (how we act in the world and in relation to others). Furthermore, as sociologist Eduardo Bonilla-Silva has argued, race and racism (and I would add class and classism as well) are *structural* phenomena: "Racialized social systems are societies that allocate differential economic, political, social, and even psychological rewards to groups along racial lines; lines that are socially constructed" and the "aggregate" of "racialized social systems" is "the racial structure of society" wherein "Blacks' life chances are significantly lower than those of whites.... Ultimately a racialized social order is distinguished by this difference in life chances" (1997, pp. 474, 470).

54. See Mills 1959.

55. As Paul Willis has written, "The difficult thing to explain about how middle class kids get middle class jobs is why others let them. The difficult thing to explain about how working class kids get working class jobs is why they let themselves. It is much too facile simply to say that they have no choice" (1981, p. 1).

56. In a recent paper, Barbara Reskin discusses this line of sociological questioning in depth and calls for future research that will push our thinking forward by asking "how" questions. She argues, "We have failed to progress because most of our research has focused on *why* ascriptively-defined groups vary on their access to societies' rewards, rather than on *how* variation is produced in ascriptive groups' access to opportunities.... I appeal, in the interests of science and justice, for research on *how* people come to be stratified on the basis of their ascribed characteristics.... Explanation requires including mechanisms in our models—the specific processes that link groups' ascribed characteristics to variable outcomes" (2003, pp. 1–2).

57. See Appendix for further information, including the general demographic characteristics of the families interviewed.

58. Since I could find no similar studies in the research literature, it was not at all clear how upper-class families would react to in-depth interviewing directly on the topic of the ideology of meritocracy and the structure of wealth inequality. Before the interviewing began, when I would tell people what I planned to do (to ask affluent families outright about this paradox), I was usually met with nervous laughter. Many friends and colleagues, in fact, told me that their prediction was that I would be "thrown out of these families' houses." I was very curious as to how it would unfold. As it turned out, the interviewed families were extraordinarily forthcoming and surprisingly

frank during our conversations. They seemed genuinely open to the interview, and—as I've found in all of my experiences with in-depth interviewing—they seemed to sincerely enjoy the experience.

59. Throughout the book, quotations from interviews appear with short descriptors of the people interviewed (usually including names, occupations, self-reported racial identity, and metropolitan area). All names have been changed. Otherwise, I have tried to keep the quotations as authentic to the interview voices as possible. Italics are used to mark parts of interview quotations that the interviewees themselves emphasized. For example, "I believe in it" is different than "I *believe* in it!" I have tried to stay true to the interviews by using italics and certain punctuation only where appropriate. When an ellipsis (...) appears, this indicates a break in the natural flow of the interview where I cut a section of a quotation to shorten it in the interest of readability. Other than these deviations, all quotations appear as they do in the original transcripts from the recorded interviews.

Chapter 2

1. Cullen 2003; Delbanco 1999.
2. In the past ten years, groundbreaking contributions have been made to our understanding of the history and origins of the American Dream. Hochschild 1995 includes an analysis of the roots and historical significance of the notion. Andrew Delbanco 1999 traces the tenet of hope so central to the dream itself. Cullen 2003 is the first book to explicitly take on the challenge of tracing in depth the origins of the American Dream and its significant role in and on American history. Jillson 2004 explores the origins, evolutions, and implications of the American Dream through the present day. McNamee and Miller 2004 provides an overview of the literature on the American Dream and focuses specifically on the principle of meritocracy central to it.
3. Cullen 2003.
4. Cullen 2003; Hochschild 1995; Hochschild and Scovronick 2003.
5. Schwarz 1997, p. 10.
6. Cullen 2003; Hochschild 1995; Schwarz 1997. Cullen is explicit about the role of *agency* in the notion of the American Dream. He notes, for example, that agency "lies at the very core of the American Dream, the bedrock premise upon which all else depends" (p. 10).
7. Cullen 2003, p. 66.
8. Hochschild 1995; see especially part 1 for an in-depth analysis of the American Dream and its tenets.
9. There are, of course, significant exceptions to this, including individuals who do not subscribe to mainstream or dominant political frameworks. It is also important to recognize that whole social groups have been discriminated against and/or excluded from sharing in

the nationalist ideology of the American Dream in the same ways other individuals and groups have historically. Native Americans, for example, are a case in point.

10. Although not the focus here, the question of how we learn the American Dream and pass it along to the next generation is important for future research. The American Dream is entrenched in daily life and culture. We are socialized to it throughout our lives. Further research is sorely needed to expand our understanding of how these things happen. How are dominant ideologies shaped, maintained, and perpetuated by us as part of our collective consciousness? How is it that we all know what the American Dream is? How do children learn the American Dream and carry it through their adulthoods? The answers to these questions are crucial to understanding how the American Dream is reproduced from one generation to the next.

11. Cullen 2003, p. 10.

12. Sennett and Cobb 1972, pp. 267, 271.

13. Sources are discussed and their citations appear throughout the remainder of the book. See especially Bowman and Ladd 1998; Huber and Form 1973; Kluegel and Smith 1986.

14. Ladd 1994.

15. See for example Gallagher 2003; 2005.

16. See DiTomaso, forthcoming; Hyde 2002; Sherwood 2004.

17. See the *Washington Post* study, cited in Hochschild and Scovronick 2003.

18. Farkas and Johnson 1998.

19. Shuman and Krysan 1999, p. 847.

20. Phi Delta Kappa 2003.

21. Hochschild 1995, p. 259. Hochschild's data regarding people's beliefs in the American Dream is an important comparison point for my own. However, I am limited in how much I can engage with the results she discussed because while her respondents were explicitly focused on comparisons between racial groups, mine were not. In fact, race—as a specific and explicit subject—was barely discussed in the interviews I conducted. While race was a major focal point of her work, class (wealth) has been more the focus of mine—especially as a central focus of the interviews. Furthermore, much of Hochschild's data is from social surveys and public opinion polls. This makes contrasting Hochschild's data with my own—purely qualitative data from in-depth interviews—challenging and problematic.

22. Sennett and Cobb 1972.

23. MacLeod 1987.

24. Nightingale 1993.

25. See the research literature on contemporary white privilege and "color-blind" racism; for example, Bonilla-Silva 2001; Bonilla-Silva 2003; DiTomaso 2000; Feagin and O'Brien 2003; Gallagher 2003; Gallagher 2005; Krysan and Lewis 2004; Lewis 2004.

26. These findings provide empirical data for a phenomenon that others, too, have observed. Cullen 2003 notes that the American Dream and the belief in equality of opportunity tend to obscure even our own lived reality. He writes, "That the circumstances of everyday life routinely belie this belief is hardly a problem as long as the principle of equality is affirmed" (p. 108).
27. See Delbanco 1999.
28. Kluegel and Smith 1986, p. 42; See also, for example, Brantlinger 2003; Lareau 2000 and 2003.
29. Hochshild and Scovronick 2003 discusses this in depth.
30. The degree to which the parents were consciously aware of the discrepancies between what they said and what they did was not clear and would require further research to explore. For discussion and analysis regarding the relationship between what people way and what people do, see Deutscher, Pestello, and Pestello 1993.
31. Holme 2002, for example, observes similar findings in her study of high-status families in California.
32 For interview data and analytic discussion on this particular aspect of the interviews, see Johnson and Shapiro 2003; Shapiro and Johnson 2005b.
33. See Johnson and Shapiro 2003 and Shapiro and Johnson 2005b for further elaboration on these points. See especially Johnson and Shapiro 2003 for discussion of the overt racism expressed by many of the white families interviewed.
34. See Bonilla-Silva 1997; Bonilla-Silva 2001; Bonilla-Silva 2003.
35. See Bonilla-Silva 1997.
36. For discussion of how class frames parents' perspectives on schools see Holme 2002. Even though Holme's study only included upper middle-class white parents, the interviews conducted for this book yielded similar findings overall.
37. U.S. Department of Education 2004.
38. For a review of the cross-disciplinary literature see Meyer 2000.
39. Farley and Frey 1994.
40. Yinger 1995; Orfield and Eaton 1997.
41. Massey and Denton 1993.
42. Iceland, Weinberg and Steinmetz 2002.
43. See Oliver and Shapiro 1995; Shapiro 2004.
44. Massey and Denton 1993, p. iii.
45. Hacker 1992.
46. Shipler 1997.
47. Jackman 1994, p. 136.
48. Hoffman and Llagas 2003.
49. Orfield and Yun 1999.
50. U.S. Department of Education 2004.
51. Hochschild and Scovroncick 2003; Orfield 1999; Orfield and Eaton 1996.
52. Orfield 1999; Orfield and Eaton 1996.

53. Steinhorn and Diggs-Brown 1999; Orfield 1999; Orfield and Eaton 1996.
54. Hochschild 2003, pp. 825–26.
55. Children's Defense Fund 1998.
56. Children's Defense Fund 1998.
57. Pagani, Boulerice, and Tremblay 1997.
58. Poor children are, for example, twice as likely as middle-class children to drop out of school, and eleven times more likely than wealthy children to do so. See Children's Defense Fund 1998, p. xiv. See also Duncan and Gunn 1997; Fine 1991; Haveman and Wolfe 1994; Haveman, Wolfe, and Spaulding 1991.
59. See Anyon 1997; Fine 1991; Hochschild 2003; Orfield and Eaton 1996; Wells 1995.
60. See Johnson and Shapiro 2003; Shapiro and Johnson 2005b.
61. See Holme 2002 for a thorough account of parents' social construction of school quality. See also Ball 2003 and Brantlinger 2003 on how middle-class families choose schools.
62. See for example, Mayer 1997.
63. See Hochschild and Scovronick 2003 for a thorough literature review on this subject. Quote here is from Hochschild and Scovronick 2003, p. 26.
64. In 1966, sociologist James Coleman and his team of researchers published a highly influential report (now known as the "Coleman Report") on school inequality. In it, the authors argued that family background, rather than schools themselves, was the major variable in determining differences in student achievement. The Coleman Report ignited much controversy and scholarly debate. Since then, numerous studies have shown mixed and varied results regarding the impact of family background on student outcomes, as well as which variables matter, how much they matter, and why they matter to student achievement. See Coleman 1966. See also the work of Jencks 1979.
65. See, for example Thernstrom and Thernstrom 2003.
66. For a recent collection of studies examining family background and factors outside of the educational sphere impacting educational attainment, see Conley and Albright 2004.
67. Rank 2004, p. 207.
68. Rank 2004, p. 210.
69. Mayer, Mullens, and Moore, 2001.
70. Oakes and Saunders 2004.
71. Darling-Hammond and Post 2000.
72. Others have reported similar findings. Warren and Tyagi 2003, for example, found that parents believed so strongly that there were real differences in school quality, and they believed so strongly that school quality translated into children's life chances, that they were willing to do whatever they could (including going into significant financial debt) to gain access for their children to the best schools possible.

Chapter 3

1. Social survey research shows that racist attitudes on the part of whites are prevalent, persistent, and at the center of much of their perspectives and decisions. See Bobo, Kleugel, and Smith 1997; Feagin and Vera 1995; Tuch and Martin 1997.
2. See Bobo and Zubrinsky 1996; Massey and Denton 1989; Schuman, Steeh, Bobo, and Krysan 1997.
3. While not the topic of this book per se, dynamics of race and class bias, prejudice, and discrimination were palpable in these interviews. Chapter 3 mentions some of the ways that racism and classism were incorporated into people's decisions about where they would like to live and send their children to school. The interviews made clear that other aspects of race and class were at play as well. For example, race identity, class identity, racial and class group formation, children's socialization, and the cultural aspects/cultural and social capital were involved with much of parents' decisions about neighborhoods and schools. While outside the scope of this book, these are all important areas for analysis in future research.
4. See Shapiro 2004. The white, middle-class families interviewed had often received help with down payments from their parents. This help had eased their entries into homeownership and helped them to access well-resourced neighborhoods. This pattern, as well policies and practices that support it, are well-documented by Shapiro.
5. Shapiro 2004, p. 167.
6. Shapiro 2004, p. 167.
7. Bielick and Chapman 2003.
8. Bielick and Chapman 2003.
9. McNamee and Miller 1998, p. 196.
10. See Blinder 1988; Cox and Rank 1992; Gale and Scholz 1994; Keister 2000; Kotlikoff and Summers 1981; Schoeni 1997; Shapiro 2004; Wilhelm 2001.
11. See Avery and Rendall 1997; Havens and Schervish 1999.
12. Keister 2000, p. 252.
13. Boshara, Scanlon, Page-Adams 1998; Page-Adams and Sherraden 1997; Sherraden 1991.
14. Havemand and Wolfe 1994
15. Axinn, Duncan, and Thornton 1997.
16. Orr 2003.
17. Forum on Child and Family Statistics 1999.
18. See Oakes and Lipton 1998; Orfield, Eaton, and Harvard Project 1996; Reimers 2001; Rothstein 2004; Wells 1995.
19. Mayer 1999, p. 3.
20. As Kenty-Drane 2004 notes, "The dearth of empirical work documenting disparities in educational conditions is also a significant problem for researchers because we have public figures in educational policy asserting that disparities in conditions are minimal or

do not exist, and furthermore that even if they do exist, they do not matter" (p. 21).

21. Haycock 1998.
22. Darling-Hammond 2004.
23. See Bourdieu 1977, 1986; Bowles and Gintis 1976.
24. See Lareau 2000; Lareau 2003.
25. Cookson and Persell 1985, p. 16.

Chapter 4

1. Keister 2000, p. 215.
2. Conley 1999, p. 26.
3. Axinn, Duncan, and Thornton 1997, p. 538.
4. Duncan and Brooks-Gunn 1997, p. 602.
5. Conley 1999.
6. Smith, Brooks-Gunn, and Klebanov 1997.
7. Children's Defense Fund 1998, p. xiii.
8. Teachman, Paasch, and Carver 1997, p. 416.
9. Children's Defense Fund 1998, p. xiii.
10. Orfield and Eaton 1996, p. 360
11. See, for example, Conley 1999; Keister 2003; Oliver and Shapiro 1995; Shapiro 2004.
12. Oliver and Shapiro 1995, p. 168. See also Conley 1999; Shapiro 2004.
13. See Blinder 1988; Cox and Rank 1992; Gale and Scholz 1994; Keister 2000; Kotlikoff and Summers 1981; Schoeni 1997; Shapiro 2004; Wilhelm 2001.
14. Survey research shows that approximately 25 percent of families who save say they are doing so for their retirement (Kennickell and Starr-McCluer 1994). More often, families save for short-term purposes; approximately 42 percent report they are saving so that they will be able to liquidate assets if needed for major purchases or in a financial crisis (Kennickell and Starr-McCluer 1994). The savings goals of the families interviewed for this book were consistent with this. In families without backgrounds of family wealth savings were being conceived of as a safety net to be used in case earned income were to become insufficient to pull a family through some situation in the future. These families were also found to be saving specifically for planned purchases, such as buying a house or paying for childrens' college education. In contrast, wealth-holding families reported their primary reason for saving was investing. This is consistent with research reported in Keister 2000 and Kennickell and Starr-McCluer 1994.
15. Stack 1974, p. 105. See especially chapter 5.
16. Chiteji and Hamilton 2002. For other discussion of what I am referring to as "intergenerational transfers in reverse" operating in black families, see Billingsley 1992; Chiteji and Hamilton 2005; Heflin

and Pattillo 2003; McAdoo 2002; Taylor, Chatters, and Mays 1988; Wilkerson 1990.

17. Chiteji and Hamilton 2005, p. 107.
18. See Hill 1972; Hill 1999; Stack 1974.

Chapter 5

1. Furthermore, as opposed to race or gender status, which are generally hard to hide, wealth privilege is almost impossible to see. It is important to analytically distinguish wealth and class as separate conceptual frameworks here: while class may perhaps at times be quite observable (in regard to such cues as attire, mannerisms, tastes and preferences), family wealth (in regard to how much assistance is being granted through intergenerational transfers, a sense of financial security, etc.) is not normally visible at all.
2. In chapter 6, the ideological conflict between meritocracy and structured inequality expressed by the families is discussed in depth.
3. For an in-depth analysis of the subject of social class as taboo in the contemporary United States, see hooks 2000.
4. Newman 1988.
5. For some of the most important work related to this see Conley 1999; Oliver and Shapiro 1995; Shapiro 2004; Sherraden 1990. See also policy work, such as Friedman 2003a and 2003b; Miller-Adams 2002.
6. See Oliver and Shapiro 1995, pp. 5 and 51, for examples regarding their use of the notion of wealth's "cumulative effect."
7. Sociologist Robert Merton coined this sort of phenomenon the "Matthew effect." See Merton 1968.
8. Valian 1998, p. 3.
9. See, for example, Sherraden 1990.
10. See Lareau 2000; 2003.

Chapter 6

1. Another thing that stood out the most here was the fact that many people (not just in families who were struggling) had regrets in life and felt that they probably should have made "more," "better," or "wiser" decisions along the way. However, one of the major benefits of the safety net provided by family wealth was its capacity to mitigate the less, worse, unwise decisions along the way.
2. As noted in chapter 2, this research finding contrasts with Jennifer Hochschild's findings. See that chapter for discussion.
3. Even in the cognitive dissonance literature from psychology and social psychology, the prevailing idea is that when faced with the tension that results from two inconsistent attitudes or beliefs, or

when faced with attitudes or beliefs that conflict with behaviors or realities, then people will attempt to resolve the cognitive dissonance they experience by adjusting or abandoning their attitudes, beliefs, or behaviors. If attitudes or beliefs conflict with reality, then people will change their attitudes, beliefs, and/or behaviors to adjust accordingly; they will come up with a way to either reconcile the two in their own minds, or adapt their attitudes to correspond and fit with the reality with which they are faced.

4. Feagin 1975.
5. Feagin 1975; Huber and Form 1973; Hunt 1996; Hunt 2004; Kluegel and Smith 1986; Smith and Stone 1989. Kluegel and Smith did note that sometimes individuals may hold inconsistent beliefs: "The ambivalent orientation to inequality ... within the same person, does not necessarily require resolution toward consistency" (1986, p. 7). However, Kluegel and Smith's work, as well as most of the work on this subject, did not focus on ambivalence but on how strongly Americans subscribe to the dominant ideology of individualistic beliefs. This is in line with the traditional scholarship that generally assumes an either/or situation regarding belief structures. Only very recently has this assumption begun to be challenged in a concrete way.
6. See Huber and Form 1973 and Kluegel and Smith 1986. Most studies of stratification beliefs since these have followed in their tradition.
7. Huber and Form 1973, p. 3
8. Kluegel and Smith 1986, p. 23.
9. Starks 2003, p. 220.
10. Hochschild 1995.
11. Bobo 1991; Hughes and Tuch 1999; Hyde 2002; Miller and Clark 1997.
12. Hyde 2002, pp. 69, 163.
13. Hunt 1996, p. 312.
14. Bobo 1991; Hunt 1996; Hunt 2004; Hyde 2002; Mann 1991.
15. Smith 1985; Smith and Stone 1989.
16. Smith and Stone 1989, pp. 103, 104.
17. Smith and Stone 1989, p. 94.
18. Hunt 2004.
19. Prager 1982, p. 102.
20. Eagleton 1991, p. 5.
21. Eagleton 1991.
22. *Hope*, according to *Webster's New World Dictionary of the American Language*, is "a feeling that what is wanted will happen ... to want and expect." Delbanco 1999 discusses hope as the ability to transcend boundaries of current reality and/or self; to understand future with unconstrained possibility; as in the opposite of melancholy.

Chapter 7

1. One interview stood out as an exception in that the family (interviewed in the second phase of interviews) insisted throughout the
interview that all good fortune, advantage, and privilege is due in
large part to pure luck. This interview was striking because it was
the only one of the two hundred wherein the interviewee took this
stance. "Being in the right place at the right time," "jumping at an
opportunity when it is presented to you," and "just plain luck of
the draw," were all themes that this couple revisited repeatedly in
their interview. And indeed, in the case of that family luck did seem
to have played some sort of role in their success. They considered
themselves lucky on many counts. According to them, however,
their most major lucky happenstance involved their having inherited a piece of land from a relative that "wound up" being rich soil
for citrus production. In their own view, the family had "lucked
out" because "who would have thought that a deserted piece of land
would produce such a ripe crop?" At the time of their interview, they
were continuing to receive quarterly checks for their profits and had
put all three of their daughters through college and graduate school
with this money. It is important to note, however, that while this
is definitely "lucky" (and they clearly perceived it as so) there are
other—quite different—ways of looking at this same story through
the lens of inherited family wealth.

2. Many people tell me that they expected families to respond in
this way. Even if they had claimed that their inherited wealth was
deserved because the relative they received it from had earned it
(which, notably, none of them did), this would still negate the fundamental values of individualism and equal opportunity at the core
of the American Dream.

3. Bonilla-Silva 1997, p. 467. See also Bonilla Silva 2001; 2003.

4. See Johnson and Shapiro 2003.

5. In an edited book on the subject of "unequal chances" and social
reproduction, Samuel Bowles, Herbert Gintis, and Melissa Osbourne
Groves present a collection of scholarly research focused on family background and children's economic success. The consensus is
that "intergenerational inequality in the United States is far greater
than was previously thought," and the editors argue that, "while the
inheritance of wealth and the better schooling typically enjoyed by
the children of the well-to-do contribute to this process, these two
standard explanations fail to explain the extent of intergenerational
status transmission." The book covers a wide range of scholarly
work on other factors contributing to the perpetuation of intergenerational inequality. See Bowles, Gintis, and Groves 2005; quotation here is from summary on book flap.

6. See Shapiro and Johnson 2005b, p. 259.

7. See Hochschild 2003. I have found Hochschild's concept of "nested
inequalities" useful in thinking through the debacle of unequal edu-

cation. She is particularly focused on disadvantages, negative consequences, and weak outcomes for underprivileged populations in regard to urban education. Similarly, I would argue, conceptualizing the opposite—*nested privileges*—can be useful in thinking through the *advantages* conferred to many students from relatively privileged backgrounds who have opportunities to attend higher-quality, whiter, wealthier, generally more suburban schools.

8. For a collection of work focused on the shift in education reform away from equity goals and reasons why we must make efforts to "bring equity back" as a central policy aim, see Petrovich and Wells 2005.

9. The presumption that white and/or upper-class families care more about their children's schools or that black and/or poor families devalue education is at the root of much of the research literature in the social sciences and was also an often-recurring theme in our interviews with middle- and upper-class white parents who frequently claimed that poor families (and often implied that black families) simply do not care about schooling and do not value their children's education as much as they do. For other data affirming this finding see Brantlinger 2003; Brantlinger, Majd-Jabbari, and Guskin 1996. Contrary to popular belief, however, studies in addition to this one have shown that poor families do indeed highly value education, show "reverence" for it, and have "high hopes for their offsprings' school success" (Branlinger, Majd-Jabbari, and Guskin 1996, p. 572). See also Rosier and Corsaro 1993.

10. Roemer 2000, p. 32.

11. MacLeod 1987, p. 266.

12. See Avery and Rendall 1997; Havens and Schervish 1999.

13. For work on reparations as a critical policy strategy, see for example, Feagin 2001.

14. For a collection of work by scholars and policy analysts focused on asset-based reform and the importance of asset building policy, see Sherraden 2005.

15. See, for example, Friedman 2003a; Friedman 2003b; Miller-Adams 2002; Shapiro and Wolff 2001; Sherraden 1990.

16. For work on kin networks, asset accumulation among poor black populations, and policy implications see Chiteji and Hamilton 2005; Chiteji and Hamilton 2002.

17. See Spilerman 2000.

18. See Muller 1988.

19. See Shapiro 2004.

20. Wahl 2003, p. 279.

21. Cannon 2003, p. 552.

22. Young 1961 portrays a fictional vision of what meritocracy might actually look like. Thought experiments such as Young's help us to imagine how a true meritocracy might play out and to consider the potentially destructive and demoralizing results, including for example ruthlessness, rigid testing, elitism, etc.

23. Bowman and Ladd's examination of survey data and public opinion polls concludes that Americans are not ready to give up on the American Dream, its ideals, or the hopes imbedded in it. Their examination also concludes that Americans do not think of the American Dream as any less practical now than they have in the past. See Bowman and Ladd 1998.
24. Ladd 1994.
25. For a thorough discussion, see Hochschild and Scovronick 2003.
26. Mills 1956, p. 21.
27. As Lareau 2000 has argued, "the strength of qualitative data is that it can illuminate the *meaning* of events" (p. 223).
28. Conley 2003, p. 2.

Appendix

1. Tesch 1991, pp. 25–26.
2. Oliver and Shapiro 1995, pp. 58–60. For extensive discussion of net worth versus net financial assets as indicators of wealth, see Conley 1995; Keister 2000; Oliver and Shapiro 1995; Sherraden 1991.

Bibliography

Alexander, Karl, and Travis Gosa. 2004. *Family (Dis)Advantage and the Educational Prospects of Better Off African American Youth: How Race Still Matters*. Baltimore: Department of Sociology, Johns Hopkins University.

Allatt, Patricia. 1993. "Becoming Privileged: The Role of Family Processes." Pp. 139–59 in *Youth and Inequality*, edited by Inge Bates and George Riseborough. Buckingham, England: Open University Press.

Allport, Gordon W. 1954 [1979]. *The Nature of Prejudice*. Reading, Massachusetts: Addison-Wesley.

Anderson, Elijah. 1999. *Code of the Street: Decency, Violence, and the Moral Life of the Inner City*. New York: W. W. Norton.

Anyon, Jean. 1997. *Ghetto Schooling: A Political Economy of Urban Educational Reform*. New York: Teachers College Press.

Apple, Michael W. 1982. *Education and Power*. Boston: Routledge and Kegan Paul.

———. 1993. "What Post-modernists Forget: Cultural Capital and Official Knowledge." *Curriculum Studies* 1:301–17.

Apple, Michael W., and Lois Weis. 1983. *Ideology and Practice in Schooling*. Philadelphia: Temple University Press.

Arrow, Kenneth, Samuel Bolwes, and Steven Durlauf. 2000. *Meritocracy and Economic Inequality*. Princeton, N.J.: Princeton University Press.

Ausdale, Debra Van and Joe R. Feagin. 1996. "Using Racial and Ethnic Concepts: The Critical Case of Very Young Children." *American Sociological Review* 61:779–93.

Avery, Robert, and Michael S. Rendall. 1997. *The Contribution of Inheritances to Black-White Wealth Disparities in the United States*. Ithaca, N.Y.: Bronfenbrenner Life Course Center, Cornell University.

———. 2002. "Lifetime Inheritances of Three Generations of Whites and Blacks." *American Journal of Sociology* 107:1300–1346.

Axinn, William, Greg J. Duncan, and Arland Thornton. 1997. "The Effects of Parents' Income, Wealth and Attitudes on Children's Completed Schooling and Self-Esteem." Pp. 518–40 in *Consequences of Growing*

Up Poor, edited by Greg J. Duncan and Jeanne. Brooks-Dunn. New York: Russell Sage Foundation.

Balfe, Judith Huggins. 1999. *Passing It On: The Inheritance and Use of Summer Houses*. Montclair, N.J.: Pocomo Press.

Ball, Stephen J. 2003. *Class Strategies and the Education Market: The Middle Classes and Social Advantage*. London: Routledge Falmer.

Becker, Howard S. 1970. *Sociological Work: Method and Substance*. Chicago: Aldine.

Bell, Derrick. 1987. *And We Are Not Saved: The Elusive Quest for Racial Justice*. New York: Basic.

———. 1992. *Faces at the Bottom of the Well: The Permanence of Racism*. New York: Basic.

Berger, Peter L. and Thomas Luckmann. 1966. *The Social Construction of Reality: A Treatise in the Sociology of Knowledge*. New York: Anchor.

Berrick, Jill Duerr. 1995. *Faces of Poverty: Portraits of Women and Children on Welfare*. New York: Oxford University Press.

Bielick, Stacey, Christopher Chapman, and U.S. Department of Education. 2003. "Trends in the Use of School Choice: 1993–1999." Washington, D.C.: National Center for Education Statistics.

Billingsley, A. 1992. *Climbing Jacob's Ladder: The Enduring Legacy of African American Families*. New York: Simon and Schuster.

Blau, F. D., and J. W. Graham. 1990. "Black-White Differences in Wealth and Asset Composition." *Quarterly Journal of Economics* 105:321–39.

Blauner, Bob. 1989. *Black Lives, White Lives: Three Decades of Race Relations in America*. Berkeley and Los Angeles: University of California Press.

Blinder, Alan S. 1988. "Comments on Chapters 1 and 2." Pp. 21–52 in *Modeling the Accumulation and Distribution of Wealth*, edited by Denis Kessler and Andre Masson. Oxford: Clarendon Press.

Bobo, Lawrence. 1983. "Whites' Opposition to Busing: Symbolic Racism or Realistic Group Conflict?" *Journal of Personality and Social Psychology* 45:1196–1210.

———. 1991. "Social Responsibility, Individualism, and Redistributive Policies." *Sociological Forum* 6:71–92.

———. 1997. "Race, Public Opinion, and the Social Sphere." *Public Opinion Quarterly* 61:1–15.

Bobo, Lawrence, and James R. Kluegel. 1993. "Opposition to Race-Targeting: Self-Interest, Stratification Ideology, or Racial Attitudes?" *American Sociological Review* 58:443–64.

Bobo, Lawrence, and Camille L. Zubrinsky. 1996. "Attitudes on Residential Integration: Perceived Status Differences, Mere In-Group Preference, or Racial Prejudice?" *Social Forces* 74:883–909.

Bonilla-Silva, Eduardo. 1997. "Rethinking Racism: Toward a Structural Interpretation." *American Sociological Review* 62:465–80.

————. 2001. *White Supremacy and Racism in the Post-Civil Rights Era*. Boulder, Colo.: Lynne Rienner.

————. 2003. *Racism without Racists: Color-Blind Racism and the Persistence of Racial Inequality in the United States*. Lanham, Md.: Rowman and Littlefield.

Bonilla-Silva, Eduardo, and Tyrone A. Forman. 2000. "'I Am Not a Racist But …': Mapping White College Students' Racial Ideology in the USA." *Discourse and Society* 11:50–85.

Boshara, Ray, Edward Scanlon, and Deborah Page-Adams. 1998. *Building Assets*. Washington D.C.: Corporation for Enterprise Development.

Bottomore, Tom. 1993. *Elites and Society*. London: Routledge.

Bourdieu, Pierre. 1977. *Outline of a Theory of Practice*. Cambridge: Cambridge University Press.

————. 1986 "The Forms of Capital." Pp. 241–58 in *Handbook for Theory and Research for the Sociology of Education*, ed. John G. Richardson. New York: Greenwood.

Bowen, William G., and Derek Bok. 1998. *The Shape of the River: Long-Term Consequences of Considering Race in College and University Admissions*. Princeton, NJ: Princeton University Press.

Bowles, Samuel, and Herbert Gintis. 1976. *Schooling in Capitalist America: Educational Reform and the Contradictions of Economic Life*. New York: Basic.

Bowles, Samuel, Herbert Gintis, and Melissa Osbourne Groves, eds. 2005. *Unequal Chances: Family Background and Economic Success*. Princeton, NJ: Princeton University Press.

Bowman, Karlyn and Everett Carll Ladd. 1998. *What's Wrong: A Survey of American Satisfaction and Complaint*. Washington, D.C.: AEI.

Bradshaw, York and Michael Wallace. 1996. *Global Inequalities*. Thousand Oaks, Calif.: Pine Forge.

Brantlinger, Ellen. 2003. *Dividing Classes: How the Middle Class Negotiates and Rationalizes School Advantage*. New York: Routledge Falmer.

Brantlinger, Ellen, Mossoumeh Majd-Jabbari, and Samuel L. Guskin. 1996. "Self-Interest and Liberal Educational Discourse: How Ideology Works for Middle-Class Mothers." *American Educational Research Journal* 33:571–97.

Brooks-Gunn, Jeanne, Greg J. Duncan, and Pamela Kato, Naomi Sealand. 1993. "Do Neighborhoods Influence Child and Adolescent Development?" *American Journal of Sociology* 99:353–95.

Broughman, Stephen P., and Lenore A. Colaciello. 2001. "Private School Universe Survey, 1999–2000." Washington, D.C.: U.S. Department of Education National Center for Education Statistics.

Burke, Peter J., Timothy J. Owens, Richard T. Serpe, and Peggy A. Thoits. 2003. *Advances in Identity Theory and Research*. New York: Kluwer Academic/Plenum.

Cancio, S. A., D. T. Evans, and D. J. Maume. 1996. "Reconsidering the Declining Significance of Race: Racial Differences in Early Career Wages." *American Sociological Review* 61:541–56.

Cannon, Laura. 2003. "The Butterfly Effect and the Virtues of the American Dream." *Journal of Social Philosophy* 34:545–55.

Centers, Richard. 1949. *The Psychology of Social Classes: A Study of Class Consciousness*. Princeton, N.J.: Princeton University Press.

Chamberlain, Sara. 1997. "Gender, Race, and the 'Underclass': The Truth behind the American Dream." *Gender and Development* 5:18–25.

Charles, Cammille Z. 2003. "The Dynamics of Racial Residential Segregation." *Annual Review of Sociology* 29:167–208.

Cheal, David J. 1979. "Hegemony, Ideology, and Contradictory Consciousness." *Sociological Quarterly* 20:109–17.

Chiteji, Ngina, and Darrick Hamilton. 2002. "Family Connections and the Black-White Wealth Gap among Middle Class Families." *Review of Black Political Economy* 30:9–28.

———. 2005. "Family Matters: Kin Networks and Asset Accumulation," Pp. 87–111 in *Inclusion in the American Dream: Assets, Poverty, and Public Policy*, edited by Michael Sherraden. New York: Oxford University Press.

Clignet, Remi. 1992. *Death, Deeds, and Descendants: Inheritance in Modern America*. New York: Aldine de Gruyter.

Coleman, James S. 1966. "Summary Report." pp. 3–28 in *Equality of Educational Opportunity*. Washington, D.C.: U.S. Government Printing Office.

Coles, Robert. 1977. *Privileged Ones: The Well-Off and the Rich in America*, vol. 5. Boston: Little, Brown.

———. 1986. *The Moral Life of Children*. Boston: Houghton Mifflin.

Coles, Robert, and Randy Testa with Michael Coles. 2001. *Growing Up Poor: A Literary Anthology*. New York: New Press.

Collins, Patricia Hill. 1993. "Toward a New Vision: Race, Class, and Gender as Categories of Analysis and Connection." *Race, Sex & Class* 1, no. 1: 25–45.

Comer, James P. 1988. *Maggie's American Dream: The Life and Times of a Black Family*. New York: Plume.

Conley, Dalton. 1999. *Being Black, Living in the Red: Race, Wealth, and Social Policy in America*. Berkeley and Los Angeles: University of California Press.

———. 2003. *Wealth and Poverty in America*. Malden, Mass.: Blackwell.

Conley, Dalton and Karen Albright, eds. 2004. *After the Bell: Family Background, Public Policy, and Educational Success*. London: Routledge.

Cookson, Peter W., Jr. 1994. *School Choice: The Struggle for the Soul of American Education*. New Haven, Conn.: Yale University Press.

Cookson, Peter W., Jr., and Caroline Hodges Persell. 1985. *Preparing for Power: America's Elite Boarding Schools*. New York: Basic.

Cox, Donald and Fredric. Raines. 1985. "Interfamily Transfers and Income Redistribution." Pp. 393–425 in *Horizontal Equity: Uncertainty, and Economic Well-Being*, edited by Martin David and Timothy Smeeding. Chicago: University of Chicago Press.

Cox, Donald, and Mark R. Rank. 1992. "Inter-vivos Transfers and Intergenerational Exchange." *Review of Economics and Statistics* 74:305–14.

Cross, Theodore, and Robert Bruce Slater. 1997. "The Commanding Wealth Advantage of College-Bound White Students." *Journal of Blacks in Higher Education* 15:80–90.

Cullen, Jim. 2003. *The American Dream: A Short History of an Idea That Shaped a Nation*. New York: Oxford University Press.

Danziger, Sheldon, and Peter Gottschalk. 1995. *America Unequal*. New York and Cambridge, Mass.: Russell Sage Foundation and Harvard University Press.

Danziger, Sheldon, and Deborah Reed. 1999. "Winners and Losers: The Era of Inequality Continues." *Brookings Review* 17:14–17.

Darling-Hammond, Linda. 2004. "Inequality and the Right to Learn: Access to Qualified Teachers in California's Public Schools." *Teachers College Record* 106, no. 10:1936–66.

Darling-Hammond, Linda, and Laura Post. 2000. "Inequality in Teaching and Schooling: Supporting High-Quality Teaching and Leadership in Low-Income Schools." Pp. 127–67 in *A Notion at Risk: Preserving Public Education as an Engine for Social Mobility*, edited by Richard D. Kalenberg. New York: Century Foundation Press.

Davies, James B. 1982. "The Relative Impact of Inheritance and Other Factors on Economic Inequality." *Quarterly Journal of Economics* 97:471–98.

Davis, Kingsley, and W. E. Moore. 1945. "Some Principles of Stratification." *American Sociological Review* 10:242–45.

Deever, Bryan. 1994. "Living *Plessey* in the Context of *Brown*: Cultural Politics and the Rituals of Separation." *Urban Review* 26:273–88.

Delbanco, Andrew. 1999. *The Real American Dream: A Meditation on Hope*. Cambridge, Mass.: Harvard University Press.

Della Fave, L. Richard. 1980. "The Meek Shall Not Inherit the Earth: Self-Evaluation and the Legitimacy of Stratification." *American Sociological Review* 45:955–71.

———. 1986. "Toward an Explication of the Legitimation Process." *Social Forces* 65:476–500.

———. 1993. "Ritual and the Legitimation of Stratification." *Sociological Perspectives* 34:21–38.

Delpit, Lisa. 1995 *Other People's Children: Cultural Conflict in the Classroom* New York: New Press.

Deutscher, Irwin, Fred. P. Pestello, and H. Frances G. Pestello. 1993. *Sentiments and Acts*. New York: Walter de Gruyter.

Devine, Fiona. 1998. "Class Analysis and the Stability of Class Relations." *Sociology* 32:1–12.

———. 2004. *Class Practices: How Parents Help Their Children Get Good Jobs*. Cambridge: Cambridge University Press.

Devine, Fiona, and Mary C. Waters. 2004. *Social Inequalities in Comparative Perspective*. Malden, Mass.: Blackwell.

DiTomaso, Nancy. 2000. "Why Anti-Discrimination Policies Are Not Enough: The Legacies and Consequences of Affirmative Inclusion—for Whites." Presented at the 95th annual meeting of the American Sociological Association, August 16, Anaheim, CA.

Doane, Ashley W., and Eduardo Bonilla-Silva. 2003. *White Out: The Continuing Significance of Racism*. New York: Routledge.

Domhoff, G. William. 1998. *Who Rules America? Power and Politics in the Year 2000*. Mountain View, Calif.: Mayfield.

Domhoff, William G. 1970. *The Higher Circles*. New York: Random House.

Duncan, Greg J., and Jeanne Brooks-Gunn. 1997. *Consequences of Growing Up Poor*. New York: Russell Sage Foundation.

Eagleton, Terry. 1991. *Ideology: An Introduction*. London: Verso.

Edin, Kathryn, and Laura Lein. 1997. *Making Ends Meet: How Single Mothers Survive Welfare and Low-Wage Work*. New York: Russell Sage Foundation.

Ehrenreich, Barbara. 1989. *Fear of Falling: The Inner Life of the Middle Class*. New York: Harper Collins.

———. 2001. *Nickel and Dimed: On (Not) Getting By in America*. New York: Metropolitan.

Ellwood, David T. 1988. *Poor Support: Poverty in the American Family*. New York: Basic.

Engelhardt, Gary V. and Christopher J. Mayer. 1994. "Gifts for Home Purchase and Housing Market Behavior." *New England Economic Review* May/June:47–58.

Evans, Geoffrey. 1997. "Political Ideology and Popular Beliefs about Class and Opportunity: Evidence from a Survey Experiment." *British Journal of Sociology* 48:450–70.

Fantasia, Rick. 1995. "From Class Consciousness to Culture, Action, and Social Organization." *Annual Review of Sociology* 21:269–87.

Farkas, Steve, and Jean Johnson with Ann Duffett and Joanna McHugh. 1998. "A Lot to Be Thankful For: What Parents Want Children to Learn about America." New York: Public Agenda.

Farley, Reynolds. 1984. *Blacks and Whites: Narrowing the Gap?* Cambridge, Mass.: Harvard University Press.

Farley, Reynolds, and William H. Frey. 1994. "Changes in the Segregation of Whites from Blacks during the 1980s: Small Steps Toward a More Integrated Society." *American Sociological Review* 59:23–45.

Feagin, Joe R. 1972. "When it Comes to Poverty, It's Still 'God Helps Those Who Help Themselves.'" *Psychology Today* 6:101–29.

———. 1975. *Subordinating the Poor*. Englewood Cliffs, N.J.: Prentice-Hall.

———. 1997. *The New Urban Paradigm: Criticial Perspectives on the City*. Lanham, Md.: Rowman and Littlefield.

———. 1993. *Racist America: Roots, Current Realities and Future Reparations*. New York, Routledge.

Feagin, Joe R., and Eileen O'Brien. 2003. *White Men on Race: Power, Privilege, and the Shaping of Cultural Consciousness*. Boston: Beacon Press.

Feagin, Joe R., and Melvin P. Sikes. 1994. *Living with Racism: The Black Middle-Class Experience*. Boston: Beacon.

Feagin, Joe R., and Hernan Vera. 1995. *White Racism: The Basics*. New York: Routledge.

Fine, Michelle. 1991. *Framing Dropouts: Notes on the Politics of an Urban Public High School*. Albany: State University of New York Press.

Fine, Michelle, Lois Weis, Linda C. Powell, and Mun Wong. 1997. *Off White: Readings on Race, Power, and Society*. New York: Routledge.

Fischer, Claude, Michael Hout, Martin S. Jankowski, Samuel Lucas, Ann Swidler, and Kim Voss. 1996. *Inequality By Design: Cracking the Bell Curve Myth*. Princeton, N.J.: Princeton University Press.

Fischer, Claude S., Gretchen Stockmayer, John Stiles, and Michael Hout. 2004. "Distinguishing the Geographic Levels and Social Dimensions of U.S. Metropolitan Segregation, 1960–2000." *Demography* 41:37–60.

Fong, Christina. 2001. "Social Preferences, Self-Interest, and the Demand for Redistribution." *Journal of Public Economics* 82:225–46.

Form, William and Claudine Hanson. 1985. "The Consistency of Ideologies of Economic Justice." *Research on Stratification and Mobility* 4:239–69.

Franklin, John Hope. 1993. *The Color Line: Legacy for the Twenty-First Century*. Columbia: University of Missouri Press.

Friedman, Robert. 2003a. "Lessons on Achieving the American Dream." *Assets: A Quarterly Update for Innovators* 4: 9.

———. 2003b. "State of the Field, 2003." *Assets: A Quarterly Update for Innovators* 4:1, 7.

Furby, Lita. 1979. "Inequalities in Personal Possessions: Explanations for and Judgments about Unequal Distribution." *Human Development* 22:180–202.

Gale, William G., and John Karl Scholz. 1993. "Intergenerational Transfers and the Accumulation of Wealth." Madison, WI: Institute for Research on Poverty.

———. 1994. "Intergenerational Transfers and the Accumulation of Wealth." *Journal of Economic Perspectives* 8:145–60.

Gallagher, Charles A. 2003. "Color-Blind Privilege: The Social and Political Functions of Erasing the Color Line in Post Race America." *Race, Gender and Class* 10, no. 4: 189–196.

———. 2004. *Rethinking the Color Line: Readings in Race and Ethnicity*. Boston: McGraw-Hill.

————. 2005. "Color Blindness: An Obstacle to Racial Justice?" Pp. 103–116 in *Mixed Messages: Multiracial Identities in the "Color-blind" Era,* edited by David L. Brunsma. Boulder, Colo.: Lynne Rienner.

Geertz, Clifford. 1983. "Thick Description: Toward an Interpretive Theory of Culture." Pp. 3–30 in *Contemporary Field Research,* edited by R. Emerson. Boston: Little, Brown.

Gilder, George. 1981. *Wealth and Poverty.* New York: Basic.

Goldscheider, Frances K., and Calvin Goldscheider. 1991. "The Intergenerational Flow of Income: Family Structure and the Status of Black Americans." *Journal of Marriage and the Family* 53:499–508.

Goodman, Mary Ellen. 1952 [1964]. *Race Awareness in Young Children.* New York: Collier.

Graham, Lawrence Otis. 2000, 1999. *Our Kind of People: Inside America's Black Upper Class.* New York: Harper Perennial.

Granovetter, Mark. 1995. *Getting a Job: A Study of Contacts and Careers.* Chicago: University of Chicago Press.

Grusky, David B. 1994. *Social Stratification: Class, Race, and Gender in Sociological Perspective.* Boulder, Colo.: Westview.

Gurin, Patricia, Arthur H. Miller, and Gerald Gurin. 1980. "Explaining Perceptions of Class and Racial Inequality in England and the United States of America." *British Journal of Sociology* 34:344–66.

Hacker, Andrew. 1992. *Two Nations: Black and White, Separate, Hostile, Unequal.* New York: Ballantine.

Hans, W. S. 1969. "Two Conflicting Themes: Common Values Versus Class Differential Values." *American Sociological Review* 34:679–90.

Harrison, Bennett, and Barry Bluestone. 1988. *The Great U-Turn: Corporate Restructuring and the Polarizing of America.* New York: Basic.

Hartman, Chester. 1997. *Double Exposure: Poverty and Race in America.* Armonk, N.Y.: M. E. Sharpe.

Haveman, Robert, and Barbara Wolfe. 1994. *Succeeding Generations: On the Effects of Investments in Children.* New York: Russell Sage Foundation.

Havens, John Jay, and Paul G. Schervish. 1999. "Millionaires and the Millennium: New Estimates of the Forthcoming Wealth Transfer and the Prospects for a Golden Age of Philanthropy." Boston: Boston College Social Welfare Research Institute.

Haycock, Kati. 1998. "Good Teaching Matters a Lot." *Thinking K–16* 3:3–14.

Heflin, Colleen M., and Mary Pattillo. 2002. "Kin Effects on Black-White Account and Home Ownership." *Sociological Inquiry* 72:220–39.

Henig, Jeffrey R. 1994. *Rethinking School Choice: Limits of the Market Metaphor.* Princeton, N.J.: Princeton University Press.

Herrnstein, Richard J., and Charles Murray. 1994. *The Bell Curve: Intelligence and Class Structure in American Life.* New York: Free Press.

Hertz, Rosanna and Jonathan B. Imber. 1993. "Fieldwork in Elite Settings: Introduction." *Journal of Contemporary Ethnography* 22:3–6.

Hill, Robert B.. 1972. *The Strengths of Black Families*. New York: Emerson Hall.

———. 1999. *The Strengths of African American Families: Twenty-Five Years Later*. Lanham, Md.: University Press of America.

Hochschild, Jennifer. 1981. *What's Fair? American Beliefs about Distributive Justice*. Cambridge, Mass.: Harvard University Press.

———. 1995. *Facing Up to the American Dream: Race, Class, and the Soul of the Nation*. Princeton, N.J.: Princeton University Press.

———. 2001. "Where You Stand Depends on What You See: Connections among Values, Perceptions of Fact, and Political Prescriptions." Pp. 313–40 in *Citizens and Politics: Perspectives from Political Psychology*, edited by J. H. Kuklinski. New York: Cambridge University Press.

———. 2003. "Social Class in Public Schools." *Journal of Social Issues* 59:821–40.

Hochschild, Jennifer, and Bridget Scott. 1998. "Trends: Governance and Reform of Public Education in the United States." *Public Opinion Quarterly* 62:79–120.

Hochschild, Jennifer, and Nathan Scovronick. 2003. *The American Dream and the Public Schools*. New York: Oxford University Press.

Hoffman, Kathryn, and Charmaine Llagas. 2003. "Status and Trends in the Education of Blacks." Washington D.C.: U.S. Department of Education, National Center for Education Statistics.

Holme, Jennifer Jellison. 2002. "Buying Homes, Buying Schools: School Choice and the Social Construction of School Quality." *Harvard Educational Review* 72:177–205.

hooks, bell. 2000. *Where We Stand: Class Matters*. New York: Routledge.

Horowitz, Ruth. 1997. "Barriers and Bridges to Class Mobility and Formation: Ethnographies of Stratification." *Sociological Methods and Research* 25:495–538.

Horton, Hayward Derrick, Beverly Lundy Allen, Cedric Herring, and Melvin E. Thomas. 2000. "Lost in the Storm: The Sociology of the Black Working Class, 1850–1990." *American Sociological Review* 65:128–37.

Houser, Robert, and David Featherman. 1977. *The Process of Stratification*. New York: Academic.

Howard, Christopher. 1997. *The Hidden Welfare State: Tax Expenditures and Social Policy in the United States*. Princeton, N.J.: Princeton University Press.

Huber, Joan, and William Form. 1973. *Income and Ideology: An Analysis of the American Political Formula*. New York: Free Press.

Hughes, Michael, and Steven A. Tuch. 1999. "How Beliefs about Poverty Influence Racial Policy Attitudes: A Study of Whites, African Americans, Hispanics, and Asians in the United States." Pp. 165–190 in *Racialized Politics: The Debate about Racism in America*, edited by David O. Sears, James Sidanius, and Lawrence Bobo. Chicago: University of Chicago Press.

Hunt, Matthew. 2004. "Race/Ethnicity and Beliefs about Wealth and Poverty." *Social Science Quarterly* 85:827–53.

Hunt, Matthew O. 1996. "The Individual, Society, or Both? A Comparison of Black, Latino, and White Beliefs about the Causes of Poverty." *Social Forces* 75:293–322.

Huston, Aletha C. 1991. *Children in Poverty*. New York: Cambridge Univesity Press.

Hyde, Katherine Ann. 2002. "Holding Disillusionment at Bay: Latino/a Immigrants and Working Class North Carolinians Expose and Reinforce the American Dream's Discrepancies." Ph.D. diss., North Carolina State University.

Iceland, John, Daniel H. Weinberg, Erika Steinmetz, and U.S. Census Bureau. 2002. "Racial and Ethnic Residential Segregation in the United States: 1980–2000." Washington D.C.: U.S. Government Printing Office.

Immerwahr, John. 2004. "Public Attitudes on Higher Education: A Trend Analysis 1993–2003." New York: Public Agenda.

Jackman, Mary R. 1994. *The Velvet Glove: Paternalism and Conflict in Gender, Class, and Race Relations*. Berkeley and Los Angeles: University of California Press.

Jackman, Mary R., and Robert Jackman. 1983. *Class Awareness in the United States*. Berkeley and Los Angeles: University of California Press.

Jackman, Mary R., and Michael J. Muha. 1984. "Education and Intergroup Attitudes: Moral Enlightenment, Superficial Democratic Commitment, or Ideological Refinement?" *American Sociological Review* 49:751–69.

Jackson, Bruce. 1987. *Fieldwork*. Urbana: University of Illinois Press.

Jacoby, Russell, and Naomi Glauberman. 1995. *The Bell Curve Debate: History, Documents, Opinions*. New York: Random House.

Jen, Gish. 1992. *Typical American*. New York: Plume.

Jencks, Christopher, and Meredith Phillips. 1988. "The Black-White Test Score Gap." Washington, D.C.: Brookings Institution Press.

Jencks, Christopher. 1979. *Who Gets Ahead? The Determinants of Economic Success in America*. New York: Basic.

Jillson, Cal. 2004. *Pursuing the American Dream: Opportunity and Exclusion over Four Centuries*. Lawrence: University Press of Kansas.

Johnson, Heather Beth. 2001. *The Ideology of Meritocracy and the Power of Wealth: School Selection and the Reproduction of Race and Class Inequality* (Ph.D. diss., University of Michigan). Ann Arbor, MI: University Microfilms.

Johnson, Heather Beth, and Thomas M. Shapiro. 2003. "Good Neighborhoods, Good Schools: Race and the 'Good Choices' of White Families," Pp. 173–87 in *White Out: The Continuing Significance of Racism*, edited by Eduardo Bonilla-Silva and Woody Doane. New York: Routledge.

Johnson, Jennifer. 2002. *Getting By on the Minimum: The Lives of Working Class Women*. New York: Routledge.

Karen, David. 1991. "'Achievement' and 'Ascription' in Admission to an Elite College: A Political-Organizational Analysis." *Sociological Forum* 6:349–80.

Katznelson, Ira and Margaret Weir. 1985. *Schooling for All: Class, Race, and the Decline of the Democratic Ideal*. Berkeley and Los Angeles: University of California Press.

Keister, Lisa A. 2000. *Wealth in America: Trends in Wealth Inequality*. Cambridge: Cambridge University Press.

Keister, Lisa A., and Stephanie Moller. 2000. "Wealth Inequality in the United States." *Annual Review of Sociology* 26:63–81.

Kendall, Diana. 2002. *The Power of Good Deeds: Privileged Women and the Social Reproduction of the Upper Class*. Lanham, Md.: Rowman and Littlefield.

Kenty-Drane, Jessica L. 2004. *First-Grade Inequality: Disparities in Educational Conditions of the U.S. Public School First-Grade 1999–2000 Cohort* (Ph.D. diss., University of Michigan). Ann Arbor, MI: University Microfilms.

Kerbo, Harold. 1983. *Social Stratification and Inequality: Class Conflict in the United States*. New York: McGraw-Hill.

Kerbo, Harold R. 1996. "The Process of Legitimation." in *Social Stratification and Inequality: Class Conflict in Historical and Comparative Perspective*, edited by Harold R. Kerbo: McGraw-Hill.

Kessler, Denis, and Andre Masson. 1989. "Bequest and Wealth Accumulation: Are Some Pieces of the Puzzle Missing?" *Journal of Economic Perspectives* 3:141–52.

Kincheloe, Joe L., Shirley R. Steinberg, Nelson M. Rodriguez, and Ronald E. Chennault. 1991. *White Reign: Deploying Whiteness in America*. New York: St. Martin's.

Kinder, Donald R., and Lynn M. Sanders. 1996. *Divided By Color: Racial Politics and Democratic Ideals*. Chicago: University of Chicago Press.

Kirp, David L., John P. Dwyer, and Larry A. Rosenthal. 1995. *Our Town: Race, Housing, and the Soul of Suburbia*. New Brunswick, N.J.: Rutgers University Press.

Kluegel, James R., and Eliot R. Smith. 1986. *Beliefs about Inequality: Americans' Views of What is and What Ought to Be*. New York: Aldine de Gruyter.

———. 1987. "Whites' Beliefs about Blacks' Opportunity." *American Sociological Review* 47:518–32.

Kotlicoff, Laurence J., and Lawrence H. Summers. 1981. "The Role of Intergenerational Transfers in Aggregate Capital Accumulation." *Journal of Political Economy* 89:706–32.

Kotlicoff, Laurence J., and Lawrence H. Summers. 1988. "The Contribution of Intergenerational Transfers to Total Wealth: A Reply." Pp. 53–67 in *Modeling the Accumulation and Distribution of Wealth*, edited by Denis Kessler and Andre Masson. Oxford: Clarendon Press.

Kotlowitz, Alex. 1991. *There Are No Children Here: The Story of Two Boys Growing Up in the Other America*. New York: Anchor.

———. 1998. *The Other Side of the River: A Story of Two Towns, a Death, and America's Dilemma*. New York: Nan A. Talese/Doubleday.

Kozol, Jonathan. 1988. *Rachel and Her Children: Homeless Families in America*. New York: Random House.

———. 1991. *Savage Inequalities: Children in America's Schools*. New York: Crown.

———. 1995. *Amazing Grace: The Lives of Children and the Conscience of a Nation*. New York: Crown.

Krysan, Maria, and Amanda Lewis, eds. 2004. *The Changing Terrain of Race and Ethnicity*. New York: Russell Sage Foundation.

Ladd, Everett Carll. 1994. *The American Ideology: An Exploration of the Origins, Meaning, and Role of American Political Ideas*. Storrs, Conn.: Roper Center for Public Opinion Research, University of Connecticut.

Lamb, Kevin. 1995. "The Problem of Equality." *The Journal of Social, Political and Economic Studies* 20:467–78.

Lamont, Michele. 2000. *The Dignity of Working Men: Morality and the Boundaries of Race, Class, and Immigration*. New York: Russell Sage Foundation/Cambridge, Mass.: Harvard University Press.

Lamont, Michele. 1992. *Money, Morals, and Manners: The Culture of the French and the American Upper-Middle Class*. Chicago: University of Chicago Press.

Lane, Robert. 1962. *Political Ideology*. New York: Free Press.

Lareau, Annette. 2000. *Home Advantage: Social Class and Parental Intervention in Elementary Education*. Lanham, Md.: Rowman and Littlefield.

———. 2002. "Invisible Inequality: Social Class and Childrearing in Black Families and White Families." *American Sociological Review* 67:747–76.

———. 2003. *Unequal Childhoods: Class, Race, and Family Life*. Berkeley and Los Angeles: University of California Press.

Leahy, Robert. 1990. "The Development of Concepts of Economic and Social Inequality." *New Directions for Child Development* 46:107–20.

Leahy, Robert L. 1983. *The Child's Construction of Social Inequality*. New York: Academic.

Lee, Valerie E. and David T. Burkam. 2002. *Inequality at the Starting Gate: Social Background Differences in Achievement as Children Begin School*. Washington D.C.: Economic Policy Institute.

Lerner, Melvin. 1980. *The Belief in a Just World: A Fundamental Delusion*. New York: Plenum.

Levine, Rhonda F. 1998. *Social Class and Stratification: Classic Statements and Theoretical Debates*. Lanham, Md.: Rowman and Littlefield.

Levitan, Sar A., and Isaac Shapiro. 1987. *Working but Poor: America's Contradiction.* Baltimore: Johns Hopkins University Press.

Levitas, Maurice. 1974. *Marxist Perspective in the Sociology of Education.* London: Routledge and Kegan Paul.

Levy, Frank. 1998. *The New Dollars and Dreams: American Incomes and Economic Change.* New York: Russell Sage Foundation.

Lewis, Amanda. 2003. *Race in the Schoolyard: Negotiating the Color Line in Classrooms and Communities.* New Brunswick, N.J.: Rutgers University Press.

———. 2004. "'What Group?' Studying Whites and Whiteness in the Era of 'Color-Blindness'" *Sociological Theory* 22, no. 4:623–46.

Lewis, Michael. 1993. *The Culture of Inequality.* Boston: University of Massachusetts Press.

Lewis, Oscar. 1959. *Five Families: Mexican Case Studies in the Culture of Poverty.* New York: Basic.

Lichter, Daniel T. 1997. "Poverty and Inequality among Children." *Annual Review of Sociology* 23:121–45.

Lieberson, Stanley. 1980. *A Piece of the Pie: Blacks and White Immigrants Since 1880.* Berkeley and Los Angeles: University of California Press.

Lipsitz, George. 1998. *The Possessive Investment in Whiteness: How White People Profit from Identity Politics.* Philadelphia: Temple University Press.

Logan, John R., Brian J. Stults, and Reynolds Farley. 2004. "Segregation of Minorities in the Metropolis: Two Decades of Change." *Demography* 41:1–22.

MacLeod, Jay. 1987 [1995]. *Ain't No Makin' It: Aspirations and Attainment in a Low-Income Neighborhood.* Boulder, Colo.: Westview.

Mann, Michael. 1970. "The Social Cohesion of Liberal Democracy." *American Sociological Review* 35:423–39.

Manning, D. J. 1980. *The Form of Ideology.* London: George Allen and Unwin.

Marable, Manning. 1983. *How Capitalism Underdeveloped Black America: Problems in Race, Political Economy, and Society.* Boston: South End Press.

Martinez, M. Loreto. 2000. *Neighborhood Context and the Development of African American Children.* New York: Garland.

Marx, Karl. 1867 [1967]. *Capital: A Critique of Political Economy,* vol. 1. New York: International.

Massey, Douglas S., Camille Z. Charles, Garvey F. Lundy, and Mary J. Fischer. 2003. *The Source of the River: The Social Origins of Freshmen at America's Selective Colleges and Universities.* Princeton, N.J.: Princeton University Press.

Massey, Douglas S., and Nancy A. Denton. 1989. "Hypersegregation in U.S. Metropolitan Areas: Black and Hispanic Segregation Along Five Dimensions." *Social Forces* 26:373–91.

Massey, Douglas S., and Nancy A. Denton. 1993. *American Apartheid: Segregation and the Making of the Underclass*. Cambridge, Mass.: Harvard University Press.

Mayer, Daniel P., John E. Mullens, and Mary T. Moore. 2001. "Monitoring School Quality: An Indicators Report 2000." NCES 2001-030. Washington, D.C.: U.S. Department of Education, National Center for Education Statistics.

Mayer, Susan E. 1997. *What Money Can't Buy: Family Income and Children's Life Chances*. Cambridge, Mass.: Harvard University Press.

Mayer, Susan E., and Paul E. Peterson. 1999. "Earning and Learning: How Schools Matter." Washington, D.C.: Brookings Institution Press/New York: Russell Sage Foundation.

McCarthy, Cameron, and Warren Crichlow. 1993. *Race, Identity, and Representation in Education*. New York: Routledge.

McDonough, Patricia. 1997. *Choosing Colleges: How Social Class and Schools Structure Opportunity*. Albany: State University of New York Press.

McLellan, David. 1995. *Ideology*, Edited by Frank Parkin. Minneapolis: University of Minnesota Press.

McNamee, Stephen J., and Robert K. Miller Jr. 1998. "Inheritance and Stratification." Pp. 193–213 in *Inheritance and Wealth in America*, edited by Robert K. Miller Jr. and Stephen J. McNamee. New York: Little, Brown.

McNamee, Stephen J., and Robert K. Miller. 2004. *The Meritocracy Myth*. Landham, Md.: Rowman and Littlefield.

Meier, Kenneth, Joseph Stewart, Jr. and Robert E. England. 1989. *Race, Class, and Education: The Politics of Second Generation Discrimination*. Madison: University of Wisconsin Press.

Menchik, Paul L., and Nancy Ammon Jianakoplos. 1997. "Black-White Wealth Inequality: Is Inheritance the Reason?" *Economic Inquiry* 35:428–42.

Merton, Robert K. 1938. "Social Structure and Anomie." *American Sociological Review* 3:672–82.

———. 1948. "The Self-Fulfilling Prophecy." *Antioch Review* 8:193–210.

———. 1968. "The Matthew Effect in Science." *Science* 159:56–63.

Meyer, Stephen Grant. 2000. *As Long as They Don't Move Next Door: Segregation and Racial Conflict in America's Neighborhoods*. Lanham, Md.: Rowman and Littlefield.

Mickelson, Roslyn Arlin. 1990. "The Attitude-Achievement Paradox Among Black Adolescents." *Sociology of Education* 63:44–61.

———. 2001. "Subverting Swann: First- and Second-Generation Segregation in the Charlotte-Mecklenburg Schools." *American Educational Research Journal* 38:215–52.

Miller, Fayneese, and Mary Ann Clark. 1997. "Looking Toward the Future: Young People's Attitudes About Affirmative Action and the American Dream." *American Behavioral Scientist* 41:262–71.

Miller, Robert K., Jr., and Stephen J. McNamee. 1998. *Inheritance and Wealth in America*. New York: Little, Brown.

Miller-Adams, Michelle. 2002. *Owning Up: Poverty, Assets, and the American Dream*. Washington D.C.: Brookings Institution Press.

Millman, Marcia. 1991. *Warm Hearts and Cold Cash: The Intimate Dynamics of Family and Money*. New York: Free Press.

Mills, C. Wright. 1956. *The Power Elite*. London: Oxford University Press.

———. 1959 [2000]. *The Sociological Imagination*. New York: Oxford University Press.

Modigliani, Franco. 1988. "Measuring the Contribution of Intergenerational Transfers to Total Wealth: Conceptual Issues and Empirical Findings." in *Modeling the Accumulation and Distribution of Wealth*, edited by Denis Kessler and Andre Masson. Oxford: Clarendon Press.

———. 1988. "The Role of Intergenerational Transfers and Life Cycle Saving in the Accumulation of Wealth." *Journal of Economic Perspectives* 2:15–40.

Monroe, Kristen Renwick. 1996. *The Heart of Altruism: Perceptions of a Common Humanity*. Princeton, NJ: Princeton University Press.

Morken, Hubert, and Jo Renee Formicola. 1999. *The Politics of School Choice*. Lanham: Rowman and Littlefield.

Morse, Janice M. 1995. "The Significance of Saturation." *Qualitative Health Research* 5:147–49.

Moss, Kirby. 2003. *The Color of Class: Poor Whites and the Paradox of Privilege*. Philadelphia: University of Pennsylvania Press.

Mulder, Clara H., and Geroen Smits. 1999. "First-Time Home-Ownership of Couples: The Effect of Inter-Generational Transmission." *European Sociological Review* 15:323–37.

Munnell, Alicia H. 1988. "Wealth Transfer Taxation: The Relative Role for Estate and Income Taxes." *New England Economic Review* Nov./Dec.:3–28.

Neckerman, Kathryn M., ed. 2004. *Social Inequality*. New York: Russell Sage Foundation.

Newman, Katherine S. 1988, 1999. *Falling from Grace: Downward Mobility in the Age of Affluence*. Berkeley and Los Angeles: University of California Press.

———. 1999. *No Shame In My Game: The Working Poor in the Inner City*. New York: Alfred A. Knopf /Russell Sage Foundation.

Nightingale, Carl Husemoller. 1993. *On The Edge: A History of Poor Black Children and Their American Dreams*. New York: Basic.

Noguera, Pedro. 2003. *City Schools and the American Dream: Reclaiming the Promise of Public Education*. New York: Teachers College Press.

Oakes, Jeannie. 1982. "Classroom Social Relationships: Exploring the Bowles and Gintis Hypothesis." *Sociology of Education* 55:197–211.

———. 1990. *Multiplying Inequalities: The Effects of Race, Social Class, and Tracking on Opportunities to Learn Mathematics and Science*. Santa Monica, CA: Rand.

Oakes, Jeannie and M. Lipton. 1998. *Teaching to Change the World*. Boston: McGraw-Hill.

Oakes, Jeannie, and Marisa Saunders. 2004. "Education's Most Basic Tools: Access to Textbooks and Instructional Materials in California's Public Schools" *Teachers College Record* 106, no. 10: 1967–88.

O'Connor, Carla. 1999. "Race, Class, and Gender in America: Narratives of Opportunity Among Low-Income African American Youths." *Sociology of Education* 72:137–157.

Oliver, Melvin L., and Thomas M. Shapiro. 1990. "Wealth of a Nation: A Reassessment of Asset Inequality in America Shows at Least One Third of Households Are Asset-Poor." *American Journal of Economics and Sociology* 49:129–51.

Oliver, Melvin L., and Thomas M. Shapiro. 1995. *Black Wealth/White Wealth: A New Perspective on Racial Inequality*. New York: Routledge.

Oliver, Melvin L., Thomas M. Shapiro, and Julie E. Press. 1995. "'Them That's Got Shall Get': Inheritance and Achievement in Wealth Accumulation." *Research in Politics and Society* 5:69–95.

Omi, Michael, and Howard Winant. 1986. *Racial Formation in the United States*. New York: Routledge.

Opinion Research Corporation. 2001. "Wealth of American Individuals and Families Survey." Storrs, Conn.: Roper Center for Public Opinion Research, University of Connecticut.

Orbuch, Terri L. 1997. "People's Accounts Count: The Sociology of Accounts." *Annual Review of Sociology* 23:455–78.

Orfield, Gary, Susan E. Eaton, and the Harvard Project on School Desegregation. 1996. *Dismantling Desegregation: The Quiet Reversal of Brown v. Board of Education*. New York: New Press.

Orfield, Gary and John T. Yun. 1999. *Resegregation in American Schools*. Cambridge, Mass.: Civil Rights Project, Harvard University.

Orr, Amy J. 2003. "Black-White Differences in Achievement: The Importance of Wealth." *Sociology of Education* 76:281–304.

Orzechowoski, Shawna, Peter Sepielli, and the U.S. Census Bureau. 2003. "Net Worth and Asset Ownership of Households: 1998 and 2000 Household Economic Studies." Washington D.C.: U.S. Census Bureau.

Ostrander, Susan A. 1984. *Women of the Upper Class*. Philadelphia: Temple University Press.

———. 1993. "'Surely You're Not in This Just to Be Helpful': Access, Rapport, and Interviews in Three Studies of Elites." *Journal of Contemporary Ethnography* 22:7–27.

Ostrower, Francie. 1995. *Why the Wealthy Give: The Culture of Elite Philanthropy*. Princeton, N.J.: Princeton University Press.

Page-Adams, Deborah, and Edward Scanlon. 2001. "Assets, Health, and Well-Being: Neighborhoods, Families, Children and Youth." St. Louis, Mo.: Center for Social Development, Washington University.

Perrucci, Robert and Earl Wysong. 1999. *The New Class Society*. Lanham, Md.: Rowman and Littlefield.

Persell, Caroline Hodges, Sophia Catsambis, and Peter W. Cookson Jr. 1992. "Differential Asset Conversion: Class and Gendered Pathways to Selective Colleges." *Sociology of Education* 65:208–25.

Peshkin, Alan. 2001. *Permissible Advantage? The Moral Consequences of Elite Schooling*. Mahwah, N.J.: Lawrence Erlbaum.

Petrovich, Janice, and Amy Stuart Wells, eds. 2005. *Bringing Equity Back: Research for a New Era in American Educational Policy*. New York: Teachers College Press.

Phi Delta Kappa International. 2003. "The 35th Annual Phi Delta Kappa/Gallup Poll of the Public's Attitudes toward the Public." Bloomington, Ind.: Phi Delta Kappa International.

Phillips, Kevin. 2002. *Wealth and Democracy: A Political History of the American Rich*. New York: Broadway.

Prager, Jeffrey. 1982. "American Racial Identity as Collective Representation." *Ethnic and Racial Studies* 5:99–119.

Proctor, Bernadette D., and Joseph Dalaker. 2003. "Poverty in the United States: 2002." Washington D.C.: U.S. Government Printing Office.

Ramsey, Patricia. 1991. "Young Children's Awareness and Understanding of Social Class Differences." *Journal of Genetic Psychology* 152:72–81.

Ramsey, Patricia G. 1995. "Growing Up with the Contradictions of Race and Class." *Young Children* 50:18–22.

Rank, Mark R. 1998. "Poverty at the .05 Level: The Limitations of Mainstream Research." *Contemporary Sociology* 27:568–69.

Rank, Mark Robert. 2004. *One Nation, Underpriviledged: Why American Poverty Affects Us All*. New York: Oxford University Press.

Reimers, Fernando. 2001. *Unequal Schools, Unequal Chances: The Challenges to Equal Opportunity in the Americas*. Cambridge, Mass.: Harvard University Press.

Reskin, Barbara. 2003. "Including Mechanisms in Our Models of Ascriptive Inequality." *American Sociological Review* 68(1): 1–21.

Risman, Barbara J. 1998. *Gender Vertigo: American Families in Transition*. New Haven, Conn.: Yale University Press.

Ritzer, George. 1992. *Classical Sociological Theory*. New York: McGraw-Hill.

Roberts, Sam. 2004. *Who We Are Now: The Changing Face of America in the Twenty-First Century*. New York: Times Press.

Roemer, John E. 2000. *Equality of Opportunity*. Cambridge, Mass.: Harvard University Press.

Rosier, Katherine Brown, and William A. Corsaro. 1993. "Competent Parents, Complex Lives: Managing Parenthood in Poverty." *Journal of Contemporary Ethnography* 22:171–204.

Rothenberg, Paula S. 2002. *White Privilege: Essential Readings on the Other Side of Racism*. New York: Worth.

Rothstein, Richard. 2004. *Class and Schools: Using Social, Economic, and Educational Reform to Close the Black-White Achievement Gap*. New York: Economic Policy Institute.

Rubin, Herbert J. and Irene S. Rubin. 1995. *Qualitative Interviewing: The Art of Hearing Data*. Newbury Park, Calif.: Sage.

Rumberger, R. W. 1983. "The Influence of Family Background on Education, Earnings, and Wealth." *Social Forces* 61:755–73.

Ruskin, Barbara F. 2003. "Including Mechanisms in Our Models of Ascriptive Inequality." *American Sociological Review* 68:1–21.

Sallach, David L. 1974. "Class Domination and Ideological Hegemony." *Sociological Quarterly* 15:38–50.

Scharf, Adria. 2004. "Wealth Inequality by the Numbers." *Dollars and Sense* 2:20.

Scheper-Hughes, Nancy. 1992. *Death without Weeping: The Violence of Everyday Life in Brazil*. Berkeley and Los Angeles: University of California Press.

Schneider, Mark, Paul Teske, and Melissa Marschall. 2000. *Choosing Schools: Consumer Choice and the Quality of American Schools*. Princeton, N.J.: Princeton University Press.

Schoeni, Robert F. 1997. "Private Interhousehold Transfers of Money and Time: New Empirical Evidence." *Review of Income and Wealth* 43:423–48.

Schuman, Howard, and Maria Krysan. 1999. "A Historical Note on Whites' Beliefs about Racial Inequality." *American Sociological Review* 64:847–55.

Schuman, Howard, Charlotte Steeh, Lawrence Bobo, and Maria Krysan. 1997 [1985]. *Racial Attitudes in America: Trends and Interpretations*. Cambridge, Mass.: Harvard University Press.

Schwalbe, Michael, Sandra Godwin, Daphne Holden, Doug Schrock, Shealy Thompson, and Michele Wolkomir. 2000. "Generic Processes in the Reproduction of Inequality: An Interactionist Analysis." *Social Forces* 79:419.

Schwarz, John E. 1997. *Illusions of Opportunity: The American Dream in Question*. New York: W. W. Norton.

Schwarz, John E., and Thomas J. Volgy. 1992. *The Forgotten Americans: Thirty Million Working Poor in the Land of Opportunity*. New York: W. W. Norton.

Sears, David O., Jim Sidanius, and Lawrence Bobo. 2000. *Racialized Politics: The Debate about Racism in America*. Chicago: University of Chicago Press.

Semyonov, Moshe, Danny R. Hoyt, and Richard I. Scott. 1984. "Place, Race, and Differential Occupational Opportunities." *Demography* 21:259–70.

Sen, Amartya K. 1999. *Commodities and Capabilities*. New York: Oxford University Press.

————. 1999. *Development as Freedom*. New York: Alfred A. Knopf.

————. 2000. "Merit and Justice." in *Meritocracy and Economic Inequality*, edited by Kenneth Arrow, Samuel Bowles, and Steven Durlauf. Princeton, N.J.: Princeton University Press.

Sennett, Richard, and Jonathan Cobb. 1972. *The Hidden Injuries of Class*. New York: W. W. Norton.

Shapiro, Thomas M. 2004. *The Hidden Cost of Being African American: How Wealth Perpetuates Inequality*. New York: Oxford University Press.

Shapiro, Thomas M., and Heather Beth Johnson. 2005a. "Family Assets and School Access: Race and Class in the Structuring of Educational Opportunity." Pp. 112–27 in *Inclusion in the American Dream: Assets, Poverty, and Public Policy, edited by* Michael Sherraden. New York: Oxford University Press.

Shapiro, Thomas M. and Heather Beth Johnson. 2005b. "Race, Assets, and Choosing Schools: Current School Choices and the Future of Vouchers." Pp. 244–262 in *Bringing Equity Back: Research for a New Era in American Educational Policy*, edited by Amy Stuart Wells and Janice Petrovich. New York: Teachers College Press.

Shapiro, Thomas M., and Edward N. Wolff. 2001. *Assets for the Poor: The Benefits of Spreading Asset Ownership*. New York: Russell Sage Foundation.

Shepelak, Norma J. 1987. "The Role of Self-Explanations and Self-Evaluations in Legitimating Inequality." *American Sociological Review* 52:495–503.

Sherraden, Michael. 1991. *Assets and the Poor: A New American Welfare Policy*. Armonk, N.Y.: M. E. Sharpe.

Sherraden, Michael, ed. 2005. *Inclusion in the American Dream: Assets, Poverty, and Public Policy*. New York: Oxford University Press.

Sherwood, Jessica Holden. 2004. Talk About Country Clubs: Ideology and the Reproduction of Privilege. Ph.D. diss., North Carolina State University.

Shipler, David K. 1997. *A Country of Strangers: Blacks and Whites in America*. New York: Alfred A. Knopf.

————. 2004. *The Workng Poor: Invisible in America*. New York: Alfred A. Knopf.

Shofield, Janet Ward. 1989. *Black and White in School: Trust, Tension or Tolerance?* New York: Teachers College Press.

Simmons, Roberta G., and Morris Rosenberg. 1971. "Functions of Children's Perceptions of the Stratification System." *American Sociological Review* 36:235–49.

Sleeper, Jim. 1997. *Liberal Racism*. New York: Viking.

Smith, J. P. 1995. "Racial and Ethnic Differences in Wealth Transfer Behavior." *Journal of Human Resources* 30:158–83.

Smith, Kevin B. 1985. "I Made it Because of Me: Beliefs about the Causes of Wealth and Poverty." *Sociological Spectrum* 5:255–267.

————. 1985. "Seeing Justice in Poverty." *Sociological Spectrum* 5:17–29.

Smith, Kevin B., and Lorene H. Stone. 1989. "Rags, Riches, and Boot-straps: Beliefs about the Causes of Wealth and Poverty." *Sociological Quarterly* 30:93–107.

Sorensen, Aage B. 2000. "Toward a Sounder Basis for Class Analysis." *American Journal of Sociology* 105:1523–58.

South, S. J., and K. D. Crowder. 1995. "Leaving the 'Hood: Residential Mobility Between Black, White, and Integrated Neighborhoods." *American Sociological Review* 63:17–26.

Spilerman, Seymour. 2000. "Wealth and Stratification Processes." *Annual Review of Sociology* 26:497–524.

Spindler, George Dearborn. 1987. *Education and Cultural Process*, 2d ed. Prospect Heights, Ill.: Waveland.

Stack, Carol. 1974. *All Our Kin: Strategies for Survival in a Black Community*. New York: Harper and Row.

Starks, Brian. 2003. "The New Economy and the American Dream: Examining the Effect of Work Conditions on Beliefs about Economic Opportunity." *Sociological Quarterly* 44:205–25.

Steelman, Lala Carr, and Brian Powell. 1993. "Doing the Right Thing: Race and Parental Locus of Responsibility for Funding College." *Sociology of Education* 66:223–44.

Steinhorn, Leonard, and Barbara Diggs-Brown. 1999. *By the Color of Our Skin: The Illusion of Integration and the Reality of Race*. New York: Penguin.

Stolte, John F. 1983. "The Legitimation of Structural Inequality: Reformulation and Test of the Self-Evaluation Argument." *American Sociological Review* 48:331–42.

Strauss, Anselm, and Juliet Corbin. 1990. *Basics of Qualitative Research: Grounded Theory Procedures and Techniques*. Thousand Oaks, Calif.: Sage.

————. 1997. *Grounded Theory in Practice*. Thousand Oaks, Calif.: Sage.

Swidler, Ann. 2001. *Talk of Love: How Culture Matters*. Chicago: University of Chicago Press.

Szydlik, Marc. 2004. "Inheritance and Inequality: Theoretical Reasoning and Empirical Evidence." *European Sociological Review* 20:31–45.

Taylor, Robert Joseph, Linda Chatters, and Vickie Mays. 1988. "Parents, Children, Siblings, In-Laws, and Non-Kin as Sources of Emergency Assistance to Black Americans." *Family Relations* 37:298–304.

Teachman, Jay, Kathleen Paasch, and Karen Carver. 1997. "Social Capital and the Generation of Human Capital." *Social Forces* 75:1343–59.

Terkel, Studs. 1980. *American Dreams: Lost and Found*. New York: New Press.

————. 1988. *The Great Divide: Second Thoughts on the American Dream*. New York: Pantheon.

————. 1992. *Race: How Blacks and Whites Think and Feel About the American Obsession*. New York: Doubleday.

Tesch, Renata. 1991. "Software for Qualitative Researchers: Analysis Needs and Program Capabilities." Pp. 16–37 in Using Computers in Qualitative Research. Edited by Nigel G. Fielding and Raymond M. Lee. Thousand Oaks, Calif.: Sage.

Therborn, Goran. 1980. *The Ideology of Power and the Power of Ideology*. London: Verso.

Thernstrom, Abigail, and Stephan Thernstrom. 2003. *No Excuses: Closing the Racial Gap in Learning*. New York: Simon and Schuster.

Thomas, William I. and Dorothy Swaine Thomas. 1928. *The Child in America: Behavior Problems and Programs*. New York: A.A. Knopf.

Tilly, Charles. 1998. *Durable Inequality*. Berkeley and Los Angeles: University of California Press.

Tuch, Steven A., and Jack K. Martin. 1997. *Racial Attitudes in the 1990's: Continuity and Change*. Westport, Conn.: Praeger.

Tumin, Melvin M. 1953. "Some Principles of Social Stratification: A Critical Analysis." *American Sociological Review* 18:387–94.

U.S. Census Bureau. 2001. "Poverty in the United States." Washington, D.C.: U.S. Government Printing Office.

————. 2003. *Statistical Abstract of the United States: 2002*. Washington, D.C.: U.S. Government Printing Office.

U.S. Department of Education and National Center for Education Statistics. 2004. "The Condition of Education 2004." Washington, D.C.: U.S. Government Printing Office.

Valian, Virginia. 1998. *Why So Slow? The Advancement of Women*. Cambridge, Mass.: MIT Press.

Vallantine, Jeanne H., and Joan Z. Spade. 2004. *Schools and Society: A Sociological Approach to Education*. Belmont, Calif.: Thomson Wadsworth.

Van, Dempsey, and George W. Noblit. 1993. "Cultural Ignorance and School Desegregation: Reconstructing a Silenced Narrative." *Educational Policy* 7:318–39.

Van-Dijk, Teun A. 1993. *Elite Discourse and Racism*. Newbury Park, Calif.: Sage.

Vanneman, Reeve, and Lynn Webber Cannon. 1987. *The American Perception of Class*. Philadelphia: Temple University Press.

Wahl, Jenny B. 2003. "From Riches to Riches: Intergenerational Transfers and the Evidence from Estate Tax Returns." *Social Science Quarterly* 84:278–96.

Walzer, Michael. 1992. *What It Means to Be an American: Essays on the American Experience*. New York: Marsilio.

Warren, Elizabeth, and Amelia Warren Tyagi. 2003. *The Two-Income Trap: Why Middle-Class Parents Are Going Broke*. New York: Perseus.

Wells, Amy Stuart. 1995. "Reexamining Social Science Research on School Desegregation: Long- Versus Short-Term Effects." *Teachers College Record* 96:691–706.

West, Cornel. 1993. *Race Matters*. Boston: Beacon.

Wilhelm, Mark O. 1996. "Bequest Behavior and the Effect of Heirs' Earnings: Testing the Altruistic Model of Bequests." *American Economic Review* 86:874–92.

———. 2001. "The Role of Intergenerational Transfers in Spreading Asset Ownership." Pp. 132–61 in *Assets for the Poor: The Benefits of Spreading Asset Ownership*, edited by Thomas M. Shapiro and Edward N. Wolff. New York: Russell Sage Foundation.

Wilkerson, Isabel. 1990, November 26. "Middle Class Blacks Try to Grip a Ladder while Lending a Hand." *New York Times*.

Wilkes, Rima, and John Iceland. 2004. "Hypersegregation in the Twenty-First Century." *Demography* 41:23–37.

Willie, Charles Vert. 1977. *Black/Brown/White Relations*. New Brunswick, N.J.: Transaction.

———. 1979. *The Caste and Class Controversy*. Dixon Hills, N.Y.: General Hall.

———. 1985. *Black and White Families*. Dixon Hills, N.Y.: General Hall.

———. 1989. *Caste and Class Controversy on Race and Poverty: Round Two of the Willie/Wilson Debate*. Dixon Hills, N.Y.: General Hall.

Willis, Paul. 1977. *Learning to Labor: How Working Class Kids Get Working Class Jobs*. Aldershot, England: Gower.

Wilson, George, and Jomills Braddock. 1997. "Analyzing Racial Ideology: Post-1980 America." Pp. 129–143 in *Postmodernism and Race*, edited by E. M. Kramer. Westport, Conn.: Praeger.

Wilson, William Julius. 1978. *The Declining Significance of Race*. Chicago: University of Chicago Press.

———. 1987. *The Truly Disadvantaged*. Chicago: University of Chicago Press.

———. 1996. *When Work Disappears: The World of the New Urban Poor*. New York: Vintage.

———. 1999. *The Bridge over the Racial Divide: Rising Inequality and Coalition Politics*. Berkeley and Los Angeles: University of California Press/New York: Russell Sage Foundation.

Winnick, Andrew. 1989. *Toward Two Societies: The Changing Distributions of Income and Wealth in the United States Since 1960*. New York: Praeger.

Wolff, Edward N. 1987. "Estimates of Household Wealth Inequality in the United States, 1962–1983." *Review of Income and Wealth* 33:231–56.

———. 1995. *Top Heavy: The Increasing Inequality of Wealth in America and What Can Be Done About It*. New York: New Press.

———. 2001. "Recent Trends in Wealth Ownership, from 1983 to 1998." Pp. 34–73 in *Assets for the Poor: The Benefits of Spreading Asset Ownership*, edited by Thomas M. Shapiro and Edward N. Wolff. New York: Russell Sage Foundation.

———. 2002. "Racial Wealth Disparities: What are the Causes?" *Indicators* 1:63–76.

Wright, Erik Olin. 1997. *Class Counts: Comparative Studies in Class Analysis*. Cambridge: Cambridge University Press.

Yinger, John. 1995. *Closed Doors, Opportunities Lost: The Continuing Costs of Housing Discrimination*. New York: Russell Sage Foundation.

Young, Michael. 1961. *The Rise of Meritocracy, 1870–2033: An Essay on Education and Equality*. Baltimore: Penguin.

Zelizer, Viviana A. 1989. "The Social Meaning of Money: 'Special Monies.'" *American Journal of Sociology* 95:342–77.

Zweigenhaft, Richard L., and G. William Domhoff. 1991. *Blacks in the White Establishment? A Study of Race and Class in America*. New Haven, Conn.: Yale University Press.

Index

A

achievement ideology, 150
Ackerman, Chris and Peter, 133–134
Adams, Amanda and Clifford, 83–84
African Americans, *see* blacks
All Our Kin (Stack), 98
American Apartheid (Massey and
        Denton), 45
American Dream
    and belief in
        by Americans, 23–24
        by blacks, 28
        by disadvantaged urban
            teenagers, 28
        by parents, 24–30
        public opinion polls and, 27–28
        by working-class, 28
    as a creed, 21
    definition of, by various individuals,
        26–27, 29
    dominant ideology of, 22–23,
        150–154, 189n10
    hope, and power of, 154–156
    principles of, 20–21
    quandary of, 169–171
    social change and, 172
    teaching of, to children, 170

assets
    asset-based policy and, 168–169
    intergenerational transfers of wealth
        and, 7–8
    as measure of family's well-being,
        177
    poverty, 6, 7, 12
    transformative, 66–67
Assets and Inequality Project, 175
Assets and the Poor (Sherraden), 5

B

Barry, Briggette and Joe, 132–133
Bethesda School District, 106
Beverly Hills High School, 102–103
Bezdell, Moira, 69–70
Bezdell, Nancy, 69–70
blacks
    belief in American Dream by, 28
    black-white inequality gap and,
        27–28
    college-educated, and wealth of
        compared to whites, 7
    commitment of, to children's
        education, 34–35, 41
    desegregation and, 39, 46
    family net worth of, 95

hypersegregation of, 45–47,
      184n19
individualistic and structuralist
      explanations for poverty,
      and belief in, 151–152
intergenerational transfers, 8–9
      of poverty, and quality of
      education, 50
   in reverse, 93–99
moving to white neighborhoods,
      and racism, 59
private school enrollment of, 72
racial wealth gap and, 7–8
test scores of, compared to whites,
      75–76
Black Wealth/White Wealth (Oliver
      and Shapiro), 7, 175
Bobo, Lawrence, 151
Bonilla-Silva, Eduardo, 42, 161,
      187n53
Booth, Carl, 91–92
Boothe, Lily, 110–111
Boothe, Lily and Jonathan, 134–135
Boyles, Regina and Arthur, 92
Breslin, Sandra, 29
Brown vs. Board of Education, 46
Bryant, Alice and Bob, 79, 80–83,
      118
Bryant, Matthew, 81–82

C

California Distinguished School, 61,
      62
Campbell, Mark, 67
Capital (Marx), 4
Carroll, Anne and John, 67–68
Chiteji, Ngina, 98
class, *see* social class
Clayton School District, 64
Clinton, Chelsea, 104
Cobb, Jonathan, 23, 28
Coleman, James, 191n64
Coleman Report, 191n64

command over future resources, 177
Conley, Dalton, 8, 173
Connor, Abigail, 115–116
Conrad, Bridger, 104
Conrad, Devon, 104
Conrad, Grace and Joel, 103–105,
      112–113, 137
Conrad, Taryn, 104
consciousness
   class, 11
   dual, 152, 153
Cookson, Peter, 77
Cromer, Ellie, 84–85
Cullen, Jim, 22
Cummings, Elizabeth, 117–118
Curley, Deborah, 43, 48

D

Darling-Hammond, Linda, 51, 76
Delbanco, Andrew, 30
Denton, Nancy, 45
desegregation, 39, 46
Desmond, Melissa, 33
Diamond, Tracei, 131–132
Doherty, Linea, 72–73
Doucette, Jen and Sam, 43
Duke University Survey of
      Elementary Schools, 62
Durkheim, Émile, 3

E

education. *see also* schools
   analysis of wealth inequality, and
      importance of, 11
   as Great Equalizer, 30–40
   high school *vs.* college, and
      income of working- age
      men, 76
   inequalities in
      Gallup Poll on, 27–28
      predicament of, 163–166

structured educational *vs.*
structured wealth, 108–109
parents' commitment to, 36–40
of blacks, 34–35, 41
and lack of family wealth,
79–85
nonmaterial resources used by,
for positive influence, 76–77
peers, and influence of, 47–51
wealth, and power in, 53–55
Education Trust, 76
egalitarianism, 10, 21, 22, 36,
161–163, 167
equal opportunity, 2, 22, 27, 28

F

*Facing Up to the American Dream:
Race, Class, and the Soul
of a Nation* (Hochschild),
22, 28
Fairburne School, 40
family wealth, defined, 5, 183n6
Feagin, Joe, 150
Ford Foundation, 175
Form, William, 150
Frohmer, Jacki, 55–58
Frohmer, Michael, 55–58

G

Gordon, Pamela and James, 26,
111–112, 143–145, 146
Graham, Daniel, 39, 146–147
Great Equalizer, 30–40

H

Hadley, Steve and Jan, 157–158
Hamilton, Derrick, 98
Harmon, Kimberly, 32
Haycock, Kati, 76
Haynes, Melanie and Troy, 60–62
Hermosa Beach, 61, 62

*The Hidden Cost of Being African
American: How Wealth
Perpetuates Inequality*
(Shapiro), 7, 66, 175
The Hidden Injuries of Class
(Sennett and Cobb), 23, 28
Hills School, 117–118
Hochschild, Jennifer, 22, 28, 46, 50,
189n21
Holden, Olivia and Nicholas, 101,
138
Holme, Jennifer Jellison, 49
Home Advantage (Lareau), 76, 126
hope, defined, 195n22
Huber, Joan, 150
Hunt, Matthew, 151–152, 153
Hyde, Katherine Ann, 151

I

inclusiveness, 1, 22, 163
individualism, 9, 20, 22, 25, 74, 150,
163
inequality
in education, 37, 44–51
income, 5, 6
individualistic and structuralist
explanations for, 151–152
intergenerational transmission of,
5, 10, 162
nested character of, and
separation, 165, 196n7
patterns of, 46
race
and sedimentation of, 96
and studies on, 12, 27, 45,
186n49
social class, 5
inherited wealth, 5
advantages of
through ascription, 141
unearned, 14, 97, 102, 120,
122, 130, 132
analyzing origin of, 178

dilemma of, 166–169
earning of, 9, 102, 196n2
hard work and, contradiction of,
    148–156
implications of, 5
intergenerational transfers of,
    62–63, 102
    and ability to buy in to "good"
        schools, 62–78, 102
    ramifications of, 75
    in reverse, 97, 98
    vs. income savings, 97
Opportunity Act and, 169
racial differences in, 8, 9
self-achievement combined with,
    136–137
interviews
    on acknowledging advantage:
        a structure of wealth
        inequality, 110–122
    on *American Dream* phrase, 19
    on an unresolved conflict,
        157–159
    on buying in: "to get the best
        schools," 55–67
    on conviction in meritocracy:
        hard work or lack thereof,
        130–140
    core questions of, 10–13
    on family wealth and
        intergenerational transfers,
        74–78
    on feeling stuck: "stuck some
        place where you can afford,"
        86–93
    first phase of, 13–15
    on a "good" school, 40–43,
        53–54, 79
    on the Great Equalizer and the
        key to the American Dream,
        30–36

on "it's not necessarily fair, and
    it's not necessarily right,"
    36–40
on making do: "the best we can
    afford" and "fudging it,"
    80–86
on opting out: "private school is
    best," 67–74
on parents' beliefs in the American
    Dream, 24–30
participants of, 13
    demographics of, 179–182
    identification of, through
        snowball sampling method,
        15
    and savings goals, 193n14
on passing along advantage: the
    schools we choose, 102–110
patterns of, 16–18
on a persistent paradox, 148–156
on realism of the American
    Dream, 129
on "running with fast horse,"
    47–51
second phase of, 15
on separate and unequal
    education, 44–47
on upholding the contradiction:
    the American Dream
    and the power of wealth,
    140–148
U.S. cities chosen for, 16
on wealth poverty and
    intergenerational transfers
    in reverse, 93–99
on wealth privilege as a private,
    public power, 122–127

J

Jackman, Mary, 45
Johnson, Elaine and Bradford,
    138–139

Johnson, Macy, 138
Johnson, Maya, 138
Jones, Karen and Billy, 35

K

Keenan, Victoria and Abraham,
    71–72, 113
Keister, Lisa, 7
Kiefer, Valerie and Mark, 74
King, Martin Luther, Jr., 1
Kluegel, James, 150–151, 152, 153
Krysan, Maria, 27

L

L.A. Unified School District, 60–61
labor market, 5, 7
Ladd, Everett Carll, 24
Ladue School District, 55–57
Lareau, Annette, 76–77, 126
life chances
    for children, 3
        and asset poverty, 6, 118
        and education/schools, 11, 20,
            33, 48, 50, 75, 77, 103, 107,
            142, 166
        and hopefulness, 29–30, 154
        and intergenerational transfers
            of wealth, 62, 116, 118–119,
            167, 169
        and racial wealth gap, 8, 146,
            161, 171–172
    family wealth and, 5
    meritocracy and, 26, 101, 132
    private property ownership and, 4

M

Martin, Faith and Carter, 37–38,
    47–48, 105–106, 119,
    130–131
Marx, Karl, 4

Massey, Douglas, 45
Masterson, Mary, 48–49
McLeod, Jay, 28
Meador, Joyce and Eliston, 30–31,
    38–39, 42–43
Medina, Yvette, 53–54
meritocracy, 20–24
    conviction in, 130–140
    disadvantaged parents on,
        130–132
    life chances and, 26, 101, 132
    net worth, and intergenerational
        transfers of wealth, 133
    wealth inequality and
        contradiction of, 141–148
Mills, C. Wright, 13, 172
Mitchel, Emily, 116, 148
Mitchel, Jacob, 32, 129

N

National Blue Ribbon Schools, 61, 62
nested privileges, 165, 196n7
net financial assets (NFA)
    defined, 177
    families of students in private
        schools vs. public, and
        student loans, 72, 89–90,
        131, 133, 138–139
    racial differences in, 185n24
net worth (NW)
    asset poverty and, 6
    defined, 177
    meritocracy, and intergenerational
        transfers of wealth and, 133
    racial differences in, 7, 8, 95,
        185n24
    for top 1% of families, 6
Nightengale, Carl Husemoller, 28

"NUD*IST" (Qualitative Solutions
        and Research's Non-
        Numerical Unstructured
        Data-Indexing, Searching,
        and Theorizing program,
        version 4), 176–177

O

Oakes, Jeannie, 51
Oliver, Melvin, 7, 96, 175, 177
Olsen, Lori and Dan, 36–37, 58–59,
        120
One Nation, Underprivileged
        (Rank), 50
open society, 22, 162
Opportunity Act, 169
Orfield, Susan and Gary, 45–46, 95
Otis, Sarah, 36

P

Panford, Iris, 87–88, 102–103
Parks, Molisa, 41
Parkway School District, 53–54
Payne, Debbie and Bill, 37
Perkins, Cynthia and Paul, 114–115
Persell, Caroline Hodges, 77
Phillips, Tallie and Marcus, 31
Post, Laura, 51
Post–Civil Rights Era, 2, 10, 20, 24,
        154
poverty
    asset, 6, 7, 12
    beliefs about, three basic types of,
        150
    breaking out of, 29–31
    children living below poverty line,
        in U.S., 44, 95
    educational attainment, and
        negative affects on, 95
    individualistic and structuralist
        explanations for, 151–152

intergenerational transfers of, 50
    in reverse, 93–99
racial residential segregation as
        reason for, 45
urban teenagers and, 28
wealth, 93–99, 102, 123, 130
of working poor, 86–87
Preparing for Power (Cookson and
        Persell), 77
Preston, Madeline and Karl, 107–
        108, 109, 120–121
Princeton University, 104
private property ownership, 4
public opinion polls, 27–28

Q

Qualitative Solutions and Research's
        Non-Numerical
        Unstructured Data-
        Indexing, Searching, and
        Theorizing program,
        version 4 ("NUD*IST"),
        176–177

R

racism, 41–42, 161
Rank, Mark, 50
reparations movement, 168
"A Report Card on Schools," 71
Reskin, Barbara, 187n56
Rice, Eva, 74
Rice University, 104
Roberts, Sam, 184n19
Roemer, John, 166

S

St. Louis city schools, 55–56, 66
Santa Monica, 84–85
Saucier, Thomas, 154–155
Saunders, Marisa, 51

schools. *see also* education
  access to "good"
    and advantages of wealth
      privilege in choosing,
      102–110
    and "blame-the-parents" logic,
      94, 108
    and "buying in," by wealth-
      holding families, 55–67
    and choosing through
      reputation, 48–49
    and "feeling stuck," by poor
      families, 86–93
    and "fudging it," 84–85
    and impact on children, 95
    and intergenerational transfers
      in reverse, 93–99
    and intergenerational transfers
      of wealth, 74–78
    and "making do," by middle-
      and working-class families,
      80–86
    and "opting out" of public
      schools for private, by
      wealth-holding families,
      67–74
    and parents' opinions of,
      40–43
    and race as defining factor of,
      41–42
    and structured wealth
      inequality, and parents'
      awareness of, 110–122
  communities, and link between,
    44–47
  differences, in terms of social
    status and, 47–51
  drop-out rate and, 46, 191n58
  funding for, through property
    taxes, 42, 44, 50
  intergenerational transfers of
    wealth and, 62–78
  quality of, depending on location
    and, 42–43
  reduced school lunches, and
    eligibility for, 46
  shaping of students' lifestyles and
    life chances by, 77
  student achievement
    and contributing factors, 27–28
    and family wealth, 75
    and quality of teachers, 76
    and social environment, 48–50
    and test scores of blacks,
      compared to whites, 75–76
Schuman, Howard, 27
Schwartz, Maryann and Joseph,
    63–64, 66
Scolari Sage Publications Software,
    176
Scovronick, Nathan, 50
segregation
  desegregation, 39, 46
  residential, 44–45
  school, 45–47, 164, 176
Sennett, Richard, 23, 28
Shapiro, Thomas, 7, 13, 41, 66–67,
    96, 164, 169, 175, 177,
    185n24
Sherraden, Michael, 5
slavery, 7, 184n19
Smith, Eliot, 150–151, 152, 153
Smith, Kevin, 152
Smith, Leslie, 40
social class
  defined, 183n7
  hidden injury, and working class
    men, 23
  inequality, 5
  measurement of, 5
  positioning in, 9, 14–15, 21, 50,
    134, 135
  race and, 7, 185n21
  reproduction of, 159–163

socioeconomic, 5, 7
stratification beliefs and, 5, 10,
    132, 151, 152, 159, 162
as taboo topic, 123
upper, and sense of entitlement,
    107, 108, 170
working poor, 4, 86–87
social construction, 12–13, 41
sociology
    fate, and meaning of, 172
    gender studies, and advantaged
        and disadvantaged, 125
    inequality studies and, 4, 17
    privileged, studies on, 12, 186n47
    of wealth, 4
South Street Elementary, 40
Spence, Abigail and Connor, 19,
    135–136
Stack, Carol, 98
Starks, Brian, 151
Staymans, Ginny and Matt, 85–86
Stone, Lorene, 152
Stone, Molly and Paul, 30, 117, 149

T

taxes, property, 42, 44, 50
Tesch, Renata, 177
Tessler, Moszela, 93
Thomas theorem, 13, 187n53
Touran, Ruby and Roland, 90–91
transformative assets, 66–67

U

Unequal Childhoods (Lareau), 76,
    126
U.S. Census Bureau, 45
U.S. Department of Education, 44,
    45, 51
U.S. Supreme Court, 46

V

Valian, Virginia, 125

W

Wahl, Jenny, 169
Walt Whitman High School, 106
Ward, Eleanor and Anthony, 33–34
wealth. *see also* inherited wealth
    accumulative advantage of, 125,
        139–140
    analyzing, 178
    beliefs, and study of, 150–153
    classical social theory and, 4
    code of secrecy and, 124
    cumulative effect of, 125
    luck and, 123, 196n1
    poverty, and intergenerational
        transfers in reverse, 93–99
    power of, in education, 53–55
    private school students and,
        70–71
    sociology of, 4
    as a taboo, 123–124
wealth inequality
    analysis of, through education, 11
    intergenerational, 4, 12, 162–163,
        196n5
    and transfer of, 3, 10, 15, 75,
        167, 178
    meritocracy, and contradiction of,
        141–148
    racial wealth gap and, 1, 7, 96
    structured, 3, 4, 8–10, 110–122
    in United States, 6
wealth privilege, 101–127, 142
    advantages of, acknowledging,
        110–122
    foothold steps of, 126
    impact on others, 121–122
    push or edge of, 111–114
    and safety-net of, 114–115

eliminating, 169
invisibility of, 17, 55, 102, 140, 147, 194n1
as private, public power, 122–127
Weber, Max, 4
Westwood Elementary, 88, 89
Weymouth, Tonya, 33
Wharton Business School, 104
Willis, Paul, 187n55
Windrow, Vivian, 39–40, 106–107

Winfrey, Oprah, 153
work ethic, 129, 138, 150
working poor, 4, 86–87
worldviews, 8
Wright, Suzanne and Drew, 24–26, 44, 121–122, 140–141

Y

Yun, John, 45–46